EXCUSED BOOTS
Tales of National Service

June Thistlethwaite

Best Wishes

June Thistlethwaite

Thyme Press

*This book is dedicated to all ex National Servicemen
and in memory of those who gave their lives.*

By the same author

Cumbrian Women Remember; First Published 1995,
Reprinted 1995, 1997 & 1998
Cumbria, The War Years; Published 1997
Molly's Story; Published 1998

Cover photograph by Keith Bales Photography, Workington

Published by Thyme Press, 5 Finley Close.
Kendal, Cumbria LA9 6DW

First published 1999

Printed by Kent Valley Printers Ltd, Kendal
Typeset by Indent Typesetters, Kendal

British Library Cataloguing in Publication Data
A Catalogue record for this book is available from the
British Library

ISBN 0 9531695 4 5

Contents

Acknowledgements

I am grateful to all interviewees for their patience and time so freely given. To: Prontaprint (Kendal) for their expertise; Mr Eastwood (Curator of the KOBR Museum at Carlisle), Trevor Furnass (Kendal) and John Curtiss (Milnthorpe) for their advice; Keith Bales (Workington) for his photography; Indent Typesetters (Kendal); Tim and staff at Kent Valley Colour Printers (Kendal) and my husband Clive for his help and support.

Most of the photographs in this book are produced courtesy of the interviewees. I am grateful for the loan of the KOBR badge by Mr Eastwood; Mr E Leech from Lancashire and Korean Veteran of 1st Battalion King's Own Liverpool Regiment for allowing me to reproduce his poem, *The Kingsman* on page 8; To Mrs Stubbs, Mrs Sullivan & Mrs Thompson, sisters of the late Corporal Mooney for allowing me to reproduce the photograph used on the front cover and page 27; RAF Leuchars for granting permission to use the photograph on page 225; and to Mr John Sewell (see Ch.3) for allowing his literature re National Service to be reproduced on pages 30, 107, 118, 119, 148, 182, 202 and 203.

Every effort has been made to contact copyright holders and I apologise most sincerely if I have failed to acknowledge anyone and would ask to be notified of any corrections to be incorporated in future editions.

Introduction

My books are based on the recollections of local people. Without people being prepared to talk to me and speak of their experiences and memories, I would have no books to write and publish. I am totally indebted to them all, especially the men interviewed for this book.

The present climate of our country often appears to ignore the older generation and their experiences of life. Most people are hesitant to talk about their past, especially a military one which seems to have no relevance in our 'correct' times. Unfortunately, to ignore such lives diminishes us all as we are neglecting a major part of our heritage. If their recollections and memories are forgotten, we are betraying future generations some knowledge of their ancestors.

The past of fifty years ago, was a very different world. During the time of National Service, school maps showed large parts of the world proudly coloured in pink representing our Empire and Commonwealth. It was a fact of life which very few queried. But the Cold War had arrived and British colonies and countries where we had interests were growing restless. Young men were deemed necessary to guard these interests.

For those who did National Service, the Second World War was still a vivid memory of when fathers, brothers and other relations had played their part. John Slater remembered, 'It was inevitable that someone from every family or their relations had served in the forces. First World War people were in their sixties at that time… . So you were always in contact with these two generations.' It therefore came as no surprise to most young men that they were also expected to wear military uniform.

Of the teenage boys entering National Service, very few had ventured beyond their locality or even slept away from home. The majority of them left school at fourteen or fifteen years of age and hopefully found local employment. Those such as Robert Jackson or John Sewell who served their apprenticeship or were going to college after leaving Grammar School could defer their National Service.

Boys of those days were usually very innocent and unworldly. Only people from the cities, especially 'down south' were supposed to be street wise. Tony Johnstone recalled, 'If a Cockney came up and spoke to me I would believe everything he said as I thought he was the fount of all knowledge.' Not every house-hold bought a daily paper. Very few homes had television and the wireless was listened to by the young only for programmes of entertainment. The Newsreel at the cinema was watched under sufferance until the start of the feature film. World affairs usually passed them by.

The first night away from familiar surroundings in the sparse conditions of a military establishment came as a shock. Tony Birkett said, '... that first night there were no brave Scotsmen and there were no brave Englishmen. All you could hear in the barracks were the sobs right down the line.' However, the young are resilient and a dry Cumbrian sense of humour helped whether they have fond or negative memories of their time in service.

National Service brings back memories of a time from which the majority of us have been excluded. They have their own vocabulary, such a 'blanco', 'jankers' and 'webbing' to name but a few. The men I spoke to needed patience and humour to guide me along. My first attempt at writing down Saighton (Camp) was 'Satan', which many ex-servicemen might say was most appropriate. On and on grew the list of my civilian 'howlers.'

I asked about the social aspect of National Service. The men obliged with frankness even about the 'ladies of the night.' Adam Kirkbride said, 'I could say to thousands of lads ... 'Who's Kipper Feet?' and they'd say, 'That lass who was on the main gate.'

No-one was gung-ho or militaristic. On active service they respected their opponents. Doug Philipson remembering Korea, recalled 'the Chinese lads.' John Irwin on speaking of his time in Malaya said, 'They were very intelligent people you were up against.'

Looking back, no-one wanted to do National Service but most are glad they did. Many recalled the comradeship and close knit links which still exist. These are some of the last men in twentieth century Britain who were called-up. They are all very special people. I hope you enjoy reading their stories as much as I enjoyed listening to them.

The 1st Battalion King's (Liverpool) Regiment

Korea 1950-53

"THE KINGSMEN"

I used to be a "Kingsman" back in fifty-one
We fought a war, in a far off land
But now all that has gone,
I just live with my memories
Of the friends I knew and lost,
Men who did their duty
Who ne'er did count the cost.

They came from every walk of life
These men I came to know,
There wasn't a place, including hell
These soldiers wouldn't go,
For every man's a "Kingsman"
The colours proud to serve,
And many the honours that they won
But none they didn't deserve.

They shared in every danger
These comrades from the past,
They stood together side by side
From first man to the last,
They heard each other laughing
They saw each other die,
They conquered every hardship
Never asking why.

I've watched them squat in fox-holes
Shell-fire all around,
The stuttering machine guns
Churning up the ground.
I've seen them tend the wounded
With a care I never knew,
But then again they're "Kingsmen"
What other would they do.

I was proud to be a "Kingsman"
I was proud to serve the Queen,
And the men I served my time with
Were the finest ever been,
And whatever in my life-time
I tend to hold most dear
The fact I was a "Kingsman"
Is my greatest souvenir.

EDDIE LEACH.

POSITIONS HELD BY THE REGIMENT IN THE KOREAN WAR:

Songdok, Samichon Valley, The Hook, Green Finger, Ronson, Warsaw, Sausage, Pheasant, Seattle, Yondong, Hills 355, 121, 166, 159, 111.

ONE

'There's movement out front'

Doug Philipson, *Served in 1st First Battalion, King's Own Liverpool Regiment 1951-53*

I was working on a farm at Underbarrow when I went for my medical. In those days we went to a place called Starch House Square at Preston for it. I don't think anybody failed a medical. You'd have to have been in a hell of a state before they failed you. I asked to go in either the Royal Engineers or the Royal Army Service Corps and was put in the Border Regiment.

It was a few weeks later that I was called up. The chap I worked for on the farm wasn't very happy about it when I told him I was finishing at the weekend. He did try and get me deferred but I didn't want that. All my mates had been called up and I wanted to go.

I went to Saighton Camp with Collin Sill from Kendal and Sammy Ireton from Storth but we were split up when we arrived. You were told, 'Right you lot, over here. You lot, over there.' You were chased about and given a billet and you just stopped there. Well, in them days the billets were called spiders. One main room and the rest shot off at angles from it.There would be about ten or a dozen of you in each spider and one little room at the end for your NCO who's in charge. All the toilets, baths and showers were in the centre of the building and you were like fleas in a jam pot trying to get ready in a morning. That was the worst thing, having to get up in a morning. Somebody shouting at you at about six o'clock, 'Come on, get your bloody feet on the floor,' that sort of thing.

The sergeant was a chap called Greenstreet. When he was drilling you, in the old army words, he was a bastard. But he was a genuine type of feller. The lad who was in charge of our billet, he threw his weight about. He had only one stripe but it was as though he was the colonel himself. Of course when you were as green as we were and it was the first time away from home and with people you didn't know, when he said, 'Jump' you jumped. Whatever they told you to do you did and that was it. It was as simple as that. You worked when you were told to work and ate when you were told to eat.

The food was rough and ready. I mean it was all good grub but lads who do the vegetables and stuff like that are either defaulters or sent to do the jobs and they're not thorough. I was a defaulter myself and you cut carrots and taties like squares because they're easier to peel like that. When you peeled them, the peelings were thicker than the potatoes. And when you shelled peas and beans, you weren't bothered if half the shells went in the pan with them.

I remember when we got bacon in a morning, it would be all on one big slab cooking, with each rasher overlapping another. Well, the top bit of bacon would be cooked and the bits underneath were raw. But it was eatable. The first week or ten days, your stomach heaved when you went into the cookhouse. For some reason it used to smell. Don't ask me why but a cookhouse had a smell all of its own and you couldn't get rid of it. After a while you were that damn hungry, you would eat anything and fight for stuff.

When you started your training, somebody would throw a big box of crusts on the table. For the first ten days or so, nobody would eat the crusts and they'd be thrown to the birds. But after ten days were up and your money had run low, you were feeling hungry and would eat anything.

At night you could go to the cookhouse and get crusts which you'd take back to the billet where there was a big pot bellied stove.You'd get this stove red hot and chuck bread on top.You used to call it toast but actually it was just burnt bread.

Normal training was six weeks but ours was crammed into four weeks. That first week, you didn't know whether you were coming or going. You started early in a morning and our training was going on till half past five or six at night. Actually, I think a lot of the training was skimped. When we eventually were on our passing out parade, we didn't appear to be as highly drilled as other lads.

Everything was new to you at camp. When you're eighteen years old, you'll have a go at anything as you're keen to learn. It was just like starting a new job, really. Whoever was teaching you, you listened to them and had respect for them. But after you've been in a while, it's like owt else, it goes over the top of your head and you think you know it all but you don't.

Everybody's in the same boat at basic training. You muck in together. Everything you have, you share. I didn't smoke but you'd see lads sharing a fag or you'd go to the NAAFI and get a plate of chips and beans between the four of you because you were so broke. It was just natural that you did share. If a lad pinched a dozen slices of bread, he'd share it with the lads in the billet.

One of the first jobs when you arrived at camp was your haircut. The next were injections which they usually gave you on a Friday night so that you were badly over the weekend in your own time and not theirs. We also had injections the night before our passing out parade so most of our lads on parade were in a bad way.

After the passing out parade, we were allowed home for the first time. We got about ten days leave and had to report back to Formby after that. Well, most of us had to. You see, one of the things the Army was always looking for were volunteers for the Military Police. They very rarely got them so they used to say, 'Right, you, you and you are in the Military Police.' So those lads went somewhere else and the rest of us went to Formby.

When we'd left Chester, we came home up to Cumbria as Border Regiment lads but when we arrived at Formby we were told we were in the King's Own. We had to cut our shoulder flashes off and stitch the King's Own ones on. You know how ham fisted eighteen year old lads are and you can imagine what these shoulder flashes looked like.

We were at Formby for about a month basically doing what we'd been doing at Chester. Normally, what they used to do, was look for lads who lived a distance away and you were the lads that finished up on guard or fire picket at night. You see, the way the trains were running, it wasn't worth it for us from up here to go home. So you were lumbered with those jobs because they knew you couldn't or wouldn't be going home. For guard duty there were two of you going round in pairs and armed with a pick shaft. I don't know what the hell you were supposed to do with that. In our spare time we went down into Liverpool or Southport a few times but basically you couldn't afford it as you were always buying polish, toothpaste or soap.

From Formby we came home for a few days before going to the King's Own in Germany. We went down by train from Liverpool to Harwich and onto a troopship across to the Hook of Holland and onto trains for Germany. The whole journey lasted a couple of days and you got iron rations or sandwiches, an apple and a bar or chocolate. When you travelled through part of Germany, the carriage blinds were drawn down and you weren't allowed to look out. Whether it was because we were going through the Russian occupied territory, I don't know. But it was night anyway, so there were no lights in the carriage and you just settled down to sleep.

'Doug, a rookie in Berlin'

Halfway through the train journey we were told that we were no longer the King's Own and were now in the King's Liverpool. I just forget where we were supposed to be going but instead we went to Berlin to join our new regiment. Once in Berlin, our uniform was taken off us and it went to the tailors who stitched our new shoulder flashes and badges on for us.

Our barracks were actually old SS barracks and were luxury from what we'd been used to. There were only about eight of us in a room and there was central heating. Toilet facilities and everything were on the same landing so you weren't scarpering across a spider block for toilets. For British soldiers, they were damn good barracks.

On our first day there we were put on an ID parade for a lass who'd been raped. Of course when she came round, she couldn't pick anybody out because we'd only arrived the day before. I think that was one of the Army ploys; fetch a load of lads in that they knew damn well she couldn't pick out. Well, it did frighten you at the time because the trouble was, you were still that green. There was a lot of fear with most things because you didn't want to be on jankers as they really made you work.

I was only on jankers once and that was in Berlin. A chair had been broken in our barracks when we weren't in and didn't know anything about it. The corporal couldn't find out who'd broken it so we went in front of the Company Commander. He asked us who'd broken the chair and because none of us spoke, it was classed as dumb insolence and we had to pay for the chair.

Once you were on jankers, you had to report to the Regimental Police and if the truth is told, they couldn't be bothered with you. They'd give you their boots to clean and buckles to polish and then the thing was to keep making you go and change your kit. They'd say, 'Right, I want you back here in five minutes in your PT kit.' So you'd chase back to your billet, get changed into PT kit and dash back to the guardroom. Then it was, 'Back here in ten minutes. I want you in your best battle dress, boot, gaiters, everything.' So back you'd go and get changed and then be told, 'This time we'll have you in your full marching order,' which was full kit, the bloody lot. They'd do that for an hour or so and you had to answer every time the 'defaulter' bugle blew.

We didn't see much of Berlin. We did a bit of cross-country running and saw some of the countryside but not actually Berlin. You could go into the American zone but not into the Russian one. We did go to the Brandenberg Gate because what was supposed to be the first Allied tank into Berlin at the end of the Second World War was there. It was a Russian tank guarded by Russians but to be honest we weren't really interested.

Across the road from our barracks was the Spandau Prison where all the top German prisoners-of-war, Hesse and them all were guarded. We never did guard there because we were only in Germany about a month and were told that the battalion had been volunteered for Korea so we came back to England. I don't think we were bothered about this news. Korea was such a long way away. When you're eighteen you just live from day to day and keep thinking how many days till your demob. To me and the lads I've spoken to since those days, that's all we thought about at the time.

Back in England we went to a place called Chiseldon, which is just outside Swindon. That had been a war-time officers' camp and it was a hell of a state. But you adapt and we tidied the place up and got it something like ship-shape before we attended the School of Infantry at Blackball Firs and a tank recognition course. That was to recognise enemy tanks as well as our own and how to look after and maintain guns.

After Chiseldon we went down to Salisbury Plain. That was hell on earth. It was the last place God invented and he hasn't finished yet. We were all crammed into Nissan huts and the joy of the orderly corporal in a morning was to go right along side of each hut with a pick shaft. As the sides were corrugated iron you can imagine the noise. The duty drummer would have already blown reveille but there's always them that won't or can't get out of bed. So after reveille and the pick shaft, your corporal would come into the hut and kick one or two out of bed as he was responsible for having you all out on parade.

We were put in the anti-tank platoon, which were seventeen pounders and I was in a support company with mortars, machine guns, anti-tank and assault pioneers. Then on Salisbury Plain we did our target shooting. Oh, you were ready for sleep at the end of the day. The thing was, in the Army, you never had any time to think. There was always something to do and I suppose right through until we came home on demob we were kept occupied.

We came back to Chiseldon Camp from Salisbury Plain and were given embarkation leave. As we were going to be sailing from

Liverpool, we spent three weeks prior to embarkation leave doing drill. That was because, as a Liverpool regiment, we were going to march round Liverpool and have an address from the Lord Mayor before we embarked. And when we did leave Liverpool it was unbelievable with all the crowds seeing their own lads off. Mind, with some of us coming from Cumbria, it was all good banter with the Liverpool blokes. Cabbage crunchers they'd call us or say that we'd only been caught for National Service when we came out of the hills for a haircut.

HMT Devonshire must have been about the biggest cattle boat I've ever seen because it was so rough and ready. I'd never been on a boat before and thought I was doing great as I wasn't seasick. Even when we got to the Bay of Biscay and you couldn't see for the height of the waves, I was doing grand. Believe it or not, we had liver and gravy for breakfast and I was just about to start mine one morning when a lad in the mess threw up. That was it, I was up and away with my hand over my mouth. I was never as badly in my life for the next three days. Then one of the lads said, 'It's no good being like that, Doug. Get yourself down to the bloody canteen, buy something and eat it.' So I went and bought a tin of fruit and a tin of condensed milk, mixed it all together and ate the lot. I was as right as rain after that.

The *Devonshire* had hammocks and it's great in one when it settles down. But it you were like I was and seasick and anybody went past and pushed it, it was bloody murder. But once we were in warmer weather, all the lads used to take their hammocks out onto the deck, roll them out and sleep there.

While on board, you obviously had lifeboat drill every day. You did arms drill and chucked rubbish like cardboard boxes over the back of the boat to shoot at. But basically, that was all, as there was no room for marching and anything like that. You had a fair bit of free time because it took us thirty five days to reach Hong Kong. Our first port of call was Port Said and then Colombo where the entire battalion got off the boat and marched round the island as a training exercise. Then we stopped for a day at Aden and Singapore. At these places, military personnel were being dropped off who were going to various regiments.

On reaching Hong Kong our Regiment was sent to Norwegian Farm Camp. That's not on Hong Kong Island but on the Chinese mainland beyond Kowloon where a little place called Fan Ling was the nearest village. While we were there, we were allowed to wear civilian clothes off duty so the lads used to buy their's from a shop. Brilliant tailors they were in these shops, no doubt about it. Oh, I loved Hong Kong. I would have loved to stop there a while but because we were there for such a short time and under intensive training, we didn't get much chance to go around. The training we had was forced marches, just marching across country for two or three days. That was to get us used to the climate and get fit because of the five weeks on board ship when you did nothing. It was one hell of an experience.

We were at Norwegian Farm Camp for about three months and then went on a troopship called the *Esan* which sailed from Hong Kong to Pusang. When we arrived at Korea, we went to Britannia Camp which was a transit camp with big squad tents, about thirty blokes to a tent. My first impression of Korea was that the whole place stank. You couldn't really say what it was, just a rotten smell and that smell was there the whole time. After a couple of days we were moved up to beyond Seoul to Bechelon as reserve brigade. We were on the train for about two days and the poverty we could see was unbelievable. Seoul at that time was just a pile of rubbish.

'Now in Korea, Doug is standing on the left.
2nd left, Jim Brownell (Windermere),
3rd left, Colin Johnstone (Kendal)
Right, George Duffield (Kendal)

The Korean War had started in June 1950. It was September 1952 when we arrived there and October when we went into the front line. By that time the front line was virtually static. The Chinese had one lot of hills and we had the other. The no-man's land was the paddies (paddy-fields) in-between. The front line wasn't straight so The Hook, one of our positions, actually went into enemy lines, maybe a few hundred yards from where the Chinese lads were. Now, I was originally in an anti-tank platoon and number two on a gun crew. But in Korea they didn't have anti-tank guns because they were so big and cumbersome to pull about. So we were attached to rifle companies and given these American Browning machine guns. Because I was a lance corporal, I was put in charge of the guns.

All of our stuff was carted up to the front and other places by these Korean porters. They were sturdy larl fellers and could walk up these mountain sides with your stuff on their back, which was unbelievable. It was all carried on what was called an A frame. That was two pieces of wood in an inverted V shape, with a bar across the front to load things onto. You'd load everything onto this A frame and these Koreans would just get under it, pick it up and walk away with it all. They carried everything – the ammunition, the food and brought water. Some of them would offer to do your washing for you.

We were given twenty American cigarettes a day with combat rations. Well, I didn't smoke and I'd give mine away but these Koreans would do your washing for cigarettes or a tin of baked beans. For anything, really. We used to trade stuff with them for doing jobs for us. Mostly it was your washing because your stuff used to get absolutely filthy as you didn't strip off unless you had to. Occasionally a wagon would come for you and you could go back to Bechelon, which was another part of the battalion further back where there were showers. The showers were big drums with water inside and underneath were fires that the Koreans kept going, while the water drip-fed down onto you. It wasn't a proper shower but at least it was something. Bill Davis from Pontypridd and me were in the same bunker together. One of us had the chance to go for a bath. I went and when I came back, Bill had been killed by a mortar bomb. He was my best mate and a great bloke.

At the front line you were dug-in in bunkers. These used to get flattened during the day with the Chinese firing mortar bombs, so we had to rebuild them at night. You dug in and timbered the bunker, putting sandbags on top because we had to stand a hell of a battering with shells. The fighting slits were connected by crawl trenches about six feet deep and you could walk along out of sight from the Chinese. In a lot of places it was solid rock, like Shap granite, so what we couldn't dig we built up with sandbags. We had in the bunker what we called a chuffer. It was an old army ammunition box with either a can of petrol, paraffin or diesel with a rubber hose leading into it. At the end of the tube was a bit of wire to slow the drip into the bottom of the box and that's what you used to light for warmth. Chuffers used to blow up many a time. I think we had as many lads hurt with them as we did with anything else.

All change-overs were done at night in the dark. You were taken from wherever you'd been on the front line and put in a fighting slit on the very front with either a gun or a machine gun. Some slits were open and others had a roof on them. Everybody had to 'stand to' for an hour just before last light at night and the hour at first light in the morning. Those were the two times when the Chinese were more likely to attack. They would think nothing of lying up in the paddies all through the day and never move. Folk used to say they could go two or three days on a handful of rice and that's all they used to carry with them. Until it was light the next morning, you didn't get a chance to look around.

In Korea it was red hot in summer and freezing in winter. One advantage of winter, even though it was cold, it was basically dry. The summer was hot and wet and the trenches used to fill with water. When you were digging, you dug a run-out for the water. Sometimes you had so far to dig you never used to bother and just put up with a bit of discomfort. I've seen lads standing waist deep in water when they had to 'stand to.' Then when the monsoons came, the trenches were full of water.

With Korea being a United Nations conflict, there were other nationalities as well as the British. There were the Americans who took an awful pasting but Yanks being Yanks always advertised where they were. They were brash but they were great and the Aussies were the same. There were Turks, French and I think the Indians worked on the medical side of things. Princess Patricia's Canadian Light Infantry was there. With their initials being PPCLI we called them 'The Ping-Pong Champions of Long Island.' I don't know if the South Africans had any troops in Korea but they certainly had pilots.

On the back slopes where you lived, you could do your washing or any jobs that wanted done. At the front of the hill, there was none of that. The land in front of you was blasted bare, blown to pieces with shells and mortar bombs. At nights, maybe two or three times a week, we would rewire it, using barbed wire. But as soon as you rewired it, the Chinese would blow it to pieces the next day and you'd do the same to theirs.

At night you might go out on what was called a standing patrol. On every front, in every position, you had these lads go right out into no-man's land and were virtually sacrificial lambs. Originally, a patrol was made up of a sergeant and four men. However, it got down to a corporal and four lads with a radio and field telephone, which in those days was on the end of a wire. If anything cut that wire you were buggered. You depended on your radio but mostly tried to maintain radio silence. Every so often, base would call you and you would just say, 'Nothing to report.' If anything went wrong, you'd get a message back to base.

When you were in the standing patrol and there was something in front, you didn't go and look. You radioed back in, saying 'There's movement out front.' and asked for a flare which was one of the big guns with parachute flares that last for nearly ten minutes and light up all the area. Well, as soon as one of them goes off, you freeze and ten minutes is a long time to keep still. Really, you were out in front and if anything came, you had first warning that the enemy was there. If you were hit and didn't get a message off or if the front called and there was no answer, somebody would be sent out to make sure you were all right and weren't asleep. That had been known because you got very little sleep. Basically, you worked during the day as well as 'stood to' or patrolled at night. There was only a few hours sleep and it was known for people to fall asleep.

I used to go out regularly on patrol and loved it rather than standing in a trench all night. You see, when you used to stand there all night, staring out into the blackness all the time, your mind plays funny tricks. I know it sounds bravado going out on patrol but it isn't. You're only nineteen years old and the furthest thing from your mind is anything is going to happen to you. Maybe it's the adrenaline but you're on a high. You're a young lad and things don't happen to you, they happen to everybody else. That's the way you think.

Before you ever went out on patrol you were given instructions about if you were captured and to give only your name, rank and number. You didn't wear a beret with your badge on or anything like that. You wore what was called a cap comforter which was just an old scarf turned inside out. We had parkas with hoods on but when you were in the front line you weren't allowed to have the hood up as you had to hear what was going on. We were fortunate because when we got to Korea, we were really well kitted out for the winter.

'At Yong Dong, Korea.
Doug is on the left, with Paddy McCorde on the right'

I was never on a patrol that caught any Chinese. It seemed a lot of the time they knew you were coming and got out of the way. To my mind they were a lot cleverer than they were given credit for even though they did attack in waves and virtually committed suicide.

Nowadays people would say they were high on drugs. They attacked us but we didn't attack them, ever. If they came and we lost a position, then we would take it back but we did not attack. We would go looking, take fighting patrols out, reccy patrols and standing patrols. With fighting patrols, you'd go out and try to snatch one of the enemy. If you got a prisoner, there was a week's leave in Japan for you but I never got one.

Out of the line we lived off fresh rations but when you were in the front line, you lived off American C7 rations. These were either meat and beans, pork and beans, ham and lima beans, cornbeef hash or ground meat and spaghetti. There was a tin of prunes, a candy bar – typical American isn't it? – chewing gum, toilet paper, a block of chocolate which you could either eat or make into a drink. Then there were sachets of powdered milk and chocolate and two little tablets that were actually fuel. You just put a match to these tablets when you warmed your tins up. These rations weren't bad and were actually better than British Army fresh rations.

There was a black market on the front line, mainly for beer. It was Japanese Asahi and you were allowed one beer a day. In the middle of winter it was a bit of a racket, really. The beer came packed in boxes with straw over the bottles. The beer was frozen and the top had come off. So what you got was a beer lollipop and had to wait until it thawed out. A lot of the lads had no money to buy beer and the colour sergeant or whoever brought the beer would lend them money to buy it. They were worse than bloody money lenders. These lads would pay nearly all their wages in what they owed.

The Chinese were hellish at tunnelling. What they used to do was, come across no-man's land and dig under your positions. During the day-light they'd be working away underneath and then they'd bring their people across at night. You'd be sat on top of a hill and you could hear them tunnelling underneath. I know their facilities weren't as good as ours but I'd say they were possibly better at living off the land then our lads. I mean, if you gave a Chinaman a handful of rice he was happy. Our lads used to complain if they didn't get their rations and the Yanks used to complain if they didn't get their ice-cream.

When our lads were in trouble they could call-up aircraft which would come in and drop napalm and stuff like that. So we could call an air strike in but the Chinese couldn't because they didn't have any. So they fought the war under a bigger handicap than us as they didn't have the firepower but they did have the man power. It's maybe a wrong thing to say but they seemed hell bent on destruction. I don't think you would get our lads doing what they did as they used to come in bloody waves.

There was just one night I had a close shave in no-man's land. It was all mined and the sappers had been out and marked a path through the minefield. We went with the Royal Engineers to blow up some caves that the Chinese were digging. The official report is that the patrol stumbled into a minefield but some of us who were there don't think that's right. You see, you walked through the mine-field that was marked off with a little bit of tape on one side and a luminous disc on the other. One of the lads says the Korean guide with us stepped over to pick a luminous disc up and stepped on a mine which killed him and the three lads behind him. That blew the whole operation up because the Chinese knew we were there. So when our party actually got to where we were going, the Chinese were waiting there for us. I was one who got nabbed to be in charge of the stretcher parties. We had about six or eight stretchers and when we got them behind our lines, we weren't allowed to go back because there was nobody to take us through the minefield. We had three killed that night and about six wounded. So we lost half the patrol as soon as we got about half-way across no-man's land. You see, when you attack a hillside, you're in an unfortunate position. If you throw a grenade up a hillside, it rolls back. So whether any of ours were injured with things like that, we don't know.

One counter attack where we went to blow up caves which was successful was lead by a chap from Portinscale near Keswick. He won the Military Cross that night. John St Maur Williams was his name but we knew him as Second Lieutenant Williams and he was a grand lad. He used to knock around with us, have a beer with us and things like that. If we'd been in Germany or anywhere else, that couldn't have happened.

Basically, a lot of the stuff we were using was what the Army had been using since the Second World War. We had lads on the front with bloody American carbines. How the hell they got them, I don't know. They'd come up with these carbines and were walking around dressed in American uniforms and all sorts.

Now, you were only supposed to be on the front line for a month but we dropped unlucky. Because we were still a support company, every time the companies changed over, we got left behind on the front because we weren't part of that company. We'd gone to the front in about October and our whole battalion was still there at Christmas. I wasn't very happy about this as we weren't getting a break. I thought I was being messed around and it griped me more for the lads I was in charge of that they weren't getting a break. We were being used as machine gunners, standing all night in the splits plus the fact we were being used as a standing patrol as well.

The last company we were with was C Company and the chap in charge of us was Major Horsford. He had spent a lot of time with the Gurkhas and was a grand chap so I went to see him. I explained to him, 'It just isn't on. We're not getting a break.' He agreed with this and asked what the solution was. I told him, 'Take us into the Company so that whenever the Company moves out, we move out.' So Major Horsforth took us out of the front line and I asked, 'If it's all right with you, I'll come off this machine gun and go in with one of your rifle companies, with one of the platoons and one of the sections.' So they took me out of the machine guns, put me with a rifle company where I was second-in-command of a section and given two stripes.

Having two stripes I became more involved with what was going on and I liked that much better. The sergeant was the top man, the corporal had the best job and the lance corporal was the lad who did everybody's running around. He was the oily rag. But when I went into a rifle company, the sergeant had three sections, a corporal in charge of each and a lance corporal was virtually the in-between man. I enjoyed that.

Normally, on the front line, if things were quiet and you didn't get hit, you would do a couple of months before they pulled you back and let another regiment take over. But if you had a clout from the Chinese, they would relieve you right away or within a couple of days. When we were pulled back, we were given a choice of rest and recuperation leave. You could go to Inchon, which was just down the road in Korea: Tokyo or Miya Jima, which is a little island off Japan. It depended on how much money you had to spend as to where you went. If you went to Japan you could buy souvenirs to bring home. In Korea there was nowt like that. You either spent your money on drink, fags or chocolate or gambled it away playing cards.

I went to Miya Jima by boat but was in bed for three days with malaria so that was my bloody leave gone. To be honest, it was just one of those things and it didn't bother me. I was better off being badly on the boat than I would have been on the front line. If I'd have been on the front when it happened, they would probably have said I was skiving or trying to swing the lead.

It might seem far fetched but once you stepped back from the front line, there was loads of bullshit. You were back to cleaning your kit, polishing your boots and cap badge. Every company was out to outdo the other. If your company did something, the next company would do something better. It's regimental pride and its unbelievable what you would do. As much as a Border man that I am, I'm still a King's man through and through and always will be.

Away from the front, you lived in big squad tents, maybe twenty to a tent and carried on like you would do in England. You've no parade ground but they try and keep you going with the same type of training as you did previously. You're just brushing up on everything and of course, all the time you've got new lads coming in and others going home. With it being basically National Service, your lads are changing all the time. So there was always new lads to teach and a lot of them came up with better ideas of weapons because they'd been on more modern stuff than we had.

When we came out of line, there were NAAFI road houses where you could go and have a cup of coffee, a bottle of beer and a snack. But you made your own beer bar which was only a tent and everything else was made out of beer boxes. The Aussies used to come to ours and there must have been a dozen of them one night when there was a scare on. One of the regiments at the front line was getting a clobbering and we were all kitted up ready to go in. These Aussies stood there and our Company Sergeant Major said to them, 'What the hell are you lads doing here?' They answered, 'If these lads are good enough to drink with, they're good enough to fight with.' I don't know if it was the drink talking but they were going to come and fight with our lads. Still, you can't knock an answer like that.

Really, any relaxation you had when you were out of the line was what you had to build yourself. There was a camp cinema, just the screen, surrounded with wood and thatch in case it rained. It wouldn't have done any good if it had got a direct hit and if you put a match to it, it would have gone up. I was never a film fan and would rather ratch about or play cards. We didn't have a big enough area for football so we mainly played volley ball. Any flat place where you could get half a dozen lads for each side, knock a couple of pickets in, shove a bit of camouflage net across and we'd have tournaments.

We did have shows and I saw Ted Ray at one of them. He was a Scouser and with our Liverpool Regiment being in the audience, the crack he started with was, 'The lads in the King's Liverpool stay where you are. The rest of you f—— off.' The shows were enjoyable, a break, a chance to get away from what you were doing but you tended to forget about it as soon as it finished.

When I think back, I didn't have an awful lot of time to myself. I know when we were pulled back, me and more lads volunteered to go on what they called, 'dig reserve positions.' This was in case hostilities did break out again. We went to the area with maybe a dozen Korean porters who did all the work. That was a bloody good scrounge for three weeks as there were no drills and bullshit. The ration truck came in the morning with our breakfasts, we had some sandwiches through the day and the truck came back again at night. That came just to see you were still there and hadn't buggered off.

As everybody who's been in the forces will tell you, the thing you look forward to is getting mail. In peace time conditions, the mail call goes and you can see everybody's spirit lift. When the corporal comes round with the mail and there isn't any for you, you're a bit deflated. In Korea you never knew when you were getting mail because there was no mail call. Possibly you'd get no mail for a month or six weeks and the following week, you'd get letters that had been posted after ones you still hadn't received.

I used to write home about once a week but I got word that they hadn't received my mail for almost two months. I'd write and the post corporal would come round to collect the letters but where they went from there, we never knew. Then we heard that mail had been intercepted at Singapore where some lads were taking mail and dumping the rest. We didn't know how true this was but mail that I sent home was still arriving after I'd been discharged.

When you went in the Army, you were asked about joining up and that persisted until we knew we were going to Korea, then it was forgotten about. But at the end of our time in Korea, the regiment was supposed to be going back to Germany. There was no way I would have signed on to go to Germany. I hated the place. It wasn't until we were in transit camp going home that I found out the battalion was going to Hong Kong. If I'd known that, I would have signed on because I loved Hong Kong.

At the end of our time in Korea, we sailed from Pusang on the *Empire Orwell* which was a top class boat for a trooper. But we got off at Hong Kong because lads who'd been prisoners-of-war and were being repatriated weren't very happy with the conditions of their trooper. They were taken off their trooper at Hong Kong and put on the *Orwell* and we were put on the *Empire Pride*. We didn't mind as them lads deserved to be on the *Orwell*. The *Empire Pride* was a bit rough and ready like the *Devonshire* we went out on but because we were coming home, it was a great boat even though I did come down with malaria again.

We sailed into Liverpool but there was no crowds waiting when we came back. The difference was, when we went out to Korea, it was a full regiment that went. But there were lads coming home every week and when we returned, there were only about twenty Liverpool lads with us. From this area, the ones who came back on the *Empire Pride* were, Malcolm Hetherington (Carlisle), Jimmy Sinclair (Carlisle), Brian Laidlaw (Gilsland), George Fisher (Cleator Moor), Brian Gilmore (Harrington), Alf Price (Keswick) and John Twigg (Penrith). Of the two local lads who joined when I did and went to Korea, Sammy was killed out there and Colin was discharged with me but was later killed working out in Zambia.

At Liverpool, the lads from up here should have got straight on a train at Lime Street and come up to Carlisle. We didn't, we went with the rest of the lads we were with for something to eat. When we did arrive at Carlisle, the Military Police were waiting for us. They weren't very happy we hadn't been on the train we should have been on. They took us by wagon to Hadrian's Camp and told us there was nowt to eat because it was late. The Military Police did show us where the cookhouse was for our breakfast the next morning. That was a silly thing to do because we broke into the cookhouse and ate the food we saw cooking. Unfortunately it was the guards' supper so with being late to Carlisle and then breaking into the cookhouse, we got off on the wrong foot.

With being in Korea we had all this leave owing to us and were supposed to be sent on leave straight away. That didn't happen and we were at Carlisle for about three weeks because they said there was no money to pay us, which was a bloody lame excuse. The Army tried to make us blanco our webbing, clean our boots and stuff like that but we told them we had no money to buy polish. Then it was back to the story that they had no money to pay us, so we said we'd go home. Us lads stuck together and said we'd get home some way and they'd better have the guardhouse ready because we were going home.Oh, they threatened to do all sorts to us but as we stuck together, they decided to give us a rail warrant to get home and send our money later. We should have been demobbed on 15 November but because of all the leave owing, we weren't demobbed until 6 December.

'Mrs Stubbs, Mrs Sullivan and Mrs Thompson at the grave of their brother, Corporal Mooney from Whitehaven. Photgraph taken by Doug during their visit to Korea with the Korean Vets'

After being discharged from the Army, we should have been on reserve for five years. We went to weekend camps at Carlisle, over to Yorkshire for a fourteen day camp and another one in Wales. After we'd done that, the reserve stopped so we didn't do our five years.

It's hard to believe but the Korean Veterans' Association didn't start up for a long, long time after that war finished. I read in the *Lancashire Evening Post* that a chap from St Anne's was forming a branch for the veterans at Preston so I used to go down to their meetings. Then the Cumbrian branch started up, which I joined and we meet once a month.

Through the Association, I went back to Korea in 1985 and 1990. I hope to go back in 2000 because that's when the Korean side of our Association will finish backing us. You see, they have a Korean Veterans' Association in Korea and when we go over they subsidise a lot that we get. I mean, their hotels are out of this world. It's about ninety pounds a day for a room and five or six restaurants to each hotel. There's no way most of us could afford that. But because we're with the Korean Vets', you're subsidised and given tokens to have your meals in whichever restaurant in the hotels you want to go to.

'Reunion in Korea,
Jimmy Kitching on the left and Doug on the right'

You just couldn't imagine the changes to Korea. When I went back in 1985 I was a little bit apprehensive but the difference was unbelievable. It had been thirty two years since I'd been there when Seoul had been just a heap of bloody rubbish but now it's one of the finest cities in the world. I was in our hotel in Seoul one day, talking to somebody when this lad came up to me and said, 'Can I ask where you're from, mate?' I told him I was from Kendal and he said, 'Shake hands, I come from up the road at Garnett Bridge.' It was Jimmy Kitching and we'd been in the same class at school. Unknown to me, he'd done his National Service in Korea and then moved down to the Midlands to live. So meeting up with him in Korea, now that was unbelievable.

TWO

'You two are frae Cumberland'

John Slater, *Served in the Border Regiment 1955-1957*

I left Workington Technical College at sixteen and went to Hornflowa at Maryport as an apprentice in the development laboratories. At eighteen everybody got the official brown envelope for their call-up medical. That medical at Carlisle Castle was a bit like a *Carry On* film, really. There was a series of six doctors, one looked down your throat, another couple looked between your legs, another one looked up your backside and then you had to hit a jar to see if you wanted to become a fireman!

9. Deferment of Call-up

Certain students and apprentices and others in a position similar to apprentices may have their call-up deferred until the completion of their training. Information regarding such deferment is contained in leaflet N.L.11 which is handed to every man when he registers.

Men employed in certain coalmining occupations may also have their call-up deferred so long as they remain satisfactorily employed in one of those occupations. Similar arrangements have been introduced for the suspension of call-up of men who at the time of registration under the National Service Acts are employed as merchant seamen or as seagoing fishermen provided the latter are enrolled in the Royal Naval Reserve (Patrol Service).

The arrangements hitherto in force for the suspension of call-up of men in certain agricultural occupations have been discontinued. In future, men born in 1933 or later, who are employed in agriculture are regarded as available for call-up, and deferment will only be granted in an exceptional case where the man concerned is the only one, or one of two workers, employed on an agricultural holding, and his immediate withdrawal would cause serious difficulty and loss to food production.

Should a man whose call-up has been deferred or suspended by reason of his employment leave such employment before he attains the age of 26 years he will, if medically fit for service, become available for call-up under the National Service Acts. Further information may be obtained at any Local Office of the Ministry.

'From 'Information about National Service' leaflet'

Basically, that was it. They looked at your teeth and if your teeth were all right you were A1. Then of course, you were interviewed very quickly. They would ask, 'Would you be prepared to sign on for three years?' and 'Which arm of the forces would you like to be in?' A lot of people would ask for the RAF but I said, 'I want to go in the family regiment, the Border Regiment.' Their eyes lit up and they thought, 'Well, here's an idiot who actually wants to be an infantryman.'

You walked out of the castle gates with your National Service pass and could go in a pub and nobody could question your age. Basically, that little bit of cardboard was our pub pass. If you were ever questioned in pubs, which were a lot more strict in those days – and even more strict about where you sat – you could produce your National Service pass and never be refused a drink.

All apprentices would be deferred until twenty-one when you expected to be called up once you had finished your apprenticeship. If you were at university of course, that could take you up to twenty-six. But I decided to pack in my deferment and go in the Army at twenty. I was a little bit tired of going to night school at Whitehaven. It meant me travelling from Cockermouth to work at twenty-to-seven in a morning, then catching a bus at four-thirty after work at Maryport to go to Whitehaven. After college I returned via Maryport at ten o'clock at night and then on to Cockermouth. So I was arriving home at ten-thirty to eleven o'clock, two nights a week. Those were long days.

In the 1950's, it was inevitable that someone from every family or their relations had served in the forces. First World War people were in their sixties at that time and Second World War people would either be brothers or uncles. So you were always in contact with these two generations, people who had soldiered. My dad was born in 1902, which meant he was in his teens when the First World War finished. After the war finished, it was compulsory that you served in the Territorial Army. So Dad was in the local Border territorial battalion. In the Second World War he was in the Home Guard. Actually, I have his notebook from those days and it makes quite interesting reading.

My parents knew National Service had to be done, there was no avoiding it if you were A1. It was obviously upsetting to my mother because two of her brothers were killed in the First World War and a third one was seriously wounded and gassed. Other relations had a bad time in the Second World War. As it turned out, I was the only one who put on a uniform and came out unscathed but my mother wasn't to know that at the time. When the day came for me to go away, my father took a day off work, which he could ill afford, to put me on the train for Carlisle.

There was nobody from Cockermouth going to Carlisle Castle when I went in December 1955. But people from different firms in West Cumberland that I knew from apprentice days were already in training there. They would be 'passing out' about six weeks before us, so there were a lot of local people about. It was an interesting period as squads were always getting demobbed. They were arriving from Germany having got their two years in and you were sweating and bashing it out on the square thinking, 'Good grief, two years is a life time'.

The first person I met at the Castle was the Provo Sergeant, called Sergeant Hutchinson. He was an old soldier, an extremely old soldier, who had obviously been a pugilist in India, pre-war, and not to put a finer pint on it, wasn't on this planet. I think if you interviewed anybody else who'd come in contact with him, they would say exactly the same.

You were apprehensive in a sense, you didn't know what you were going to face at all. It was a completely new experience. It could be exciting I suppose but to some people it could be quite daunting. There was the apprehension on the first day, especially the usual carry-on, 'experience of and receiving kit for soldiers use of' and 'housewife.' The housewife was a nice little piece of daunting equipment for people who weren't used to sewing buttons on overcoats. That was your first job on your first night. You were given a handful of buttons and you had to sew them on. Later, we were rescheduled and put in the East Lancs Regiment. So we had to cut off the buttons and all the insignia, hand them all in and stitch on new buttons for the East Lancs. A week later we were back in the Border Regiment, had to cut the buttons off once more and re-sew all the Border ones back on. Thank God for that!

It's more than likely that ninety-per-cent of people had never slept communal unless they'd been in the scouts or something similar. You weren't allowed out for about three weeks. I think it's as near to being in prison as you can imagine at that age. Lights out, which the bugler played every night, was at eleven o'clock so if you wanted to read you had to read by torch. You were lying in bed with these stone-cold sheets and hairy blankets. And lying there, you could hear what would be the Flying Scot and the steam trains hurtling past, either coming from Glasgow or going to Glasgow. Carlisle in the fifties had a very,

very busy train station and there was always this constant noise of trains.

Of course, the next morning is extremely exciting because this is the first time you actually put your kit on. It starts with the rock-hard boots which you haven't started to polish yet, you've been so busy sewing buttons on to hold things up. There's your webbing belt of course, and just learning the technicalities of putting all these things together and putting them on right. Being December, it was pitch black, so we walked across to the canteen in a sensible group. The squaddies who had been in six weeks in front of us were quite organised by then, obviously knew exactly what they were doing and marched across.

Your first breakfast was interesting. As with all army meals, each one of them was interesting every day. Breakfast would be a full fry or possibly scrambled eggs. You were issued with your plate (porcelain) and your knife, fork, spoon and mug. The problem was that after you'd eaten, you had to return your knife, fork, spoon and mug to your locker in a very, very clean condition. That meant dipping them into a tank of boiling water, the same tank as everybody else used. The great secret, which you learnt very quickly was to scoff your food down, get to that tank before anybody else and get your utensils really clean. If you dropped your plate, that would cost you money and a lot of aggro to get a replacement. Lots of National Service people will have very deep and fond memories of those large galvanised tanks with absolutely screaming hot water, fat and grease.

Injections were given at the same time as another medical.So we were injected and inspected at the same time.Because most people were quite ill with injections, you weren't given duty but were kept lightly moving all the time. I suppose it was to pump the contents round the system. Anyway, if the National Health system gave everybody those injections, doctors' surgeries would be empty.

The routine started from there. How to march and how to halt. You were introduced to your rifle and anybody who'd never handled a Lee Enfield was quite shocked by the weight of it. Then we went through the process of taking guns to bits and putting them back together again. For anybody who wasn't country orientated and hadn't been near guns, it could be quite alarming. It got more alarming when it came to actually taking them on the range and starting to fire them.

There was a .22 range just outside the Castle gates on the green and all you basically did was learn siting of targets and then went on the open range where you first felt the kick of the 303 rifle. As you progressed, you went through the sub-machine gun, light machine gun, Bren gun along with the fascinating Mills hand grenade.

'John enjoying (?) a break'

We were also lectured on the history of the Border Regiment and were given a Free From Infections lecture. For that, the MO gave his talk, the Education Sergeant gave his talk and the Recruitment Officer gave his talk. They talked about everything bar what was happening in the world that you might get involved in.

I think it was after about five weeks of training we had Parents Day, when parents and sweethearts would come, get a meal with you and saw you training. The Army laid on training, marching and use of weapons for that. I remember my parents and wife-to-be came and by that stage I had a stripe on my uniform, which gave them quite a surprise. Actually, it was quite a surprise to me.

From my own experience later, the system for getting stripes relied on your platoon's corporal, sergeant and officer, who were taking you through those ten weeks. They would spot people with leadership potential and in the first three weeks of training, you got a lanyard, which meant you were a marked man. If you carried on all right, they would make you up to an unpaid lance corporal. They wouldn't say, 'Would you like to be one?', they'd just tell you that you were a lance corporal. So I passed out after ten weeks with this stripe on my arm.

After the passing out parade, you got your first leave. You went on fourteen days leave right after the parade. After that, you came back to the Castle for maybe a couple of days while kit was being sorted out and the movement orders for the squad to disembark by train from Carlisle en-route to Germany. The First Battalion was stationed at Gottingen in West Germany, which was obviously enjoyed by a lot of National Servicemen. It was a nice town and there was a lot of feedback from it.

My fate was obviously sealed as I'd already received movement orders before I passed out. I was going down to Brigade Headquarters at Formby on the NCO course, with a view to taking up the position as training NCO. It's always a great pity to see acquaintances who you'd chummed up with disappear. You don't know it at that time but you won't see them again till the day you get demobbed. But it's a big world, you have no control over the situation so you just had to go along with it.

To say Formby was a big camp was an understatement. It was a huge, massive camp and the training depot for the King's Regiment, which is the Liverpudlian Regiment so you can imagine the characters I came across. It was the Brigade Headquarters covering the Lancastrian Brigade, which in turn covered the regiments of the Lancashire Fusiliers, the King's, the King's Own, Borders, East Lancs and South Lancs. Formby was also the headquarters of the boy soldiers. These were young teenagers, around about fifteen or sixteen years old, who were aggressive little buggers to say the least. You had to watch them, you really had.

We were shown basic training and instructed on how to teach it. You had to make notes but the training manuals were part of army life. So if you were instructing on how to fire a rifle, the lesson was already laid out in the manual. Basically, the system was learning the lesson and being able to stand up and instruct and you were judged against the manual. Your ability to stick to the manual was the standard format of lecturing. I think what the Army discovered in me, or I discovered in myself was that I was capable of doing all that. I'd never before stood up anywhere and talked publicly. That was certainly brought out in me, there was no question about it and that held me in good esteem later in life.

Besides lecturing, we might also be given a task; maybe you had to take the morning drill parade. We were drilled by the Brigade RSM, who was a big Irish Guard SM and had been involved in the Victory Parade at the end of the war. He was the only guy I could hear across this huge square at Formby because it was so massive. As the camp was so big it was difficult to police and there were many, many escape routes for getting out of the place. Also, it was right next to the Southport, Liverpool railway line and therefore very easy to get down into Liverpool.

At that time it was quite difficult to get to West Cumberland when you had a pass. You just couldn't do it. But I was familiar with Manchester as we had some relations there so I'd stay with them. On a Saturday I'd get a train and go down to Liverpool then straight across to Manchester and come back on a Sunday evening. That was always a very interesting journey walking in uniform through Piccadilly at Manchester as all the girls of the street were extremely active then. You had exactly the same procedure with the street girls when you arrived at Liverpool to change stations. In those days you could walk through the streets of cities in uniform. I think it would be very rare that you got into any bother. Nobody bothered you at all, except for the street girls. I used to walk through the back streets of Liverpool and Manchester in uniform but in this day and age, you just wouldn't attempt it.

I would be at Formby for about a month to six weeks and then came back to Carlisle Castle where you were swept into the normal squad NCO. As a lance corporal you'd go with a corporal, sergeant and an officer who was over the two squads. An intake was already there when I arrived back, so I was just added onto the squad under a sergeant called Sergeant Saville. He was a memorable character to say the least. He'd fought in the Western Desert, landed in Sicily, fought all over the place in the last war and was as mad as a hatter.

It was very strange within such a short period of time to find myself on the other side of the system at Carlisle. Things had happened so quickly but I soon settled in. As I was on permanent staff I shifted from Ypres block to Arroya block where you only got your own bunk when you were a corporal, not a lance corporal. But you all mucked in together, even with PTI's.

Now, when I'd been conscripted, in PT every single day, there was no way I could touch my toes. No way. So I always got a lot of umpty off these PTI's. When I was on permanent staff, I remember asking the best PTI. 'Are there some people who can't touch their toes?' 'Oh yes,' he said, 'So why did you keep hitting me when I couldn't touch mine?' I wanted to know.

I knocked around with a local lad, a PTI who lived at Crosby Villa so we played tennis and badminton at nights. We had a lot more free time when a squad finished their training before the next intake but you obviously had other duties. Getting home was no problem. There was an exit of permanent staff from the Castle on a Friday night for the five o'clock train down to West Cumberland. We had a ticket scam going for that. Originally, when somebody went home on a weekend, they would buy a ticket and avoid handing in it or getting it torn. This ticket was passed on nightly and eventually there was a permanent set of tickets flying about for people to use. On a Monday morning we used to come up to Carlisle on the very first train. Bleary eyed, we all walked together down Castle Street and into the Castle, which in memory was always dark.

I was made up to a corporal by mid '56 and in August was sent to The School of Infantry at Hythe, outside Folkstone. I can remember two of us getting on a train at midnight. In them days these were steam trains with corridors and this one was quite full so I slept sitting up all the way down to London. I was carrying all my gear and what still amazes me, carrying my rifle and bayonet.

This was the first time I'd been further south than Manchester and fortunately, Ian Banks who I was travelling with had been to London and knew the underground system. This was a new experience for me and I didn't like the underground – only foxes and rats go down holes. When we arrived at Waterloo, we left all our kit except rifles in a locker and went onto the streets of London. Still carrying our rifles and bayonets we asked a policeman where we could get a cup of tea and a sandwich. This policeman said, 'You two are frae Cumberland' and it turned out he was Cumbrian. He came with us to a cafe and had a cup of tea with us before we continued to Folkstone.

The camp at Folkstone was based on a spider system with facilities, beautiful washrooms and showers, in the middle of the building. I was split up from my mate Ian, and walked into the billet that I'd been allocated to. Once inside, I opened the window, which overlooked the English Channel. The view was amazing and I could see big ships in the Channel and across to France.

My two companions who had beds on each side of mine were most interesting. They were both Nigerians, both well educated and talked perfect English. One was a huge feller, at least six feet four inches tall with tribal scars across his face. He had three wives back home, one he'd got for three goats and a wheel barrow. Later, they wanted me to transfer from the British to the Nigerian Army. There was no chance of that! Another three beds were occupied by Gurkhas, who to me, all seemed to have the same name. They were immaculate, really beautiful people.

Also in the billet was Jock, a sergeant in the Highland Light Infantry, a nutter of the first order but a great character. Jock had been brought up pre-war in the slums of Glasgow and was fascinating. It was the first time I'd ever met the traditional Scottish kilt that he wore. Every time we went out, I held his kilt while he wound himself into it. Jock never wore anything under his kilt, to the great hilarity of a lot of people. Especially when he was going upstairs on a bus or we were having a few jars together and he was sitting on a settee. I'll never forget him, Jock McLaine. Brilliant.

At first I felt extremely out of it because it was obvious I was the only National Serviceman there. It was also a huge cultural shock to me, meeting other people from all over the world who spoke understandable English. Other people had a problem with the accents of Jock and myself. The ongoing problem was people couldn't place me and thought I was Scottish, Irish or a Geordie. They couldn't make head nor tail of broad Cumbrian.

However, it was a very, very interesting course. We learnt to instruct on all infantry weapons from the revolver to the flame thrower, British machine guns, the three-inch mortars and anti-tank weapons. We were on the ranges firing at tanks, we fired at balloons going across ranges, we did night firing and how to run a range. Now, a rifle range is hard enough to run in the day light with an ordinary intake when you've got hooligans with guns. But in the middle of the night, with flares, it was quite something. Most of us never managed to hit anything but the Gurkhas hit everything.

Wednesday afternoons at Carlisle or any other camps I was on, was sports afternoon and it was the same at Folkstone. Hockey was always predominant in the Army and when at Carlisle it was really rough playing on the tarmac. But to play hockey with the Gurkhas was a totally new experience as they were all the equivalent of Pele with ball control. They fascinated me as they even played football in bare feet which brought a total new vista to my life.

At Hythe I was adopted by two guys in the SAS. One, Sergeant Eastwood was an expert parachutist into trees. That was his speciality. The other guy was full of steel plates. Obviously he hadn't been very good at parachuting into trees. I'd read about the SAS but never gave them any thought. I found they were very, very special people. They were regulars, with money far in excess of a corporal but they taught me a lot. It was their general attitude that I liked and they were very professional people. Even out socially, they were never in any trouble. If trouble was brewing, they were away. As far as weapons were concerned, they were superb.

Looking back on the course, it was the self discipline that I liked. Except for me, they were all senior NCO's and there was no regimentation, so I found that very good indeed. There was an influx of young professional soldiers who were very predominant and the older ones were getting re-educated. You see, at that time, the main weapon of infantry was changing. The automatic FM rifle had only been issued to one battalion in the UK and the Sten gun was being replaced by the Sterling hand-machine gun. There were various other pieces of new equipment and modifications to existing weaponry. Basically, we were learning how to instruct the instructors on these new weapons.

When the course finished, I came away with a C grade which, because of being a National Serviceman was received very well by the higher authority. Ian got a B grade which meant he was allowed to wear the insignia of cross rifles on his sleeve. So we went to a shop in London to buy these before returning to Carlisle.

At Carlisle, I was now in the delightful situation as corporal to my old Platoon Sergeant from when I'd first arrived for National Service. This Sergeant was RSM Cresswell, who was a professional soldier, an ex-Arnham veteran and always immaculately dressed. As we shared an interest in the history of the Border Reivers and pele towers, often in the evenings we borrowed a car and off to pele towers. And with now being a corporal I had my own bunk at the Castle. It was a delightful bunk back in Ypres block, right at the top, and had the finest view of Carlisle Castle and the Keep.

'On manoeuves at Otterburn

I carried on taking the odd regiment. We did a lot of training with them on the Bitts Park and Sheep Mount area. In the first ten weeks of training, we took them out on what we called a night patrol in the dark, wading through the River Caldew and Eden. The fitness level actually came very quick. We used to run the squad in boots and PT kit every morning. There was the quick march down by the river near Carr's biscuit factory, then up the road past the crematorium to the four roads ends where you'd turn and run back to the Castle. After that we'd start drill procedures and weapon training.

When instructing on how to throw live hand grenades, on numerous occasions I'd be standing next to a guy who'd already primed it, opened the pin too far, pulled it out and dropped it at his feet. I can remember picking up live grenades, lobbing them over the wall and pulling everybody down and listening for the grenade to go off. Then there's the alarming experience of a guy who primes a grenade wrong, goes through the stages, throws it on the tarmac or the badly cratered area and it doesn't go off. The procedure was, the sergeant and officer walked out with the plastic explosive, locate the grenade, laid the explosive next to it, cut and lit the fuse, and then walked back. You had to walk back but you certainly moved very quickly once you got parallel to the safety wall. Later in the course, the squad was introduced to the phosphorous grenade which is basically like a tin of Brasso and causes mayhem. Personally, I didn't like those.

In between squads, I was instructing NCO courses back down at Formby and other camps in the northern counties. On one occasion my squad and soldiers from other regiments were sent to Otterburn to take part in a war game. The opposing team had set up camp there and we were the terrorists who had to avoid capture at all costs. My patrol was designated to attack the other team but what we weren't told was that we'd be doing it in the middle of the night in one of the fiercest rain storms I've ever been in my life. We had to manoeuvre our way up the banks of a river into the battle area. Each man had to hold his mate in front because it was so dark and wet. We hit the camp about two-thirty in the morning and I think the occupants were a bit pissed off to say the least to be suddenly set upon by these hooligans and gorillas. However, for the young trainee National Servicemen, it gave them an inkling what they could be facing over the next two years. But when you think, Border Reivers used to sweep down from Scotland and across Otterburn on similar wet November nights. They must have been mad!

At the Castle we had a regimental day, Arroyo Day. Every year the Border Regiment and Battalion celebrated Arroyo Dos Molinos when the captured French drums from that battle were paraded. As it's a celebration day senior NCOs of the sergeants' mess always invite the officers' mess to a binge. Usually visitors of the Chelsea Pensioners arrive for the regimental weekend at the Castle. During my time there,

I was twice allocated to look after a Chelsea Pensioner, a very senior citizen, which was always a great privilege for me.

These Chelsea Pensioners would have been ex-Border Regiment so could have been from any of the thirteen battalions in the First World War. They were very interesting old chaps, obviously well trained and well versed in the art of knocking back pints – or shorts I should say. Our main task really was to make sure you picked these gentlemen up from the mess at the time they wanted to go to bed. So with their sticks and medals dangling, and various degrees of staggering, you'd get them to their bunks.

Now Ypres block where my bunk was, always had this traditional ghost situation associated with it. And there were quite a few of these visitors who would not go and sleep in Ypres block at all. They always asked for other accommodation. I had no bother at all with Ypres block and have slept in the whole of Carlisle Castle. I've paraded the wall, been in the nooks and crannies in the dark and never came across the Grey Lady or anything what-so-ever. However, at a later date when I had finished, the bunk I used was closed because it was unoccupiable. Presumably because of a poltergeist or spirit but it certainly had never bothered me.

I was made up to sergeant in early '57. It wasn't unknown for a National Serviceman to become a sergeant but it wasn't a regular thing. I know of others who were physical training instructors or engineers who were made up to sergeant but no-one from the infantry.

You never forget your own experience coming in to do National Service. It's full of the spectrum of human life of eighteen to mid-twenty year olds. And with instructing intakes, it was still the broad spectrum you would expect. They came to the Castle because that's where they'd been allocated to come. You see, that was the way it was. Numbers were made up in the squads that were still available and you could get allocated anywhere. So we had a few Scots, a few lads from Lancashire and a few from London besides all the local ones. One university student was from the Shetland Isles and of course, had very great difficulty getting home at weekends.

We could see the extremes of people from different walks of life. We had educated people as well as those less fortunate in life. The older ones who were coming back from college to complete their National Service would see it as a complete waste of time. If you think about it logically, as far as their careers were going, yes it was. But they hadn't any choice and just had to get on with it. That was the secret of National Service, just get on with it.

*'Outside the Officers' Mess at Carlisle Castle 1957.
Front row, 2nd right, Lennie Oughterson (Mossbay), 4th left, John,
5th left, CSM Small, 4th right, Sergeant Hewitson.
2nd row, 3rd left, Bobby Harper (Salterbeck)
3rd row, 3rd left Jackie Hull (Parton)*

On recapping, I now find it strange that I used to go and instruct at a local boys institute. It was probably a very good recruiting area for the Army and I used to go there and instruct them in arms, shooting and things like that. But you had to look after your cigarettes and lighters because they would nick anything would those lads. Later on some of them that I'd met came into my squad. Two of them were the best squad people ever to have because you didn't have to tell them to do anything. They were up at the crack of dawn, their boots and their faces shone. They were immaculate. These lads made real good soldiers because obviously they were used to that type of discipline.

You met other young fellers who were more than timid. They were in permanent shock and terror and needed culturing. That could be achieved by understanding their needs and leading them, rather than an old sergeant using the blunt end of a hammer to terrify people. I think I might have been the only sergeant never to have put anybody on a charge. There wasn't any need. There are other ways of doing things. I always remember one young guy in my squad, a young farm hand and a delightful chap. He'd probably never travelled further than Keswick or Cockermouth Fair and was probably still in shock after his third week at Carlisle and absolutely shaking. I helped him along his way quietly and nurtured his better points because he was an absolutely marvellous shot. That lad won the intake shooting competition which gave him great esteem and settled him down quite well.

My last squad was a delightful squad of people. One day working with them for their final parade, I got the distinct feeling that things weren't going right on the square. Then I realised that the problem was a coach load of Asian beauties had arrived and were distracting them. So I immediately marched the squad nose to nose with the beauties and gave them three minutes to chat them up. After that they looked a proper Guard's squad and put on a huge demonstration for the girls. It was totally unathordox and caused some remarks but the squad was delighted with it.

With Carlisle Castle being a public castle, everything had to be spick and span and therefore the first ten weeks of training were pretty horrific for everybody. But visitors to the Castle also added a nice little zest to life on passing out parades. They saw the colours flying, soldiers marching and the band playing. I remember once arriving home at Cockermouth and found my mother very distressed. A local school had been on a day trip to Carlisle Castle and one of the teachers had recognised me. She commented back home at Cockermouth what a horrible person I was on the square, which upset my mother who was rather sensitive. I had to explain to her that ninety-nine per-cent of instructing drill was purely acting.

I didn't stay on in the Army after I'd served my two years. I was very close to doing it but having served my time, for me, marriage was obviously the next step in life. And the one thing about the Army I didn't like was the married quarters which I had observed on my travels to various camps. That was not how I envisaged my life to be. So that's how it was, I left the Army and carried on with my normal West Cumbrian life.

However, for my very last parade, Uncle Ernie* came up from Manchester to the Castle and that was superb for me. He was my mother's brother, the one who'd been shot through the neck, gassed and had his thumb blown off during the First World War. Ernie was more than chuffed to say the least at being back at the Castle and had the day in the sergeants' mess.

'John's last parade. The smile says it all'

Later that day I returned to Cockermouth with Ernie. Though he had lived in Manchester for many years, he returned to Cockermouth every November so he could lay a wreath on the Cenotaph. This time I was with him and I lay the wreath wearing full regimental uniform. It had been Ernie's mother, my grandmother who laid the first British Legion wreath at Cockermouth Cenotaph's official opening in 1922.

After leaving the army I was on recall which lasted for six or seven years. However there was nothing to do and no annual camps to attend. In an emergency, because I was a specialist I would obviously have been one of the first to go and start instructing again. Years later I went to the Castle for a veterans' social night and that was really something. People seemed to recognise me and kept coming up to me. I presume they never forget their sergeant. That was really a nostalgic night. Occasionally people still stop me and say, 'You're Sergeant Slater?', even though I'm over sixty. You just can't remember them all and we're all a lot greyer now.

I think most people would say, yes, they enjoyed their National Service because they'd done it. But if you were able to go through a time warp and given a choice of doing or it not doing it, the majority of people would say, 'I don't want to do it.' A lot had bad experiences and others really enjoyed it. Now, you hear people say, 'Oh, all these young ones should be made to do National Service.' The last thing the Army now needs is National Service. They need professionals.

* *Sergeant Ernest Hetherington served in the 5th Battalion of the Border Regiment during the First World War. He was mobilised in August 1914 with 'D' Company in which he had served since 1908. He was in France two months after the outbreak of war and received severe wounds at Ypres in 1915. He ended his military service as Staff Sergeant at Military Hospital, Heaton Park, Manchester.*

Of Ernest Hetherington's two brothers:
Dixon also served in 'D' Company, 5th Battalion, The Border Regiment, and was killed (sniped) in action at the Battle of Loos, September 1915, six months after enlistment. Dixon was nineteen years old.
William Hetherington was killed in action at the Battle of Thiepval, 27th September 1916 after arriving from the Dardanelles with the 6th Battalion, The Border Regiment. William was twenty-three years old.

THREE

'Excused boots'

***John Sewell**, Served in the Royal Artillery 1953-1955*

MINISTRY OF LABOUR AND NATIONAL SERVICE

NATIONAL SERVICE ACTS

APPLICATIONS FOR DEFERMENT OF CALL-UP OF STUDENTS WISHING TO REMAIN IN FULL-TIME ATTENDANCE AT SCHOOL

1.—**A student wishing to remain at school until the end of the term in which he reaches the age of 18 years 3 months** should have Certificate A below completed by his Headmaster and present it to the Medical Board Clerk on attending for medical examination.

2.—**A student wishing to remain at school until the end of the school year in which he becomes 18 years of age to take or retake an external examination** should have Certificate B below completed by his Headmaster and present it to the Registration Clerk on attending for registration under the National Service Acts.

3.—**A student wishing to remain at school for a further year** (**i.e., until the end of the school year in which he becomes 19 years of age**), **or for part of that year, to take or retake an external examination,** should have Certificate B below completed by his Headmaster and send it to the Local Office, whose address appears on the reverse of his Registration Certificate (N.S.2), quoting the Registration number shown on that Certificate.

4.—Any application for extended deferment as in para. 3 should be sent to the Local Office not later than two weeks before the expiration of the period of deferment already granted. If a student wishes to await the result of an examination before making his application for extension of deferment, he should inform the Local Office by letter, stating the date he expects to hear the result. Unless a further letter or a completed Certificate B is received within seven days after the date on which notification of the examination results is expected, the Local Office will assume that the student does not desire further deferment and arrangements will be made for his call-up as soon as practicable after the expiration of his period of deferment.

5.—Deferment of call-up to take or retake an external examination cannot be extended beyond the end of the school year in which the student reaches 19 years of age.

6.—**A student wishing to remain at school until the end of the school year in which he becomes 18 years of age who is not sitting an external examination but:—**

(1) **has been provisionally accepted for a University or comparable course in the following October, or**

(2) **wishes to fit in his service with entry to a University or comparable course after completion of his whole-time National Service,**

should have Certificate C below completed by his Headmaster and hand it to the Registration Clerk on attending for registration under the National Service Acts.

N.S. 291.

Application for deferment

In the summer of '53 I was in the upper sixth form at Ulverston Grammar School doing my A levels and had a student deferment until 31 July. A place was promised to me at Chester College for teacher training and I thought, 'Shall I go to college first then maybe into the Education Corps in the Army?' On the basis that I was more likely to enjoy my two years at college than I was the two in the Army, I decided to do my National Service first and didn't apply for further deferment.

On 14 July 1953 I was called to Barham Barracks at Lancaster for my National Service X-rays. After that, it was down to the Majestic Buildings in Starch House Square, Preston on 19 August for a medical and again on 1 September for a second one. Then came the question of which service to go in. I'd been in the combined cadet force at school, first in the Army section and then the RAF one. The Recruiting Officer said, 'Sign on for a minimum of three years and you can go in the RAF.' I thanked him and said I'd do my two years like everybody else so he told me I'd go in the Army and which branch did I prefer. I'd always fancied driving a tank and said I'd prefer the Armoured Corps but was put in the artillery!

About a fortnight after my second medical I was called up to the 17 Training Regiment, Royal Artillery, Oswestry. Some of the chaps from the local youth club I attended had been called up prior to me and one of them gave me a tip. He said, 'Wear old clothes when you go in the Army. Your civvie stuff is taken off you after a couple of days, parcelled up and sent home. But staff have been known to go through it and fit themselves out with any really nice gear.' So for travelling down to Oswestry I wore a rather battered old brown suit, one of the early drip-dry shirts which when dried a couple of times went like rubber, a tatty green tie, and a pair of crepe soled, patterned, brown leather shoes, a type specifically forbidden for army wear. I thought, 'If I lose this lot, they'll be doing me a favour.' Little did I know how it was all going to turn out.

The camp at Oswestry was a collection of wooden huts. We were there for a fortnight and it was mainly designed to knock you into shape. I'd never really been away from home before on my own but met a chap called Bill Simpson from Calder Bridge, where I was born, who was in the same billet. The meals we had are now a blank. You see, you were used to rationing and when you went into the cookhouse, food was slapped onto your plate and you ate it. I'd got used to eating what was in front of me with having grown up through the war years. You just accepted it.

We were in our civvies for a couple of days then were issued with our uniform. First, you stripped down to the waist and they threw all this gear into your arms. Secondly, as you stepped through the door with all your gear, they wiped something onto your arm, then inoculated you. I have an intense fear of needles but discovered when one comes at you unawares, you're totally relaxed and it doesn't hurt. I though, 'I'll have to remember that for the next time I have an inoculation.'

Now, the uniforms you're given are your working outfit made of denim plus a best and second best khaki uniform. I was six feet, one inch tall but if you were my height you were supposed to have a forty inch chest and mine wasn't. I was tall and thin and apparently an awkward shape. The uniform hung on me like a sack so I had to have a best uniform tailored specially, which took weeks. Everybody was given a great coat but mine was a 1918 one. Normally, with a great coat, there's a pleat in the back which comes from below the collar to the waist-band and then starts again. I looked like a tent pole because my pleat just went from top to bottom and spread out. As one sergeant said, 'Sewell, you're the only bloke who could get two women into camp underneath there and nobody would know.'

Besides being issued with our uniform we did square bashing. One afternoon after we'd done some marching and drill our pay-books were taken off us. These were collected because we were going out to do some real training and the results would have to be recorded in the pay-books. We marched out then fell out for tests of elementary training in rifle, Sten and Bren. Now, this was a squad of about thirty people and there was only three or four rifles. The Bombardier said, 'Anybody know the stoppages on a Bren gun?' Foolishly I said I did and managed to take a gun to pieces but neither of us could put it back together. Somebody else had to do that for us. Then we marched back to the barracks, got our pay books and on them was stamped, 'Passed elementary training in rifle, Bren and Sten gun.' This proved to be typical of the standard of intensive training we received because of course, we were going to be artillery men. Had we been an infantry mob, it would have been a lot different.

On the second weekend in camp, we were allowed to go down to Oswestry in our best bib and tucker. As I didn't have a best uniform, I was allowed to go in my civvies and brothel creepers as those particular shoes were called. I remember getting to the main camp gate and thinking, 'Are they going to let me out?' But being in civvies I was mistaken for a member of staff and they just waved me through. I had to go round the corner and wait for my two mates who were being checked out by the guards to see if their uniform was correct. When they eventually came round the corner, they said, 'You lucky bugger, Sewell.'

After our fortnight at Oswestry we were transferred to various other places. I went over the road with two chaps to 17 Training Regiment, 53/19 Squad at Parkhall Camp. We were considered ORI's or Potential Officer Cadets. Some chaps there were from public schools and some were working class like myself who'd been to a grammar school. Others were from universities and had been deferred earlier and were now in their twenties. We all gelled together quite well and I think we took the attitude we were in a special squad only because the others didn't have the schooling.

'A typical barrack-room at Oswestry'

The father of Gunner Vinegrad, an Oxford student, had been an officer in the Tsarist Guard in Russia, spent some time in Siberia, then left and come to England. When the Revolution had broken out in 1917, Vinegrad's father had gone back to Russia full of fervour, took one look at what was happening then got the hell out of there with his family. He came back to England where his son was born a British subject and the family name anglicised from Vinegradoff to Vinegrad.

At one stage in our training we were trooped down to a cinema where a sergeant from the Intelligence Corps took us through the forms we'd have to fill in when applying for the chance of a commission. He said, 'Now, you're father's birth certificate. That doesn't mean we want a copy of it. We just want to know where it is, such as at your home address.' A voice from the back of the room said, 'Would 'lost in the Revolution' do, Sergeant?' The Sergeant looked canny and said, 'Name?' 'Vinegrad' was the reply. 'Anglicised from Vinegradoff?' enquired the Sergeant. 'Oh, how clever of you, Sergeant' said Gunner Vinegrad. Like me, he didn't get his commission.

Unfortunately, I still just had my denim uniform. In the barracks there'd be nineteen best uniforms hanging up in the locker along with my civvie suit. There were nineteen pairs of best boots and my brown brothel creepers. I was never quite sure whether Bombardier Fountain who was in charge of us regarded me as a curse or somebody to be protected.

There was also Staff Sergeant Walker who was quite a nice guy. When he came into our barracks and saw the expanse of floor we'd tried to scrub he said, 'Come of fellers, that's no good. Club together, buy two packets of Tide washing powder, throw a bucket of water on the floor and then the Tide. Use your yard brushes to sweep all this mass of foam in front of you then when you get to the loose floorboard near the door, sweep all of it under the floorboard.' That was a damn sight better than hacking away with the old scrubbing brush. Then we moved our bed-ends in line and lay our kit in the approved manner.

The scrubbing was done because there was going to be a CO's inspection. So I polished my brasses, got everything kitted up same as everybody else and folded my huge great coat as best I could in the approved manner. We were all out on marching drill when the CO's inspection took place. But we knew that when we returned to barracks, if your great coat was on your bed, you'd passed the inspection and if not, it would be hanging on the wall. When we returned, there were two great coats hanging up and one of them was mine. So I went up to Bombardier Fountain and said, 'Sorry Bombardier, what was the problem?' Without a word he took my great coat off the wall and threw it out of the window. Now, when the inspection took place, there was Bombardier Fountain, the Captain, the Lieutenant and the CO. And as our Bombardier banged the locker open with his stick, there were all these uniforms and my brown suit with drip-dry shirt and tatty tie, all these boots and my brown shoes. So the CO was asking, 'What's this? What's this?' only to be told each time, 'They're Gunner Sewell's, sir.' 'Who the hell is Gunner Sewell?' the CO wanted to know. At first they'd thought it was all Bombardier Fountain's kit and he'd found it very upsetting they'd all believed he would wear such gear.

'At Old Park Hall Camp. John is standing on the far right, still in his denim uniform'

After that we went on the Officers Selection Course. We had lectures and had to write an essay and prepare a short speech on some topic to demonstrate how we could analyse it. Being naive, I thought the thing to do would be to talk on some military topic. As I interested in tanks I prepared a short dissertation along the lines of comparing our superior tanks with the inferior ones of the Soviet block but how we would be swamped by their greater numbers. Having delivered this dissertation, from the questions the officer asked me, I realised he was a tank man and knew a damn sight more about the subject that I did. So I didn't get many points for my talk on armour.

Then came the practical tests where we were put into groups of six or seven and in turn each of us had a small problem to solve. In my case, I had to get my men and equipment across a river. Now, this river was entirely fictional, with a wooden platform marking the river bank, so many feet of open ground and then two wooden posts marking the opposite bank. Supposedly, half-way in the river were two trees with hanging branches and a rope dangling from each tree. The nearer rope could be reached if you got hold of each other and cantilevered one chap out to grab it. Then you would swing out on the first rope, grab the second one and swing back and finally swing across the river.

This all seemed straight forward enough except that your equipment was represented by a forty gallon oil drum full of stones which you also had to get across the river. One of the blokes eventually managed to swing across to the other side and swung the rope back to us. We just didn't quite catch it and all had to cantilever out again. Eventually we got the rope, tied the drum to it and let go. The weight of the drum stretched the rope down and it hit the ground meaning all our equipment was in the river. Somehow we got the equipment back and I thought, 'An arc. Swing the drum in an arc across the river and it'll stay above the ground.' So we swung it in an arc and it hurtled towards Duggan on the other side who was standing there with his arms stretched out to catch it. I think that was the part where I got my only good point as I shouted, 'GET DOWN' and probably saved Duggan's life. This huge forty gallon oil drum filled with stones hurtled towards his head, zoomed back to us and we all jumped out of the way. I still have and can show you the form which says, 'Not recommended for officer training.'

The final morning we did an assault course and were in competition with the TA chaps who knew the course backwards. It was the usual thing, you crawl through tunnels, swing across gaps on a rope and so on. There was also a tall timber fence made up of logs which must have been at least ten feet high. We decided to have somebody lying on the top of the fence so that he'd give the rest of us a hand up. We picked Cyril, the lightest guy, cupped our hands for him to stand on, went 'One, two, three' and threw him up. Unfortunately we tried too hard and most of him went right over the top but his left foot didn't quite make it. His foot caught on our side of the fence which acted like a hook, slamming him upside down against the other side. We heard this terrible scream and thud so we ran round the other side of the fence where this guy lay in a heap. Instead of sympathy, some guy turned to me and said, 'Not quite the same effort next time, Sewell'.

After that we did our five mile route march in an hour with full kit and I ended up with blisters on my toes. The following morning I was on fatigues in the cookhouse all day washing and scraping pans. When I got back to the barracks that night my feet were like hot irons. I took my boots off and one foot just ballooned out. I had a poisoned foot like nobody's business and that meant I had to report sick the next morning. Now, you've got to be a fit man to report sick because you've got all your kit to take to the stores so nobody could pinch it while you're away. I hobbled to the Medical Reception Centre using my rifle as a crutch while two mates carried my gear to the store. My foot was looked at and it was, 'Right, seven days in the Medical Reception Centre.' I ended up lying in a bed with nice, clean sheets having penicillin jabbed into me and missing our training right in the middle of the twelve week's session.

To receive our pay we walked to another building, went up three steps into the corridor and then turned left to face the Pay Officer. The Officer sat at his table facing the doorway with the Sergeant standing behind him. Well, I had come out of the MRC and was standing in the queue wearing my denims, hat and brown pattered leather shoes instead of the regulation boots when Bombardier Fountain comes along and says, 'You're not going to salute an officer in that condition. Take your hat off.'

Now, the Pay Officer calls out a person's name. He hears the crash, crash from the soldier's boots as he come up the stairs, then boom as he comes to attention and salutes. But when he called out, 'Gunner Sewell', he heard, shuffle, shuffle, bump and there's no salute. He looked up and saw this apparition which was me and then he looked down and saw the shoes. I'm not joking, the Pay Officer opened his mouth twice before a sound came out and then he said, 'Where did you get those shoes?' I honestly can remember that it shot through my mind that if I said, 'Wilson's Shoe Shop, Tudor Square, Dalton-in-Furness' that I wouldn't see day-light for a long time. Well, he wasn't for paying me even when I produced my chitty which said, 'Excused boots.' The Pay Sergeant said, 'This is Gunner Sewell, sir. You have to pay him.' So somewhat grudgingly he parted with ten shillings while the rest of the squad were standing cross legged in the corridor trying not to laugh.

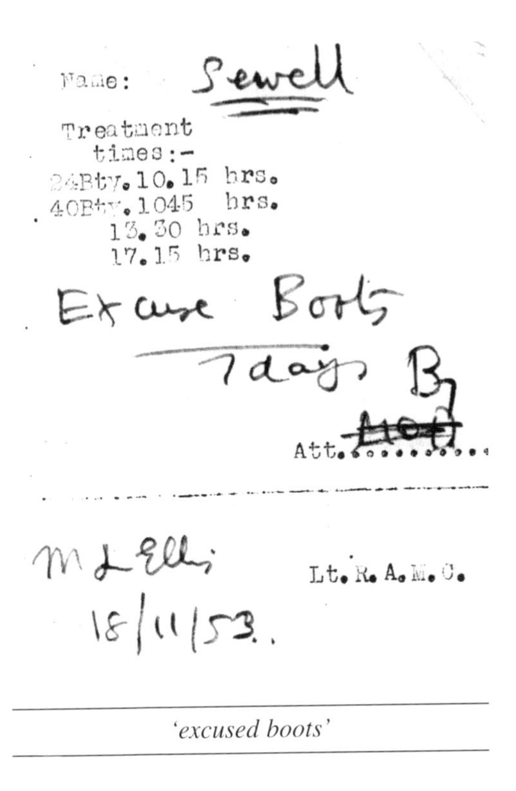

Name: Sewell

Treatment
times:-
24Bty. 10.15 hrs.
40Bty. 1045 hrs.
13.30 hrs.
17.15 hrs.

Excuse Boots
7 days By

Att. ....

M L Ellis Lt. R.A.M.C.
18/11/53.

'excused boots'

Coming out of MRC I'd been given the chit which said 'Excused boots for seven days.' The rest of the guys were doing gun drill with a twenty-five pounder. Previously I'd been number two, sight-setting and doing the fuses but I was still in my denims and wearing shoes. Now, the Army wasn't going to risk me dropping the trail of a twenty-five pounder on my toes and having to pay me a pension for the rest of my life. So I had to stand in the gun sheds watching the others doing their drill which put me even further behind. Then came the day I was signed off and could wear my second best boots. We were still on gun drill and I was determined not to let the lads down because the final passing out parade was nearly upon us.

Everything was lined up and it was, 'Stand by your guns.' We rushed to the guns but found our limber was slightly cock-eyed to the trail and the release clips were stuck. To save time I said, 'We won't mess around, we'll just yank it' which we did. The muzzle of the gun smacked into the parade ground as the trail shot past the point of balance and up in the air with me and another chap hanging on the end of it. From the ground below came a bellow from the Sergeant, 'Sewell, PUT THAT GUN DOWN.'

When it came to the morning of the passing out parade, we scrubbed the barrack-room floor as usual, got everything squared up, had our kit organised and I'd even beaten my great coat into some semblance of order. The Sergeant came in and said, 'Right, 5319A Squad is going to win the passing out parade. Gunner Sewell, report sick.' I told him there was nothing wrong with me but he answered, 'Find something lad, find something. Use your initiative.' 'Well' I said, 'There's still a blister on one of my toes.' 'Right' the Sergeant told me, 'that'll do but don't take your kit into store, leave it here.'

Off I wandered to the Medical Centre and sat in the hut letting everybody go in front of me because I didn't really want to see the MO. I sat there until the parade was over and slipped out to join the crowd while they waited for the results. Then a great cheer went up, 5319A squad were the champion squad and they were all going to celebrate. As I turned to walk away, three of the guys came up to me and said, 'Come on.' 'But I didn't do anything to help you win' I told them. 'Yes you did,' they said, 'You weren't on parade.' So off I was whipped along with the rest of the squad for a celebratory drink.

'A typical passing out parade at Old Park Hall Camp'

On the night of the passing out parade, the gunners of F Troop had gone out and got drunk. While they were out, the squad across from them had gone into F Troop's barracks and dismantled everything. They'd taken out the light bulbs, stacked the bed ends, bed springs and small packs all in different corners. F Troop had come stumbling back in the dark, couldn't switch a light on or find their beds. Some of them slept on the floor, some had found a mattress and dragged that out to sleep on and some had been sick. So the next day they were in a bolshy mood trying to find out who'd played the trick on them.

The following night F Troop stormed the block of the chaps who'd dismantled their barracks and were going to tear them apart. They hurtled in, tipped over the first two beds and started chucking mattresses about. The guilty blokes acted dead cool and instead of trying to defend their barracks, said, 'What the devil's going on? What's the matter?' The lack of opposition made these fellers stop and say, 'You did our room over so we're going to do yours.' 'No, no, it wasn't us,' was the reply, 'It was that snooty officer cadet lot that did it' and convinced the gunner section it had been us.

At that time most of our barracks were still out celebrating but a few of us were still in. Ted, a university chap was strolling towards the door with his towel over his shoulder and shaving kit in his hand, going for a bath and shave. He got to the door, opened it and turned to us, saying, 'Gentlemen, we're about to have visitors. GET THE LOCKER AGAINST THE DOOR.' We leapt to it as this lot of gunners came rampaging down the corridor. Outside the door there was a fire point with buckets of water, buckets of sand, a hose and stirrup pumps. Well, those were vulnerable. The gunners grabbed the water and went running round the outside of the hut. We locked the door and got all our windows shut. One feller was lying on his bed and there was a tiny window open above him. 'Oh,' he said, 'Nobody can get in through there.' He was right but a bucket of water could and did. It poured all over him and his bed. We were all safe but in the morning myself along with two other fellers had to clean up the fire point in the corridor. There was sand and water everywhere, along with the hose.

We had more injections at camp after our passing out parade. From my experience at Oswestry I'd thought if you're totally relaxed it didn't hurt. But how can you be relaxed when you know you're going to get an injection? The rest of the squad knew I was nervous, so of course it was, 'Oh Sewell will faint, that's what's going to happen.' A batch of us at a time went into a hut for our jabs and the feller in front of me was a big, broad-shouldered chap and at least two inches taller than me. When the doctor went up to this chap and stuck a big needle in his arm, the chap just keeled over and hit the floor with a crash. Unfortunately, the needle which was still in his arm snapped. 'Damn,' said the doctor and pulled the broken end of the needle from the bloke's arm who was being carried out by six other guys. Then the doctor started fitting a new needle and refilling his syringe. By the time he turned to me, I was totally petrified. Having turned to stone, I didn't feel a thing and walked out of the hut like a zombie much to the amazement of the rest of the squad who thought it had been me who'd fainted.

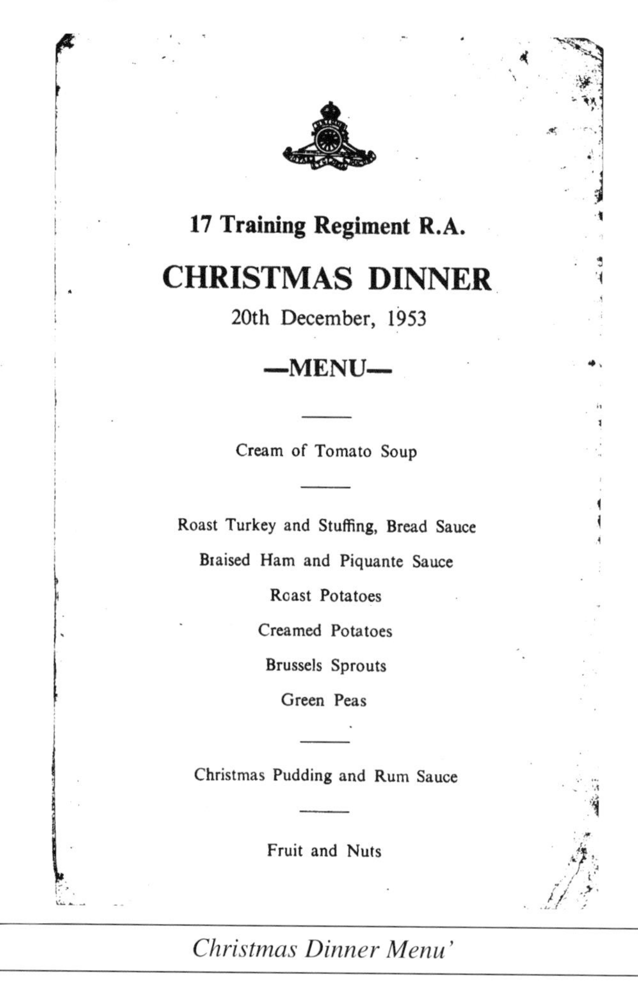

17 Training Regiment R.A.

CHRISTMAS DINNER

20th December, 1953

—MENU—

Cream of Tomato Soup

Roast Turkey and Stuffing, Bread Sauce
Braised Ham and Piquante Sauce
Roast Potatoes
Creamed Potatoes
Brussels Sprouts
Green Peas

Christmas Pudding and Rum Sauce

Fruit and Nuts

Christmas Dinner Menu'

Our postings had come through by this time and I was sent on a clerks course at Woolwich. I arrived there on 22 December 1953 when it was snowing and blowing a gale. There were only three of us in a four bedded section. That night, after taking off our battle dress blouse and boots, we put on our pyjamas and another pair of socks over the rest of our kit, then plundered the fourth bed for extra blankets before we got into our bunks. Rumour had it that we were going home on Christmas leave but we were on guard duty the following night. I remember trudging round with my rifle listening to a lone piper practising the bagpipes at two in the morning and thinking, 'I wonder why nobody's murdered him yet?' The next day I did get Christmas leave and arrived home at Dalton late on Christmas Eve.

On returning to Woolwich Barracks I started the clerks course and in theory we learnt the work of a regimental office. We had to learn how to file, prepare signals, amend Army orders and do routine office work. We were given big sheets of instructions on what we had to learn, most of which I still haven't read. Finally I passed the typing exam with the fantastic speed of fifteen words a minute which was the Army maximum. At the end of the course I was told, 'You have two choices of where you want to go but don't bother saying England.' As I had been trained on twenty-five pounders I volunteered for either Hong Kong or Germany, so it was inevitable that I was posted to a heavy aircraft battery in Egypt!

I got embarkation leave and then reported to Gooch Street at London. That was part of the unfinished section of the underground and we were sleeping in bunks in the tube tunnels. From there we went to Stanstead Airport where we flew to Malta and then on to Egypt. We landed at Fayid Airport in the Canal zone and on the run-down to the 71st Ack-Ack Regiment we passed what looked to me like one of those abandoned Mexican villages in western films. What I honestly thought were cattle pens I later discovered were where the Egyptians lived. The word poverty took on a totally new meaning to me.

Fayid camp was on the west side of the main road. We were in tents but there were walls and roof girders of the half-built NAAFI and Officers Mess to the north of us. Let's face it, the building wasn't finished because it was 1954 and the British were thinking of pulling out of the country. We were signing peace treaties with the Egyptians who were officially friendly. The Egyptians who were still unfriendly occasionally used to set up a Bren gun on the nearby railway embankment to fire at the girders. Bullets that hit the girders sprayed out in all directions and sometimes hurt somebody. One night there was a rattle of firing as we lay on our beds and I saw two holes appear in the tent roof as bullets ripped through it.

Our Battery Sergeant Major was Big Joe Orwell and he was tough but fair. I asked him, 'How do you feel about National Servicemen, sir?' 'You're a bloody nuisance,' he replied. Persevering, I said, 'I know what you mean. You get a new batch in every fortnight and by the time you get us into shape as soldiers, we disappear back into civvy street.' 'Yeh,' he agreed, 'although I don't think you'll make it!'

Of course being new boys it appeared we couldn't march properly and guard duty in England had consisted of carrying a pick-handle in case the IRA attacked. So we were trained in what was needed for an active service role. The sergeant who was training us said, 'Right, no pick-handles here. It's rifle, real ammunition, full gear and proper service conditions. The Egyptians are still a bit unfriendly so we're not taking any chances.' For two evenings we turned up for marching drill but on the third night our sergeant wasn't there and his replacement came along. He asked, 'What did the other sergeant tell you?' then gave us ten minutes arms drill before saying, 'Bugger off.' And that was the end of our course of training in how to handle ourselves in an active service zone.

Once in the battery office, I was instructed in my duties as filing and despatch clerk. Within a week or two we went into the desert in a three-ton truck and with 3.7 inch anti-aircraft guns on the one and only practise camp I was ever involved with. We were practising just in case the Russians came down through Syria, Palestine and across the Canal, which of course people were worried about in 1954. However, I learnt that although it's supposed to be very hot in Egypt, in March the temperature falls at night to almost freezing. So the trick of sleeping in the back of a three-tonner is to put three blankets on the steel floor and sleep with one over you and wear your uniform so that you don't freeze. I also learnt that shaving at night puts you on a charge of being unshaven on next morning's parade.

Back at camp I was duty clerk one night and sleeping quietly on the bunk in the back room when I was awoken by shots and then a hammering on the door. It was Battery Sergeant Major Orwell. As shots had been fired at a nearby camp he was turning out the IS (Internal Security) pickets and I was ordered to ring and inform the

Battery Major. After instructing me to stand by the phone in case they had to report in, the IS roared off into the darkness in a Land Rover with machine guns on the front. Next day I found out what had happened. An officer going round a nearby camp decided to test the reaction of the guard to a sudden emergency and ordered a sentry to fire some rounds into the eaves of the store house. This action of course had echoed all around and thinking the place was under attack, the usual procedure was put into place. IS pickets at neighbouring camps had turned out in force to re-enforce the camp believed to be under attack. I suspect there'd be a very chastened officer having a sharp, unpleasant interview with his CO for his impromptu methods.

'Soldiers of the Queen 'clean up'
the situation at Fayid, Egypt 1954'
(John is standing on the left. Behind both men is their tent, with beds visible to the left & right of them.)

Further along the road from our camp was Kensington Village, which was the married-quarters area for British families. The previous day a guard had been patrolling on the streets at Kensington and seen a large furniture van pull up outside a major's house. Egyptians had tumbled out of the van, smiled and waved at the guard, shouting 'Hello Johnny,' as they all called us. Into the Major's house had gone the Egyptians, loaded the furniture into the removal van and driven off with the guard assuming this was perfectly all right. When the major returned home he found the entire contents of his house had been stolen and the guard was, not surprisingly put on a charge. Several other people who allegedly hadn't instructed the guard properly were also in the dog house.

The following day we were on parade and were going to do guard at Kensington Village. Big Joe Orwell told us the tale of the previous day, ending with, 'AND if any of you blunder like that, may the Lord have mercy on your soul because I won't.' It was made clear to us that any bo-boos would incur the wrath of hell. We were duly driven to Kensington where we were paraded and our duties explained. Myself and a friend were detailed to guard the NAAFI.

In front of the NAAFI was a bus stop where several of the wives and children were standing. British women were a rare sight of course and I looked at them with interest. Now, the first thing my mate and I had to do was fix bayonets. I watched to see what my mate Bill was doing and he was watching me so we were standing there trying to get these damn bayonets fixed. Suddenly, my bayonet clicked and Bill eventually managed to fix his. It was fortunate for us that we had our backs to the ladies and children so they weren't upset and worried by seeing our standard of bayonet practise. Then we proudly shouldered our arms and walked around as if we knew what we were doing.

For guard duty we were kitted out with our rifles and five rounds in the magazine and forty-five more in a bandolier. At night we would also have a live round ready up the spout but with the safety catch on. On our left side was slung a large square box with three green and three red cartridges. On the right side there was another pouch containing a Very pistol which took two hands to break open. But when opening the pistol, you hadn't to put your rifle down so you'd undo the rifle sling and fasten it to your wrist. You'd have a whistle around your neck and a bike lamp clipped to your belt. If you were fool enough to switch the torch on to see if somebody is coming, he's got a perfect mark to aim for at your stomach.

The drill was, if you were patrolling and heard shots, you broke open your pistol and in the dark, pick out a green flare which you fired to indicate you were OK. If you were fired on by a single shot, you blew your whistle to summon assistance. But if you were fired on by automatic fire, you fired a red flare. All this was done so that from the guard commander's position, he could see all round the perimeter to where the trouble was. In actual fact, what it really meant was, they looked for green flares and where there was a gap in the flares, you were already dead or still lying on the ground fumbling around with these damn flares. To challenge anyone, was to shout, 'Halt, stanna, (which is Arabic for halt), who goes there? Halt, stanna or I fire.'

When you did guard duty, it was two hours on, then four hours off. So me and my mate plodded around until it began to get dark and then we were relieved. We went to the barrack block, lay down for four hours on our bunks and then back on duty but this time in the dark. I was carrying my rifle in the port position and walking towards a corner when I heard a foot-fall behind me. It flashes through your mind that you must have imagined it. So I did a check step not putting my left foot down and I definitely heard this foot-fall behind me. 'There is somebody behind me,' I thought, 'I hope it's not my mate playing silly beggars. No, it can't be.' Then I realised that could have been the last thought of many a sentry who was stabbed in the back. So feeling I didn't want to make a melodramatic fool of myself, I carefully pushed the rifle safety-catch, stepped to the corner and dropped down into a crouch and whipped around almost bayoneting a little dog that had been following me. The dog panicked, raced past me and the cat it had been stalking in front which I hadn't seen, shot down a back alley and to the dustbins. The dog crashed into the dustbins, which all went flying and created a heck of a noise. My mate heard all this, he dropped down into a half crouch and was shouting, 'Is that you, John?' I'm shouting back, 'Is that you, Bill? Everything is all right, it was only a dog and a cat. Don't fire, I'm coming round the corner now.' Oh boy, did I breathe a sigh of relief.

The second night I was on duty with the aid of a Sudanese soldier who was a huge, coal black Negro. He seemed a foot taller than me and was a big, broad feller. My great coat would have fitted him beautifully. 'Hello Johnny,' he said. He was my Arabic interpreter who spoke a smattering of English. We were walking along by the wire doing our beat and we could hear a radio giving the news about a mutiny in the Sudanese Defence Force in the Sudan where some British officers had been held hostage. It went on to say that a couple of officers had been wounded in the skirmish and the British were flying in troops to quell the mutiny on behalf of the newly independent Sudanese government. And all the time we were listening to this I was conscious of me guarding a British installation in a semi-hostile Egypt with a Sudanese. I looked at this feller to see how much he'd understood of the radio and he said, 'Oh, those were bad men, Johnny. Me, good man.' I thought, 'I'll take your word for it, mate.' Then we heard a couple of shots and I asked, 'Where did they come from?' He answered, 'I think that-a-way, Johnny.' 'They didn't come near us, did they?' I asked anxiously. 'Oh no, Johnny,' I was told. I thought about all the paraphernalia we would have had to go through with the pistol and then the flares and said, 'We didn't hear a thing,' to which my Sudanese friend answered, 'No, Johnny.'

We continued with our patrol and along the road came Captain Pickles, the Quartermaster in a Land Rover checking the guard. Now, I'd never challenged anybody before. I'd been told what to do but given no demonstration and unfortunately allowed Captain Pickles to get too near to me. I stood there saying, 'Halt, who goes there,' going through all the drill and feeling a right nerd as I could see perfectly well who it was. Captain Pickles was shouting, 'Useless, I'm far too near you. You should never have let me get this near. You'll hear about this in the morning. What's your name?' 'Now I'm for it,' I thought.

The next morning Captain Bates is there as Big Joe pulls me to attention and inspects my kit. He says, 'What happened last night? You have been reported to Captain Bates.'

'I let Captain Pickles get far too close to me because I had no idea what to do.'

'What do you mean? You got some training when you came here.'

'Yes sir, but we only did two nights marching drill and some arms drill before the Sergeant-in-Charge was called away.'

The Captain looked at Big Joe who said, 'Gunner Sewell is correct, sir.'

I was then asked if I received training in England and I told them about the passbook episode. Captain Bates turned to Big Joe and said, 'I'll leave it to you, Sergeant Major.' In turn Big Joe told me, 'You know better now, don't you? Lucky for you Captain Bates is a reasonable man.'

That night I'm on guard duty with my Sudanese friend and there's an officer coming along the road with a lady. So when he was a good hundred yards away I shouted, 'Halt, stanna, who goes there?' 'Er, excuse me, Gunner,' said the Officer, ushering the lady over the road, 'What do you mean challenging me?' 'Sir, you are between the road and the fence,' I said, 'I didn't challenge the Inspecting Officer correctly last night. I don't want to make the same mistake again, sir.' So muttering away, off went the Officer. I turned around and the Sudanese was grinning all over his face. 'Good, Johnny, good,' he told me, 'That lady was not his wife.' I felt better after that. I'd learnt something.

One day Big Joe come up to me and said, 'Sewell, you're going to get posted. They want a despatch clerk up at Headquarters so I've recommended you.' Off I went with another two fellers to my new posting at 2 AGRA (2nd Army Group Royal Artillery). This was at Tyne Camp on the road just above Timsah Lake in sight of the Canal. At 2 AGRA there were some permanent buildings and what were called canal cottages. Myself and three others, Les, Pinkie and Johnny shared one of these cottages.

'Canal Cottages, Tyne Camp, Timsah'

I was installed as despatch clerk in the offices and reported for duty at half-past-seven every morning. We knocked off at half-past-twelve to one o'clock and the rest of the day was ours. We had no guard duties and only paraded once a week for our pay. I hadn't been there long when I fancied going out of camp but you couldn't do that without an armed escort. I was told, 'If you want to get out, volunteer for something.'

'Hard at it' as despatch clerk at 2 AGRA 1954'

Jonah Jones who was a driver came into our tent one day and said, 'Major Carr wants someone to go down to the officers' club so we want an escort.' I volunteered and was told to go down to the armoury and draw out a Sten gun. So, armed, off I went in the back of a fifteen hundred-weight truck, with Major Carr sitting in the front beside

Driver Jones. Now the Sten gun is a handy little gun but if you don't look after them properly they tend to go off by themselves. That was why the rule was to remove the magazine on entering the gate at the officers' club at Ismailia.

We drove along the south bank of the Sweetwater Canal then in through the gate into the compound of the officers' club. Once in the car-park the Major went away and Jonah said, 'I'm going for a cup of char. You look after the vehicle.' I'd forgotten to take the magazine off the gun and was sitting looking around. Suddenly I realised that I'd cocked the action of the Sten gun which was between my knees. I thought if I squeezed the trigger I could catch the bolt with my left hand as I was concerned about not damaging the firing pin. But as I moved my hand I saw the magazine sticking out and made a futile attempt to unclip it. The next thing I knew, the machine gun was firing away nine rounds up into the air, straight in front of my face.

All hell broke loose. The siren went off, squaddies tumbled out of the guard room and ran across the parade ground. I could hear, 'Number One pit ready, sir,' 'Number Two pit ready, sir,' as they whipped the covers off their Bren guns wondering where the Egyptians were who were shooting up the place. And I'm sitting there thinking of the punishment camp at Tel-El-Kebir where people were up at the crack of dawn with a full pack of stones running around the perimeter track. You really do say 'Oh Mother' at a time like that.

Then the Sergeant Major came over shouting, 'WHAT DID YOU DO?' I replied, 'Accidental discharge of the machine gun, Sergeant Major.' I won't go into what he said but it did cover my ancestry for quite a few generations back. Then Jonah and Major Carr turned up and I thought they would nail me to the gate there and then. Though Major Carr hardly knew me, he stuck up for a man out of his own unit and said, 'Prepare a charge sheet but we will deal with him.' The charge sheet was signed by a lieutenant, a captain and a major. It was quite something, really.

Before leaving for our own camp, Major Carr said, 'Leave the magazine off, Sewell.' They let me keep the gun as it looked better if the Egyptians thought they had an armed escort. But Major Carr and Jonah felt safer with me having no bullets than worrying about any Egyptians who might be nasty. On reaching our camp, the Sergeant Major of the signals unit who was in charge of discipline was waiting for me. That march towards him was one of the longest of my life. He asked if the gun was loaded and I assured him it wasn't and was told to cock the action and give the gun to him, which I did. The Sergeant Major banged the butt on the ground causing the action to jump forward. Actually, he banged it so hard I was surprised he didn't bend it. The Sergeant Major looked at me straight faced and said, 'This weapon is faulty.' 'If you say so, Sergeant Major,' seemed the only appropriate reply.

'Some of the drawings which helped to win the Best Kept Canal Cottage competition

The next morning it was, 'left, right, left, right, prisoner and escort, shun,' and I was in front of Major Carr. He gave me a telling off about how dangerous the situation had been and that I might have killed myself. The Sergeant Major from the signals regiment was standing there and gave his evidence, including 'I examined the weapon and found it faulty, sir.' I was given seven days confined to barracks, then marched out of the room still a bit bewildered. But that's the Army, they look after their own.

While I was at Headquarters, the officers called us together and said, 'We've decided to smarten the camp up. We're going to hold a series of camp inspections every Sunday morning for a month. At the end of the month, we're going to award a prize to the best kept canal cottage.' Well, of course, what we all wanted to now was, 'What about our pin-ups, sir.' We were told, 'Oh well, we hope you'll keep them up and see that they look presentable and the standard of decoration will be taken into consideration.' Now lots of tents had pin-ups and I went to one tent that had a wooden arch like a shrine in one corner. Behind the arch were pictures of a particularly lithesome lady somewhat scantily dressed. Our cottage decided to make an effort and do something different so we didn't have photos of pin-ups, we drew our own. When the officers came round to judge they said, 'There are some interesting displays but we think that the personal effort put into the competition by one particular cottage is well worth the prize.' So our cottage won a crate of beer. I wasn't a hard drinking man but it was nice to win a prize for once.

'At the Arizona Cafe, Fayid, November 1954.
John (right) has a last drink with Ted Bamford (left) who off to Fayid Airport and then demob'

Life as a despatch clerk in 2 AGRA, a pleasant and easy-going camp was coming to an end. The Canal zone garrison was being wound down, units disbanded, people started to leave and we were burning files. One mate, Ted, was due to go home so a few of us went in a Land Rover to take him down to Fayid airport. On the road down to the airport we stopped at the Arizona Cafe, a small concrete building with a little veranda and two palm trees. It was there we saw one of the exotic ladies of the East, who every soldier hears tales about. This was the exotic Peg-leg Annie. She was grey haired, smoked a pipe and had a wooden leg. Images of the Arabian Nights? Forget it!

As our camp was being wound down, the roofs from our camp cottages were stripped and we ended up kipping down on our mattresses in corners of permanent buildings. Thinking that our camp was almost deserted, an enterprising Egyptian began stealing the angle irons out of the camp fence which slowly started to collapse. So Gunner Baker, the best shot in our group was placed in a little corner to keep an eye on the fence. One morning I heard the flurry of shots. Baker had put several shots over the Egyptian's head who was now lying flat on the ground clutching an angle iron. When the shots stopped, the Egyptian bounced up and ran off. Following him was our Land Rover which had two machine guns on the front and our sergeant inside shouting, 'Halt, stenna.' The terrified chap fell on his knees still clutching his angle iron and was arrested. I think at first the chap thought we'd massacre him straight away when we got him to the guard room. But when everybody went to have a look at him and offered him cigarettes and chocolate, he realised everything was all right.

Unfortunately we had to ring up the Egyptian police about the incident and they came along and started knocking the prisoner about. Our guard commander, holding his rifle, ordered them to cut it out. If he'd had his way he would have let the Egyptian go instead of letting him be hauled off by the Egyptian police. Seeing how they treated a prisoner, we were almost sorry we caught him.

One Friday myself and two other staff, Ginger and Pinkie were called into Major Carr's office. He said, 'We are going to promote all three of you to lance bombardiers so that when you are posted to a new unit, you may be able to keep your stripe.' The next morning our promotions to lance bombardiers, local acting, unpaid, duly appeared on battery orders. On the Sunday Major Carr received a request from

49 Field Regiment in Cyprus for two office clerks. He told us about this and said, 'Before saying anything, I suggest you look up the unit movement file.' The file told us that the 49th were due home to Blighty in January. As Ginger had only a few months of his National Service left to do, he preferred to stay put so Pinkie and I promptly volunteered for Cyprus. As our transfers were as gunners, our brief promotions were duly rescinded.

'Still at 2 AGRA. Pete & Scouse, 'crashing the ash"
Later, Scouse had to dig up his uniform

I was due to fly to Cyprus a day before Pinkie and set off round the camp to say my good-byes. Walking round the end of one tent I saw its occupant, Scouser, digging in the sand. Now, when Scouser had arrived in Egypt, his kit which had been blancoed green in England had to be blancoed a sand colour. Having scrubbed his kit, he lay it on the sand to dry and thought, 'I'll have to scrub it clean again when we get back to England.' So he buried his kit and when inspections came along, he borrowed another set of kit and hung it behind his bed. Now faced with returning to England he was digging his gear up.

'Enjoying Lyons ice-cream at Karalos Camp'
Back row, left to right, 'Daisy' Day, Trevor Sprittlehouse, John and 'Dutch' Holland.
Front row, ?, Johnny Hebditch and Ted 'Pinkie Beeching'

I flew to Cyprus in a twin-engined Vicker's Viking and on arriving at 49 Field Regiment was greeted with great friendliness by the office staff. They introduced me to others and I met up with Bill Simpson from Calder Bridge again. The chaps from the office kept me company and laughed and smiled at my jokes and stories. Suddenly I felt the friendliness was too much and there was something I couldn't put my finger on. When Pinkie arrived the next day I asked him what he thought of the situation. He said, 'It's strange, they even laughed at that terrible joke of yours.' He found it even more strange when I told him I'd deliberately cracked that same joke four times and they still laughed.

It wasn't until a long time afterwards that the chaps in the office told me the reason for all their friendliness. Before I arrived at Cyprus, my personal file had come ahead of me and they decided to read it. They read, 'National Serviceman. Nine 'O' levels and two 'A' levels. Charge sheet. Accidental discharge of machine gun, officers club, Ismalia. Given seven days CB.' Their response to this information had been, 'Good grief, who does he know just to get seven days CB?' So before even seeing me they formed the opinion that I was some sort of political hard-case who might gun down the first person who crossed them. Hence, they were all friendly and laughed at my jokes. I asked, 'How long did it take to figure out that I wasn't an intellectual hard-case?' 'Oh, only two or three days.' I was told.

The Eoka troubles were just beginning in Cyprus and we were fortunate that our unit moved out before things got too nasty. I remember one night there'd been a riot in Famagusta with school-girls at the front of the crowd shouting the Eoka slogans. The heroes of the revolution were standing well back, behind the school-girls, throwing the odd stone and waving revolvers. Our chaps on IS picket were having to grapple with these seventeen year old girls who they would have preferred to meet under more friendly circumstances. But the ladies in Cyprus were usually watched by one or two knife-carrying brothers and relationships were usually strictly formal.

'Ships in Famagusta Harbour'

'A welcome sight. The SS Georgic standing off Famagusta, as seen from Karalos Camp'

Christmas 1954 was spent in Cyprus with the traditional Christmas dinner which the officers and CO's served to the troops. Then just after New Year's Day there came a most welcome sight, the *SS Georgic* anchored off the breakwater at Famagusta, standing by to take us home. It was a lovely sight but it took us a week to get on board. All the gear had to be loaded and finally we packed it all and marched out of the camp.

One young soldier had wanted to marry a local girl who worked at a souvenir shop but as he was under age the CO refused to give his permission. However, the lad spent the last night in her company while his mates covered for him until he returned well after hours. The following morning we all marched down to the dock and waited our turn on the lighter to take us out to the ship. As we stood waiting there was a commotion. It transpired that the young soldier in the ranks was right opposite the shop where his girl friend worked. So his mates held his rifle and pack and the sergeant looked the other way while the lad had a last reunion with his young lady.

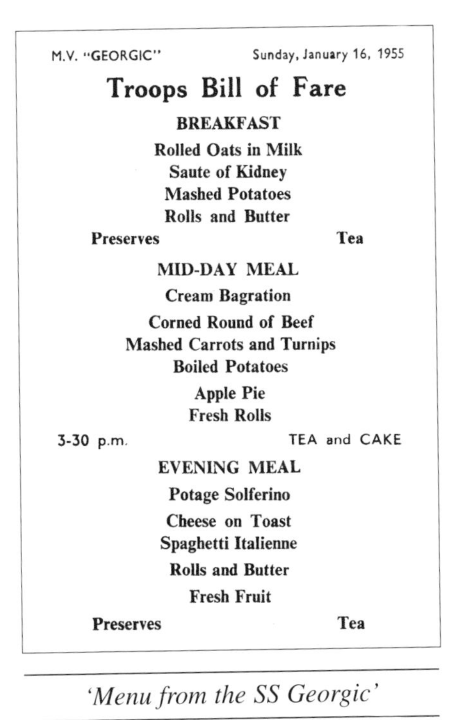

M.V. "GEORGIC" Sunday, January 16, 1955

Troops Bill of Fare

BREAKFAST

Rolled Oats in Milk
Saute of Kidney
Mashed Potatoes
Rolls and Butter
Preserves Tea

MID-DAY MEAL

Cream Bagration
Corned Round of Beef
Mashed Carrots and Turnips
Boiled Potatoes
Apple Pie
Fresh Rolls

3-30 p.m. TEA and CAKE

EVENING MEAL

Potage Solferino
Cheese on Toast
Spaghetti Italienne
Rolls and Butter
Fresh Fruit
Preserves Tea

'Menu from the SS Georgic'

In George Bernard Shaw's play, '*Arms and the Man*', the soldier loads his pack with chocolate and wine. Taking my cue from that character, my presents for home and the young lady I intended to see in Barrow were in my pack and ammunition pouches The kit bags were left behind in Cyprus and many of my contemporaries were moaning like hell because their presents for home were in the bags. I had my presents with me as I'd stacked all my army gear into my kit bag. Unfortunately, by carrying my presents I had very little room for anything else and had only two changes of underwear. So I was more than a little smelly on the voyage home.

On the voyage home I remember walking down the companionway which had a dip in it and the walls of the bulkheads were twisted and had bends in them. I thought, 'They build ships at Barrow and I'm sure they don't finish them in this rough and ready manner.' Then it dawned on me that the *SS Georgic* was a troop ship in the 1930's and then in 1942, while in Port Said harbour had been bombed by the Luftwaffer and gutted by fire. Later she was raised, repaired and put back into service and there she was in 1955, still in service.

We arrived back at Liverpool late one night and were bundled into a train and travelled in the darkness across country to Colchester barracks. Most of the regiment went on leave the next day but the chief clerk asked if he could have some volunteers to stay behind and help man the office. Working on the theory that while the bulk of the regiment were on leave, discipline was likely to be slack and parades non-existent, I volunteered to stay behind for an extra fortnight. That worked out fine and when the others returned back to barracks, I was looking forward to my leave as I'd been writing to the young lady at Barrow and wondering how things would work out. As you know, things did work out and we celebrated our fortieth wedding anniversary this March.

I was demobbed the following September and went to Chester College that same month on a two-year teacher training course where I studied English, history and RE (Religious Education). Actually, I had taken some books into the Army with me as I told myself I was going to study. But quite honestly, I was more inclined, especially in Egypt, to lie on my bed in the afternoons and swop the same tales over and over again with the other chaps, of civvie life and the girls we'd known.

I said that I'd joined the Army reckoning to get it over with and then enjoy college. As it turned out, they were equally cheerful and I'm glad that I saw a little bit of life beyond school, college and then teaching. I hit Chester College at one of the best times. It was still an all male college and most of the chaps there had been in the forces with just a sprinkling doing their deferment. We all had to be in college by half-past-ten at night but blokes who'd done guard duty and covered for their mates had no problems getting around that. The window in my room was one at which stones occasionally rattled and I'd get up and open the main door for chaps at two or three in the morning. Later on, in the sixties, when students kicked up a fuss about the rules, they didn't understand the slogan, 'Rules are for the guidance of wise men and the protection of fools.' Chaps who had been in the Army knew when not to make a fuss about things.

Looking back, I know I had an easy time during National Service and I've played it for the laughs when recalling those two years. My best friend was on a mine sweeper at Suez. College friends served in Malaya against communists and in Kenya against the Mau-Mau. Their experiences were somewhat different to mine. And in teaching I met men and women who having risked their lives for King and country during the Second World War were foremost in striving to improve the common lot in the new world of the 1950's and 60's. Many of them are gone now and I feel priviledged to have known them and to have shared something of their world and their dreams.

But the one thing I learnt about the Army was when-ever I was told that I'd been given a choice about something, I found that I wasn't. It made me realise that's how we'd been on the winning side of so many wars because if we confuse our own troops, how the hell was the enemy to work out what we were going to do next?

FOUR

'Ballykelly, is it in the Far East?'

***Ron Starkey**, served in the Royal Air Force 1954-1956*

I left Workington Grammar School when I was sixteen and went straight into the police as a cadet. Police cadets weren't deferred or exempt from National Service. They all had to go at eighteen and that was it. You got your papers and off you went up to Carlisle for your medical.

For me, National Service wasn't too bad, with having those two years with the police. It was just another uniform and dealing with people in uniform. I chose to go into the Royal Air Force and you had to say which trade you wanted to follow; Whether you wanted to be a cook, clerk, mechanic or whatever, so I put down RAF police.

Within five or six weeks of the medical I was sent down to Cardington. That's when you were kitted out, given your boots and uniform and shown how to wear it. Going down to Cardington wasn't too frightening. Certainly, you had to pick your friends when you went there as they were all a lot of strangers and with two hundred lads on your intake, it was difficult to find anybody from your own area. Most lads had never been away from home or worn a uniform before and you more or less helped each other out.

The food we were given was eatable. A lot of people complained about the food but I don't know what they were used to at home because it was eatable. Nobody was going to be ill with it. The one thing I can remember were the eggs. Fried eggs in the morning that used to float in oil or fat. I could hardly face eating an egg after that.

You went to Cardington for two or three weeks to be given your uniform. Then it was home for a Christmas break which I spent in bed being ill with flu. After that, it was onto what they called 'square bashing camp' at Hednesford on Cannock Chase. We were there for about eight to ten weeks and the RAF service was really drilled into you. How to march, looking after uniform and weapons. Nearly everybody enjoyed going out for weapon training with .303 Lee Enfield rifles, machine guns and Bren guns.

'Ron and Howard Pickthall (Cleator Moor) weapon training at Hednesford'

It was a corporal who looked after 'the flight' as a group of young airmen were called. He was responsible for taking you right through the ten weeks' training. I suppose these corporals were good at their job but they were disciplinarians, very sarcastic and you went in fear of them. For example, every other day the billet had to be inspected. The floor had to be gleaming, beds correct and kit laid out. On one occasion all our billet had spent about two hours polishing this floor and you could see your face in it. Our corporal had been to the NAAFI and come back worse for wear with drink. He walked into our billet and said, This floor is a – -'. There was a bucket of coke standing nearby and he kicked it the full length of the billet. Then he walked right through the coke, trampling it with his boots and when he got to the far end said, 'Right, you can get that cleaned up for tomorrow morning.' So we had to set to for another hour or so and clean all that mess up.

The bucket of coke I mentioned was for the two pot-bellied stoves we had in the billet. Being there in January and February, there was a routine that everybody who went into the billet any time of the day had to check the stoves. These had to be kept going twenty-four hours a day. You could open the vents on these stoves and the wind went through them so they glowed cherry red. We used to get a metal coat hanger, put a slice of bread of it and lay it on top of the stove. Within a few seconds, one side of the toast was ready for turning. Oh, it was beautiful was that. But you were in trouble if you were caught. This corporal used to walk in, sniff the air and shout, 'Who's making toast?'

It was bloody freezing on Cannock Chase. You got these very low mists at night. In the mornings we used to be taken for cross-country runs, wearing our heavy nailed boots, a pair of shorts and a vest. You were running through the snow and ice, through the wood and across the Chase at seven or eight in the morning. That used to give you an appetite.

While we were at this camp we'd get a pass, maybe a forty-eight hour or seventy-two one. You really had to work out your train times so a lot of lads used to thumb lifts as that was often faster. In those days you could wear your uniform out of camp and most lorry or van drivers would stop and give you a lift.

Later when I went to my next RAF camp at Netheravon I remember me and a Scotch lad started to hitch-hike from way down there near Salisbury. We got a lift on the back of a lorry carrying oxygen cylinders and he took us about two hundred miles to north of Birmingham where we got off. We were frozen sitting on the back of this open lorry among the cylinders but it was cheaper and sometimes faster getting home that way. You see, the motorways hadn't been built then and you had to pick your route and keep to the west of the country. You were all right on the main roads but getting to West Cumberland could be difficult.

Once you arrived at Carlisle, if it was after ten o'clock at night, that was it. There were no trains down to West Cumberland until the first milk train in the morning, which was about six o'clock. So there you were stuck on Carlisle station all night. Later on, at my next camp, I was lucky as a lad called Howard Pickthall was there. He was from Cleator Moor where his folks had a haulage business. If we either thumbed a lift or came by train to Carlisle, his mother picked us up in her car at the station and drove us home. By the time you got home you were only there for a day and a night then had to start off back to camp.

'Ron on duty'

You had your passing out parade at Hednesford and everybody was then a basic airman. I know now-a-days it's a big thing for parents to go to a passing out parade but they never did then. It was just a formal parade with two or three hundred men in uniform. The CO gave a little speech, we all saluted and marched off. That was it.

By that time you were given your instructions for wherever you were going. Mine was to Netheravon near Salisbury, which was the main training centre for the RAF police and dog handlers. There you became a non-person, did as you were told and learnt how to follow orders. We thought we had a rough time at the square-bashing camp but if moved up three or four levels at Netheravon. Everybody one rank above you was your boss. It didn't matter what they were doing, they were that one rank above you. Oh, the discipline was tremendous. Some lads couldn't take this intense discipline and within a couple of weeks they applied to move out.

At the same time you had some laughs because the lads who were with you all wanted to be in the RAF police. About a dozen lads would be sleeping in a billet and you became a unit. Your pals were in that unit, you used to look after each other and you knocked around with each other.

In the eyes of the Air Force you were going to be their disciplinarians on their camps and establishments all over the world. You had to represent that image all the time and they were instilling it into you. The initial training you got, hopefully, would carry you all over the world to which ever camp you were sent. No doubt it would be developed if you went over-seas or wherever.

We were taught how to handle different situations, sort of basic police patrol training. They also taught us how to deal with minor thefts, accidents and incidents all involving RAF personnel. Besides a lot of physical activity such as cross-country running and gym, we learnt self-defence which was really to protect yourself if the situation arose. When bed-time came, you just used to conk out with tiredness.

There was also written work on how to prepare a report if you put somebody on a charge. If somebody was caught committing a minor offence, they would be given a small charge sheet called a 252. You were given instruction on how to make out these reports. They began with '*at – on – at, I was …*' meaning 'at such and such a time, on such and such a date, at such and such a location, I was on patrol …'

Again, at this camp our instructors were corporals. Some of them were young but they were regular RAF men who had signed on for fifteen or twenty years. This was their career and they were good at their jobs. They had to be as they got raw recruits from all over the country, from all sorts of backgrounds and had to shape them.

We weren't allowed off camp for the first three weeks. When we were eventually allowed out, we had to march down the road towards the main guard room where the RAF police staff were watching you. They'd deliberately stop you and pick faults with your uniform. It was maybe because a collar wasn't straight or for dirty buttons or shoes and they'd send you straight back to the billet to clean up or put things right. I've seen lads turned back two or three times just because the feller on duty thought he would use a bit of authority.

There was a big RAF police dog-training section on the camp which had kennels for about a hundred and fifty or two hundred dogs. At that time the American Air Force were living somewhere else but they used to come onto the camp for their dog training. Us new recruits would be lined up in rows, gleaming and disciplined for our morning inspection when these Americans would stroll into camp. Their caps would be on the back of their heads, cigars in their mouths, dog leads round their necks and hands in pockets. It was an entertainment watching them.

At the end of our training we were all lined up on parade and they shouted out your name and your posting. I wanted to go abroad, to travel and be in foreign parts. In those days, lads in the RAF were going to the Middle East, Far East and all over the place. So there we were, waiting for our posting and when they came to me it was, 'Starkey, Ballykelly.'

Now, the big film at that time was *South Pacific* and one of the hit songs from it was *Bali High*. So when they shouted out, 'Ballykelly' we all looked at each other and it was, 'Ballykelly, oh you must be going to Thailand or somewhere like that'. Eventually when we were dismissed, we all dashed to the library where the maps and charts were and looked through the index for Ballykelly. But we were looking for it being spelled B-A-L-I and couldn't find it. There was somebody else in the library and we asked, 'Ballykelly, is it in the Far East?' 'You daft buggers,' he said, 'Ballykelly is in Northern Ireland.' I was a bit deflated at that response.

Northern Ireland was classed as a home posting, especially for people from Wales, Scotland and the North of England. Sometimes when you went abroad, depending where, you got a little extra pay or allowance but not for Northern Ireland. In those days, we went across by ferry from Liverpool in our uniform and carrying our kitbag.

There was very little trouble in Ireland so we could travel in our uniform. On arrival at Belfast, we had a train journey to Limavady, the little town near the camp. The one thing I'll always remember on the train was a little old lady in a black shawl came along begging from the passengers. She'd got on at one station and wandered along the train holding her hand out. That was the first impression things were slightly different over there as I'd never seen anybody begging before.

My first impression of Ballykelly was the noise and all those aircraft. They flew RAF Coastal Command patrols twenty-four hours a day from there. The Cold War was on so they used to do round-the-clock patrols in the North Atlantic. It was a very noisy place but after a couple of months you got used to it. The camp was large in area because of the airfields. As a lot of the buildings were connected with running the airfields, we had two guard-rooms where the RAF police operated from.

The lads soon made you welcome in the billet. If I remember rightly, at that time me and another lad were the first non-regular RAF policemen at the camp. I suspect I got in because of my previous police experience in the cadets. On the camp there were lads from all over the Commonwealth – Cypriots, Maltese, and some of the regular lads were southern Irish. They were from Dublin and other parts of the Republic and some had been in the Second World War. In fact, later, I went on leave to Dublin and stayed with friends of one of lads from there. In the main, it was lads from England, Scotland and Wales at the camp. Surprisingly, my nickname was 'Geordie' because as far as they were concerned, with my accent I was a Geordie.

As RAF police we were responsible for the security of the camp which was patrolled twenty-four hours of the day. Outside the camp, towns and villages were looked after by the Royal Ulster Constabulary. However, there was a branch of the RAF police called the Provost Section. These were men who'd joined-up for fifteen to twenty years as career men. They were similar to the Army Military Police and patrolled towns and villages outside the camp when servicemen were around. However, all the RAF police wore exactly the same – white caps, arm bands, webbing, boots and gaiters. There was no difference what-so-ever.

The idea of police on the camp was to maintain good order and discipline within the service. People could have property stolen from their billets, accidents or incidents happened, or there might be a little bit of trouble at a dance on camp. But there wasn't as much trouble as you'd see in civvy street. There was always corporals, sergeants or officers around as well as the police, who had the power of discipline over junior ranks.

'Ron in his military police uniform in Ireland'

Discipline in the camp was very good and there were few incidents. Maybe the odd fight but I can hardly remember any incident connected with drink, although my first arrest was a Royal Marine who was drunk and incapable. There was never anybody protesting that they shouldn't be doing National Service. In those days you just had to accept it. It was a way of life and everybody had to do it.

We were in charge of the guards and patrols and about that time it was decided to issue the guards with arms. So we were armed and had to supervise the issuing of arms to the guards who came on duty. Then we were responsible for the guards turning up for duty, seeing they got their refreshments and rest.

One of our duties was to go on bank escort. Wages were drawn from the local bank and we used to send a patrol into town to lift the cash. In those days we were lifting great bags of money because there were no credit cards or bank accounts. Everybody was paid in cash so we used to go along to the bank as escort and armed to the teeth.

There were always people guarding the perimeter of the airfield. This was on the coast, where the railway line ran from Belfast to Londonderry. Local people who wanted to take a short cut, rather than take a bus or go the extra six miles, would chance going along the railway line. So now and again, dog patrols would bring in suspects as it was illegal to be along the shore or railway line. But these suspects would be locals, say a farmer who was wanting to see a relative.

Civvies worked on the camp and one of our duties was to pick out one or two for a search, especially when they were leaving camp. That was to make sure they weren't taking RAF property with them. It was a regular thing but the civvies knew they could be called up for a search. So, if there were half-a-dozen of them going home, you'd say, 'Right, Sammy, it's your turn today,' and they had to accept it. We never had any problems with the civvies.

Actually, the only one caught in a search was an RAF cook. He was going home on leave one bank holiday and came trundling past the guard house with his suitcase which was nearly pulling his arm out of its socket. Now, if you're going home for a weekend, it's a couple of shirts and a pair of shoes that you take with you. So we asked what he had in his case and it was, 'Oh, it's just weekend things.' When we got him to open it, it was packed with tins of meat and fruit from the cookhouse. But apart from that incident, there was very little else.

Another of our duties was controlling the camp radio network. We had a big wireless-set in the guardroom and could switch it on or off in various billets. We'd tune in to the American Forces' Network which I think was transmitted from Germany. Every night when we were on duty, everybody would gather round the wireless as there was this guy on called Elvis Presley. He used to sing a new type of music and Elvis became THE bloke. Everyone on night duty would ask, 'Can we have the radio on?' and there was Elvis.

In the evenings, Bridie sometimes used to ring the camp. She was one of the local girls and a well known character who used to meet the lads off duty. Anyway, Bridie used to ring the camp and ask the police on duty if she could speak to a certain lad. Her call would be put through to the guardroom and of course, conversations would develop. She would probably never pay for the phone call as the civilian operator would just leave her on the line. On our RAF exchange we used to plug her in to various depots round the camp so that on the line there would be Bridie, the police, the fire service and the cooks all talking. There would be six or seven conversations going on with Bridie while some of the lads would be making dates. 'See you on Friday night, Bridie.'

On camp you got your meals in the mess and the NAAFI was where you went to relax. One of the NAAFI's benefits was the cake or gateau as they called it, as you never got cake in the mess. There was always soup, main course and pudding but never cake. So I developed a taste for gateau and if we got the chance of a coffee break, I finished up with a plate of gateau. Also in the NAAFI on a Sunday night surprisingly, we had some entertainment. Imagine all these lads, maybe two thousand and they're from all walks of life and there were good entertainers amongst them. Now and again, somebody would get up and play the piano or sing so we used to get our own entertainment from inside the camp.

There was a NAAFI dance once a month when ladies from Derry or other spots came in. I only went to one and had enough of it after half an hour. It was just the fact you were on the camp base and some of the lassies that came were, shall we say, looking for husbands or somebody to take them away. Then again, we worked shifts and sometimes you were on duty at some of these events or else preparing for duty.

For most of the camp, unless you were a shift worker or on call, all meals finished with your main meal at about five or six in the evening.

So the only people who went to the mess after that were shift workers such as policemen, firemen or duty mechanics. That little group always hung around together. It was important to know the lads you were on duty with and we knocked about together on and off duty.

At night what the cooks used to do was go around 'borrowing' bikes for us which we'd hide in our billets. When we finished night duty at eight in the morning, we'd have breakfast, wait until everybody had gone on duty, then change into civvies and off on the bikes. These were all RAF bikes and some lads would have got up in the morning expecting to see their bikes where they had left them. It was either a two mile walk down to the airfield where they worked or they had to go and nick another bike fairly quickly.

Actually, no matter what trade you were in, you used to knock about with the lads in your billet. So the cooks used to go about together, the mechanics or whatever group you were in. Life revolved around the billet but you also had one or two mates like the cooks who you sometimes went out with. For example, one of the cooks used to organise taxis or hired cars to take us to Derry at weekends to go to the dances.

It was the time of these Irish show-bands of twelve to fourteen fellers and could they let rip. They also used to get musicians like Chris Barber and Lonnie Donnegan to play, long before they became famous in England. There was one little village just outside Northern Ireland, in the Irish Republic, and it looked nothing. But they had this great big dance hall and Sunday night was the night for dancing. A coach-load of us used to go to this dance and there'd be about six hundred people there. The entertainment was fabulous.

There also used to be two dances in Limavady, the small town near the camp. They had a dance at St Patrick's Catholic Hall and one in the Protestant Orange Hall, each on different nights. So there'd be two dances a week at which servicemen were welcome to both. The locals of different religions never mixed but we could go to either dance. Off duty we went out in civvies to these dances, local events and bars in the town.

Religious parades took place and if you were on the street, you'd just stop and look at them. In those days you didn't fully know what it was all about. To us, it was just like a carnival event. In places, Londonderry especially, there was strong religious areas. Again, as young National Servicemen from England, we didn't know a lot about that.

We never got briefings on it and it was all low profile. So there was always an undercurrent but it was a very low degree. But the Irish were great people who used to enjoy themselves and have a good laugh. You had to get to learn the dialect but you soon understood their accents. A great people.

'A religious parade at Limavady, the village near Ballykelly'

I didn't manage to get home too often from Ireland, just the occasional bank holiday. Even with a three-day pass it was quite a journey. You took the train to Larne and caught the ferry to Stranraer. From Stranraer it was train to Carlisle and you arrived there about one in the morning. So again, no transport at the station and you had a long wait. In fact what some lads from West Cumberland used to do was get a lift in Menzies (John Menzies Ltd) paper van. Newspapers used to be piled up on Carlisle railway station platform late at night and by word of mouth, it became a regular thing, you went and gave the van driver a hand to load all his papers. When he set off at about half-past-five in the morning, he'd give you a lift. He did his 'drops' and you would give him a hand dropping these papers off. Hopefully, at half-past-seven or eight o'clock in the morning you'd get into Workington. As you'd set off from Northern Ireland at about eleven o'clock one morning and arrived home at eight o'clock the next day, that was nearly twenty-four hours of your leave already gone.

I managed to get home for Christmas both times during National Service. You see, during basic training we were all sent home. And in Northern Ireland, by popular request they tried to work it that the English lads came home for Christmas as the Scots lads looked forward to getting home for New Year.

I had one or two pals at home who hadn't done their National Service for various reasons. Also, another pal was at university so usually it worked out that when I was on leave on these bank holidays, he was home so I went out with him. But as time went on, old school friends became further and further removed from you. They'd moved on to different things and you had gone in the forces.

Coming up to the end of your service, you went for a little interview with the education officer. He told you briefly about what you'd done over the last two years and asked whether you had a job to go to when you left the forces. I had the police to go into so my interview was very short. He said, 'You won't be interested in signing on,' but it was available if you wanted it, with extra pay and better conditions. Then you had to decide whether you wanted to be a regular RAF policeman but very few opted to stay on. Most lads who were National Service like me, more or less had their future lined up.

I came out of the forces in early December, 1956 and had a Christmas break until 4 January when I went to Warrington. That was to start my police training and we were in billets from the American forces days. These billets had hardboard walls but every man had his own room. As twelve of us had been sharing a billet in Ireland, the police training ones were a luxury. At Warrington, most of us were ex-service men, so again, discipline and the wearing of uniforms were readily accepted.

National Service gave me the chance of travelling and getting away from West Cumberland. In those days, and prior to National Service, very few people left the county unless they went to a particular job or joined the services. You see, there were the pits and steel works and lads leaving school usually got jobs there. There was a lot of industry then so there was no need for anybody to go out of the county to look for jobs. So I think National Service helped a lot of lads to open their horizons. I don't regret doing mine.

FIVE

'We want steak, steak and more steak'

Anthony (Tony) Birkett, *Served in the Catering Corps 1953-1955*

'At Aldershot, Tony is on the right.'

I was working in the offices at K Shoes opposite Curry's in Kendal when I was called up. My eighteenth birthday was on 22 June 1953 and I went to Preston for my National Service medical in July. Physically, I was grade two because I was underweight. Grade one, you were perfect, grade two and you were physically not so perfect, grade three meant you were worse but they still took you in and grade four, they didn't take you.

At Preston I was asked if I had any preferences for what I wanted to do in the forces and I said 'Yes, I want to go into the Catering Corps.' I wanted to be where the food was. Anyway, on 20 August I got my railway pass to go down to Aldershot. I was courting Joan at the time and she saw me off at the railway station and I went down to London with two other local lads. One was from Kendal and the other was from Staveley. It was frightening as I'd never been as far away as even Carlisle before. I parted company from these two lads at Euston station as they were going to other regiments and corps and I had to go to Aldershot in Hampshire.

Aldershot was a huge military complex with rows and rows of long avenues or barracks, all named after famous battles. These avenues seemed to stretch forever and I'll always remember, right down every avenue, there were conker trees with some of the biggest conkers I'd ever seen in my life. I actually got to Aldershot at about eight o'clock in the morning and as I was the first to arrive, a drill sergeant said, 'Seeing you are here, you can make yourself useful,' and I helped him to make the beds. It was seven o'clock at night when I got my first meal. I can remember it now, it was yellow fish and mashed potatoes. All these Scottish lads who arrived were saying, 'Oh God, I canna eat this. Aw, it's rubbish.' I thought, 'What have they been eating all their lives?' as it was manna from heaven to me. It was the best food I'd had in years and these Scottish lads couldn't face it. It wasn't that we were poor at home. My dad had a good job as an accountant at the Provincial Insurance Company but he was just mean as regards food. He was all right while my mother was alive but she died when I was thirteen and father just pulled the horns in.

Mind, that first day everybody was supposed to arrive at Aldershot by twelve noon but some of these lads were still coming in at nine o'clock at night and were absolutely sloshed. You see, they had older brothers who knew the score in the Army and that you couldn't get court-martialed while doing your basic training.

There were about twenty or thirty lads to each barrack. I went into Ramillies Barracks where all the catering corps lads went. A lot of the intake were big, Scottish lads and most of them had never, ever been to England before. But that first night there were no brave Scotsmen and there were no brave Englishmen. All you could hear in the barracks were sobs right down the line. Everybody had a good cry that first night. It was a bloody shock.

Before I went down to Aldershot I only shaved my top lip. Well, I'd been there about three days and we were on parade with this sergeant looking at us all. He decided, and quite rightly so, that three of us had bum fluff. We were singled out and marched to the ablutions where he told us to shave. We lathered up and I started shaving. I got right down one side of my face and realised to my horror, that I hadn't put a razor blade in the razor. I dare'nt tell the sergeant because he'd think I was taking the piss. When I dried my face off, he looked at me and said, 'Aye, that's much better.' But I tell you, every night I made sure I did have a shave because I wasn't going to be caught again.

Basic training was just rifle drill, marching, saluting, standing at ease, standing at attention, right wheel, left wheel and the rest of it. Any time we did anything wrong on parade, the drill sergeant would come screaming across, shouting 'I'll see you go to Korea, lad.' That was the one place you did not want to go, where the 'Glorious Gloucester's had held out against thousands of Chinese.

On the rifle range we fired Sten guns and .303s. Most National Service men fired Bren guns as well but we didn't. I believe the Catering Corps, while in action, a cook's gun was a Sten gun. But with the training, some were hopelessly slow learners and some tried to make out they weren't compatible with the Army. These were fly boys who I think deliberately didn't try to pick it up, hoping they could work their ticket and try to get out. But it didn't work, they had to come into line eventually.

At night you went to the NAAFI and had coffee or you could get a beer and listen to the wireless. That's where I got my first love of music because we used to listen to AFN, the American Forces Network. I didn't even know what I was listening to, all this weird style of music. There would maybe be a request on AFN from somebody serving in Dusseldorf and he would be asking for music to be played for his mother at Baton Rouge, Louisiana. Then you'd hear these weird blues sounds with harmonica and slide guitar. Captivating.

After six weeks at Aldershot I was sent to what was called a Fitness and Conditioning Course near Salisbury. I went on Number 1 Conditioning Course as I was only six stones, four pounds in weight. A few other lads from Aldershot went and lads from other regiments. Oh, it was lovely. We got excellent food and malt and cod-liver oil. You didn't do any work as they were trying to build you up. We did running, playing football, hockey, lots of gym work and even boxing.

'On the Fitness and Conditioning Course. Tony is on the front row, far right'

I got my first forty-eight hour pass from there. But I couldn't get home in forty-eight hours, because in those days, it was all steam trains. It would be about six or seven hours from London to Oxenholme, so I went to stay with an auntie who lived in Edgware at London. And being on the course at Salisbury I missed the passing out parade.

At the end of the conditioning course, I was sent to a military hospital at Virginia Water for an X-ray and to be weighed. Actually, my weight had gone up to six stones thirteen pounds but the officer who weighed me said, 'You're a pound underweight.' I asked if that was allowed and he answered, 'No, but it's up to you.' I could have got out of the Army. I could have got out that day if I pressed by case but I did my National Service.

I was sent back to Aldershot for a fortnight and put in a holding platoon. Well, I just messed about. I was an office boy with a bike, a runner for one of the offices. They used to send me with bits of paper all over Aldershot to different barracks and officers' mess's, delivering this, picking up that. It was great. I went all over on my bike.

After that, I got posted. There were six CICs (Cooking Instructional Camps) throughout the country and I was sent to Number 5 CIC, at Glencorse, which is at Penicuik, just south of Edinburgh. A lot of us went from King's Cross station up the east coast to Edinburgh at night time. Now, almost all the others who were travelling were Scottish lads. Knowing they were heading back to Scotland, every time we crossed a river from the south of England onwards, they all leapt to their feet shouting, 'We're crossing the Clyde, we're crossing the Clyde.' Their hats went up in the air and they all cheered. At every river this happened. Well, you don't cross the Clyde on the east line so we never crossed the Clyde yet. But they were going home you see, going back to Scotland.

Oh, this cookery course was all right. All in all, it took fourteen weeks' training. There was elementary cooking, different types of pastry, keeping a larder, butchery, standing camp when you were cooking outdoors under war conditions, cook house and then petrol burners. Petrol burners phase were when you went out in a field, dug a trench and used petrol burners that blasted a flame along. Above these flames you put your cooking utensils to heat up. After that course you were an army cook. It was simple stuff as you were cooking for a lot of people.

We did have machines that peeled potatoes but the rest of the vegetables were washed and peeled by hand. Usually, what happened was, there was always somebody who'd been naughty and they were confined to barracks and put on jankers. At night time these lads on jankers came in the cookhouse and prepared a lot of the vegetables for us.

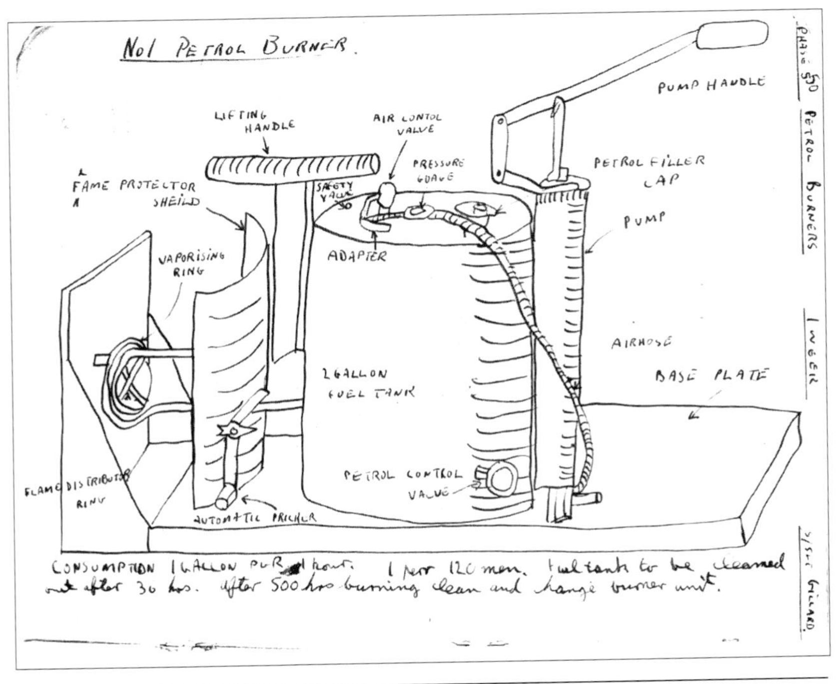

'Drawings from Tony's manual of the petrol burners used for cooking in the field'

Everybody got three cooked meals. Breakfast was usually porridge then you would get bacon and egg and fried bread. But at ten o'clock in the morning, lads could go to the NAAFI and get themselves a cup of tea and slice of toast or something similar. Then the proper meal was at dinner time. At night it was what was called a tea meal, which could be poached fish or mince and mashed potatoes or something like that. It certainly wasn't sandwiches and sausage rolls. There was no choice, none at all. If you didn't want the meal, you didn't have it and that was it.

It was while I was at Pennycuik I heard the rumour that if you lived way down south, you were given seventy-two hours leave instead of the usual forty-eight. So I went to see an officer and asked for a seventy-two hours pass. He asked where I lived and I told him, 'Westmorland.' 'Westmorland, where the bloody hell is that?' he wanted to know. I said it was quite a long way off, to which he replied, 'It must be,' as he stamped me a seventy-two hour pass. If he'd known Westmorland was just below the Scottish border, I wouldn't have got it. And the funny thing was, I got home faster than lads going north of Aberdeen as they only got a forty-eight hour pass. I had both my Christmas's at home during National Service. They let us English lads home because the Scottish lads wanted New Year off.

It was on my second Christmas at home, Joan and me went to Johnston and Court, the jewellers and I bought her an engagement ring. Now, in those days every bank in Scotland produced their own different coloured pound notes and that's all I got paid in. The girl in the jewellers had to take these pound notes to the manager to see if they would accept them as currency because they'd never had that amount before in Kendal. Obviously they'd had the odd Scottish currency but never that amount and all from different banks. Anyway, the manager looked through his door into the shop and when he saw I had my army uniform on, that clinched it.

I was at Glencourse from October 1953 until April 1954. By that time I'd completed the course and I volunteered to cook at summer camps, TA camps, which were for a fortnight or a month at a time. I went to Cultybraggan near Crieff in Perthshire then to Buddon Camp near Dundee. From there, on to the TA centre at Bell Street, Dundee to cook for the Dundee Tattoo. After that it was back again to Buddon and Cultybraggen.

'Cultybraggan Camp'

The TA lads would be under canvas but cooks weren't. We were in huts, permanent dormitories and with permanent cookhouses for us. Most of the camps are still there as the Army is very reluctant to give up anything. And I'll tell you what, I've cooked for some quite famous colleges. I don't know whether you've heard but there's some quite famous public schools in Scotland and they all had Army cadet forces. I cooked for Fettes College which is very famous as a lot of MP's went to that, and Dollar Academy. Now in these cadet forces they had their own little sergeants and corporals. So if you had a big pile of potatoes that wanted peeling, you addressed one of these lads as sergeant or corporal. Well, when a soldier called him by his rank, he was over the moon. 'Yes sir, I'll see to it', he would say and then haul his mates onto jankers and they'd have to peel potatoes. Instead of taking the mickey out of these lads, you could get anything done if you just addressed them properly.

After the summer camps I went to HQ Scottish Command at Edinburgh for two months and cooked for the 1954 Edinburgh Tattoo. We were cooking for the people who were performing in the Tattoo but the castle itself was rather austere. A lot of the crowned heads of Europe were there in '54 and would be sitting in the royal boxes. Seats were saved every night for the castle staff to attend the Tattoo, which was more militaristic than it is now. Either the Gurkhas or somebody like them were appearing so every night we would dash down to the show and take our seats when we knew they were coming on. Then when the act was finished, we'd leave and go back to the castle.

I left Edinburgh Castle in September and as the summer camps had finished, I went to a military hospital in Glasgow as a sergeants' mess cook. While I was there, I was sent on a B2 course, which was the next step up for advanced cookery and fancy dishes. I passed that, having the highest grades of anybody on my course and then it was back to the military hospital at Glasgow.

With cooking in the sergeants' mess, I got a messing allowance for being on duty from seven in the morning, right through to seven at night. There would be about five sergeants to cook for at breakfast, maybe twelve for dinner and again, five of them at tea-time, so I had it cushy. With being on duty long hours like all cooks were, I earned some good money. The waiter with me was a lad from Wigan. What we used to do, he did the cooking and waiting on one weekend and I did it all the following weekend. So that meant both of us could get home once a fortnight. It was all right was that, as I left the hospital by Friday dinner-time and was home by the tea-time.

Mind, while at Glasgow I overstayed a home leave. I was in love, you see and always with Joan. The police arrived at home to find out why I hadn't returned to camp. I told them I'd sent a letter to camp as my dad was very ill and for them to go upstairs and see him. Now, my dad was fine but looked shocking when he was still in bed. The police took one look at him lying there without a shave and said, 'Oh yes, we can see that he's ill.' But I was marched up to the police station on Lowther Street and sat there while they made a phone call to camp. Eventually a message came back from Scotland to say, yes they had received the letter but it had got mislaid. I'd never written a letter. Some clerk fearing a backlash said, 'Oh yes, we've got his letter' so I got an extra fortnight at home and another travel pass to go back with.

Now back at the military hospital a certain quartermaster sergeant fell in love with a WRAF sergeant and together they decided she was eligible to come into the sergeants' mess. This was one of the first instances that I know where women's lib succeeded as ladies had never, ever been involved in the sergeant's mess. It was a men-only domain with snooker and darts but a meeting was held and it was decided, yes, she could be admitted.

Once in the sergeant's mess, this WRAF sergeant decided she'd do something about the food they were getting as she wanted a greater variety. Now, in a sergeant's mess, they didn't get their food free. They paid messing fees except the duty sergeant who would get a free evening meal. The next thing this woman wanted to know was, what happened to the messing money. Nobody seemed to know and eventually somebody was found who said, 'Oh, it just goes into an account.' Well, they looked into this account and it had umpteen hundreds of pounds in it which all the sergeants decided to spend on food. So I was told, 'We want steak, steak and more steak. The money's there, get it bought.'

To buy food I had to walk across a couple of fields to a shop similar to a Co-op. Well, as you can imagine, this shop welcomed me with open arms. I never paid any money, it was just put on the slate and the steak, steak and more steak was bought. As the WRAF sergeant also wanted fruit in profusion for the mess table, that was put on the slate as well. It was such a large order the shop had to deliver it all by van. As I ate the same food as the sergeants, oh we lived off the fat of the land.

This went on for a number of weeks and I approached the quartermaster sergeant one day and said, 'You know, we're spending quite a lot of money.' I was told, 'You cook, you don't interfere in mess activities. You're here as a cook, do your cooking and that's it.' So I stepped back and didn't interfere. Two or three weeks later, the RSM landed with a book-keeper and found that the sergeants' mess was about a hundred pounds in debt. That was a lot of money in 1954. There were all sorts of carrying's-on and a court martial. I was lead into this court martial, not marched in, and asked the circumstances of the affair. I told them exactly what had happened and how I'd approached the quartermaster. He was in the room when I was saying all this and was his face sour. He looked as though he had a lemon in his mouth.

Nothing happened to me. It was, 'Right ho, Private Birkett. That's it.' But I mean, crickey Moses, when twenty-eight shillings worth of steak's delivered by van, that's a lot of money when steak was about two shillings a pound in those days. Remember, at that time, you could buy a meal of fish and chips for three and a half-pence. Anyway, the whole of the sergeants' mess was taken over to sort things out and I was posted to Strathearn Road Medical Reception Station in Edinburgh.

Strathearn Road station was a very small medical reception station for anybody who'd had an accident or been taken ill. It was the equivalent of a cottage hospital and had three cooks, a duty sergeant, an officer and matron in charge because there were three of Queen Alexandra's Nursing Corps there.

I'd only started at Strathearn Road when the head cook said to me, 'By the way, you're doing breakfasts in the morning, aren't you? Well, we always take the nurses a cup of tea up to their room on the top floor. Now, when you take the tea up, the first door on the right is where the matron sleeps. For Christ's sake, make sure you go past there silently because if she comes out, you're for it.' So the next morning I went up the stairs quietly with these three mugs of tea. I was expecting the nurses would be sat in their room and it would be, 'Oh, a cup of tea. Well done' when they saw me. But they were fast asleep in their beds. How do you wake-up three naked girls? None of them had a stitch on with it being summer and there were knickers and bras and stockings hanging all over the spot. I was petrified. Things are different nowadays but then, I'd never touched a girl like that in my life. I stood and coughed but nobody moved. Eventually they woke up and it's laughable now how embarrassed I was. But after that first time I was all right. I just used to go into their room in the mornings and give their beds a kick to wake them.

From Edinburgh it was back to Cowglen, a fortnight's leave, then back to work for one day. A new sergeant had taken over and asked, 'Do you know anything about special diets? No? Well, it's never to late to learn. Tomorrow morning, first thing it's diet cooking.' 'I don't think so' I told him. 'I'm getting demobbed tomorrow.' Well, he went into orbit but I only worked in the main cookhouse the next day. Then I went from Glasgow to Crowborough in Sussex to get demobbed which took nearly three days.

'Tony in his cook's uniform'

When we started our National Service, we got twenty-one shillings a week. Out of that, if you allowed your parents seven shillings a week and you got a bullet through your head doing active service, they got compensation. So I was reduced to fourteen shillings a week. Then they always took something off for barrack room damages and that left me with twelve shillings. With being a cook and working in a sergeants' mess for a lot of my service, I earned quite a lot of money with extra messing allowance. And being on duty from seven in the morning right through to seven at night was more money. Then when I passed my B2 that gave me a hefty pay rise.

Actually, I was quite well off and went to the pictures a lot when I was at the CIC. In them days there were picture houses in every little village like Dalkeith, Lasswade, Bonnyrigg or Penicuik. The reason why I could go to the pictures was that I didn't smoke. I had my last cigarette the night I started courting with Joan on 12 July 1952. We got paid on a Thursday and by Monday, nearly everybody who smoked was absolutely bankrupt. They'd take it in turns to go round the ashbins of the officers' and sergeants' mess looking for cigarette ends so they could roll themselves cigarettes. So me and two others who didn't smoke used to go to the pictures. We weren't very popular because it was peer pressure, you see, we weren't fitting in because we didn't smoke and had money. Then again, I had sixteen postings in twenty-four months, so I didn't experience the same comradeship there was with other servicemen.

We hadn't been in the Army long when we had to go and see an officer. He told us all the benefits of signing-on for twenty-one years, all the extra money we'd get and we'd be out by the time we were forty with a pension. Everyone of us thought he was a lunatic because none of us was ever going to reach the age of forty. Our parents reached forty but not us. At eighteen it was too far into the future. Yet time goes by. I remember when I reached forty and the years had gone by, just like that. And I thought, 'I could have had a pension now, a good army pension,' but when you are eighteen the idea is a non-starter.

I was very proud to do my National Service. I wouldn't actually say I enjoyed it because I didn't. I would rather have been at home but as I say, I'm proud now that I did it. With being under-weight I always had the satisfying thought at the back of my mind that if I ever got into a load of bother or got somebody nasty in charge of me, I could have pulled the carpet from right under their feet by going to the MO.

When I was eighteen I had stroppy ideas and thought Kendal was a bum place. I wanted to see the lights and see the world but after I'd seen London, Glasgow and Edinburgh, I knew where I wanted to be for the rest of my life. But National Service made you appreciate the finer points of home life even though I didn't have much of one after my mother died, I knew I was going to marry Joan and things would get better. With being on good money in the Army, I'd saved it all and that furnished our house when Joan and I got married.

Now, when I finished my National Service, I was an AER reservist and was called up again in 1956. I should have gone down to Bedford in the spring of 1956 but that was the day my daughter Susan was born. So I rang and asked if I could be let off and went down to Bedford in the May. There were hundreds and thousands of us on the camp and all the lads did was march up and down. I was cooking of course, so it wasn't so bad. I remember we did some cooking for a lot of local dignitaries. We had to come running into this wood with leaves stuck on our helmets and faces blackened. Then we dug trenches for the petrol burners and cooked a meal for all these dignitaries. It was a lovely summer day and all these officers and their ladies sat down and ate this meal we prepared. Apart from us cooking, it was a complete waste of time.

A couple of months after I'd come home for being an AER reservist, the Suez Crisis erupted and the lads on standby were kept in for six months. I missed the Korean War by three weeks and the Suez Crisis by a couple of months. But I wasn't really sorry. Rather than go abroad, I wanted to get home to Joan. I'd written one hundred and fifty letters to her in two years as I was in love, you see.

SIX

'Harsh discipline'

Jim Mattinson, *Served in the Welsh Guards 1952-1954*

I went to Dent school and then when I was eleven or twelve I was sent to a boarding school between Leeds and Bradford at a place called Apperley Bridge. My father had died and I think my mother sent me to boarding school because she thought being brought up by herself and my two sisters wasn't good for me. But I was never an academic person and as soon as I was old enough, I left school and went to work at Gilbert, Gilkes and Gordon's, the engineers at Kendal.

At seventeen we used to have to register for National Service and then got word to go for a medical. Well, you see with Dent being in Yorkshire, I had to go to Leeds for my medical. I remember the recruiting officer was a big Coldstream Guards sergeant and he asked me what I wanted to do. I said I wanted to go into the Navy and was told no. If I went into the Navy I had to sign on for five years as a medical man. So I asked, 'What about the REME?' and the sergeant replied, 'Well, if you sign on for three years you can go into REME.' I wasn't going to sign on for anything like that and when he said, 'We want hundred-per-cent fit men like you for the infantry.' I told him, 'I'll do my two years in the infantry.'

I got my calling-up papers in February 1952 and had to report to the Guards depot at Caterham in Surrey. Imagine, me a country yokel never having been to London and going down there. But the journey wasn't so bad. I went down on the overnight train and got into Euston about five o'clock in the morning. I wandered round London and as I'd heard all about Lyons' tea houses I went into one of them. After lunch I decided I'd make my way to Caterham and on the train were quite a few lads going there.

When we reached Caterham we went into the camp and there was this sergeant-of-the-guard at the gate. It was 'Come on in lads, come on in.' Well, as soon as we were inside, it was a different atmosphere. There was a young recruit on picket duty and he had to take us down to the receiving room. That was a distance of maybe a quarter of a mile down a long drive. This recruit was marching at one hundred and eighty paces a minute with his arms flung high and there was the rest of us trying to keep up with him. I even got a stitch doing that. On the receiving room wall was a list of regiments. Our names were under which one we were going into. I looked down the list of regiments and no, I wasn't in the Grenadier Guards or the Coldstream Guards, or the Irish Guards and I eventually I found my name under the Welsh Guards.

MINISTRY OF LABOUR AND NATIONAL SERVICE

NATIONAL SERVICE ACTS

Medical History

1. When you attend for medical examination you will be required to furnish details of your personal and family medical history. The Medical Board will give careful consideration to any medical evidence which you may bring with you regarding any illnesses or disabilities from which you have suffered. You should also be prepared to answer the following questions:

In what parish and town were you born?

Are you a British subject by birth?

Are both your parents British subjects by birth? If the answer is in the negative, information will be required regarding nationality at birth of your parents.

Are you or is either of your parents a naturalised British subject? If so, the date of the naturalisation certificate in each case will be required.

Service Preference

2. As indicated in the leaflet N.L.2. which is issued to all men who register under the National Service Acts, while as far as possible arrangements will be made to allow men to serve in the Service for which they express a preference, it may not always be possible (e.g., because of the limited number of vacancies or because of medical grading) to post an individual in accordance with his preference.

3. Accordingly, whether or not you originally expressed a preference for service in the Army, you may find yourself being interviewed by the Military Interviewing Officer with a view to service in the Army. Among other questions, you would be asked whether you have a preference for any particular Corps or Regiment, and if so, whether it was based on a family connection, e.g., because your father or brother was serving or had served therein.

N.S.32 [P.T.O.

Ministry of Labour & National Service Act

From the receiving room, a training soldier came and collected us and took us to our respective barracks. The first night was a bit rough and some of the lads couldn't hack it but fortunately I was used to being away from home. The following day we were issued with all our equipment and uniform, bought our blanco, had our hair cut, our teeth examined and the discipline really started.

As you know, the discipline in the Guards is very strict. We started square bashing and after doing that all day, we'd go back to our billet, put a ground sheet and a board across our beds, then sit for an hour and a half working. You filled your mug up with water for blancoing and you just blancoed and spit and polished your boots. All this stuff was on your beds and while you worked away, you weren't allowed to speak to each other. The qualified guardsman in charge, 'Training Soldier' as you had to address him, fired questions as you polished. He'd ask you a question and you sat to attention to answer him on the regimental history, company mottoes, and battle honours.

All that was before tea. After tea, which was our last meal of the day, you could talk and smoke then it was back to your work. For the first few weeks, you never got to the NAAFI. On a Thursday, which was pay-day, one guy was allocated to go to the NAAFI to buy your boot polish and stuff you needed but the rest of us couldn't go. We continued working and at ten o'clock at night Training Soldier would inspect all our kit. If it wasn't up to what he thought was the standard, he'd put your boots in the coal bunker and you had to walk all over them. All the polish would be cracked on your boots and as lights out was at ten thirty, you had to go onto the landing and spit and polish all over again.

Now, Caterham Barracks were very, very old and big cold buildings. You went up big circular stone steps like the inside of a tower, with rooms off between each landing. These steps had vent holes or slots just like an old castle and this was where you had to sit and do your kit after lights out. I know we had a bit of snow that year and it was blowing through these holes when we were sitting there freezing and cleaning our boots for the next morning. Because when you went on parade, you got inspected and got booked if something was dirty, then it was the training soldier in charge who got into trouble.

On the drill square if you made a mistake or got out of step, the sergeant would come across, stare into your face saying, 'You're a dozy bastard. What are you?' All the time he was saying that, he'd be rubbing the bottom of his boot on your toe-cap, breaking the film of polish you had on it. Then all the platoon would do what was called 'a chasing.' They'd have us going hell-for-leather left, right, left, right, right turn and sweat would be pouring out of you. The sergeant was blaming you and saying, 'This is all because of Mattinson.' He was trying to get the others on your back but that never happened in fact I think it created goodwill.

Really our time at Caterham was PT and mostly square bashing. I must admit I found all the square bashing very difficult at first and thought I'd never learn or remember it all. But once you got the hang of it, it was all right. You see, with the square bashing you had to learn everything by numbers because the Guards would be on duty for royal funerals, the Trooping of the Colour and even the Coronation. However, while the Guards are trained to do ceremonial duties, they are foremost infantry soldiers and have good fighting records and quite impressive battle honours.

When you were out drilling, they'd do an inspection of the barracks. Now, your overcoat was hung up in your locker because it was very rarely used. But it had to be folded in a certain way with all the buttons to the front and showing. If you had forgotten about this, when you got back to the barracks, all the buttons would have been cut off. It was a hell of a job sewing buttons onto an army coat. Then it was back to the blancoing all night until ten when you had a smoke and then bed.

Oh, it was harsh discipline. I've always said, if I hadn't had a good home, I'd have been over that army wall and off to Canada. Kit inspections were once a week and before the Officer came round, training soldier would have a look at the kit. If he didn't like the look of it or was in a mood with you, he'd just tip it on the floor. You just had to set it all out again properly as it all had to be laid out in a sequence.

All the time you were going to the mess room or the barracks you had to go at one hundred and eighty paces to the minute which is quite fast. Even when you had your knife, fork and mug in your left hand, your right arm had to swing up to shoulder height. The thing was, say you'd been on the square doing drill and it was PT next, you were marched to the door of your billet, then you raced upstairs, changed and the last one outside when you reformed had to clean the toilets that night.

There was one horrible thing I witnessed. There was this lad and Training Soldier reckoned he was dirty so six guys were picked out to give him a bath. Bloody hell, they got brushes and scrubbed him with them. It was barbaric and cruel. Now-a-days they would be sued if they did things like that. But when you looked through the museums of the Guards and saw some of the punishments that had previously been carried out, I suppose that's how they kept discipline and their good name.

After four weeks' training you'd have a parade and if you failed that, your whole parade was put back a week and you had to do it all again the following week. The same thing happened after eight weeks and twelve weeks. You really suffered if you failed one, as it was bad marks against your drill NCO.

Eventually, you were allowed out of camp on a Saturday afternoon and could go to Croydon. However, you'd get the sergeant-of-the-guard to sign you out and he would inspect you. Sometimes, if he was in the mood, he'd find something wrong with you. Then you'd have to go back to the barracks and rectify it but you knew you were wasting your time trying to go out again as he'd still find something wrong so you just didn't bother.

Our wage was ten shillings one week and one pound the next week. I don't think anything was taken off for barrack room damages but one time I had to pay for a new kit bag. They'd told me to light a fire in the barrack room one day. You know how you used to hold paper over the fire place to cause a draught and get a fire going? Well, I used my kit bag instead and that caught fire.

It was while we were at Caterham that the King (King George V1) died. We were the only recruits at Caterham at the time and we had to line Fleet Street in London while the proclamation for the Coronation was read out. I'll never forget that. We weren't qualified to wear our red guards' tunics and wore our khaki uniform. We were all lined up on the street, then formed up, have fixed bayonets and space out. One of our lads dropped his bayonet while he was fixing it. Well, that night, it was in one of the London papers, 'Guardsman looses his bayonet,' because guardsmen aren't supposed to do anything like that or faint.

I did get home for a weekend. We could get up to London and catch the overnight train to Oxenholme. In those days it was called the mail train and sometimes the mail man from Sedbergh would be at Oxenholme and give me a lift home. But in the forces, you just got home the best way you could.

After Caterham I was moved on to Perbright in Surrey for field training. We were in huts at Perbright and only had two drills, one on Wednesday and the other on Saturday. The rest of the time you were in denims learning how to take guns, 303's and Lee Enfields apart. After six or eight weeks we went up to Yorkshire on manoeuvres. We stayed in huts at the castle at Pickering and went upon the moors near Filingdale using live ammo. First, there was a demonstration of what to do and then off we went by truck onto the moors to do what we'd been shown. Later that day we were supposed to come back to Pickering by truck. But we had a platoon commander, a smashing little feller but he had us either walking or force marching both ways, every day. That got you really fit.

After that we got embarkation leave before going to Germany and then sailed from Harwich. The journey was bloody awful as it was a pretty rough crossing and a lot of people were sick. When you went up on deck the next morning, all the toilets were full and swilling all over the decks. On reaching the Hook of Holland, we travelled by train into Germany and through the Russian zone. It was night when we travelled through the Russian zone and there hadn't to be a light showing from the train. If the Russians were that way inclined, they'd stop the train and send us back. At the time there was a lot of tension between the Russians and the other three powers and that's why they made it difficult. Just prior to us arriving, there had been the Berlin air-lift to get food in because the Russians had stopped people travelling into Berlin.

We were stationed at the Wavell barracks in Berlin and they were beautiful. These had been German barracks during the war and Hitler must have looked after his troops as we had none like them in England. I mean, some rooms just had two people in and the most to a room was six.

The first thing they did when you'd been in Berlin a couple of days, was take you by coach, showing you around and where all the sectors ended. That was so you didn't get into the Russian zone by mistake. Now, the western sectors, they'd rebuilt their sectors a hell of a lot but the Russian one was still in ruins. Even though the Brandenberg Gate is in the British sector, there was two Russian tanks guarded by two Russians. It was quite hilarious as our sergeant was showing us round these tanks and calling the Russian guards all sorts of names but they hadn't a clue what he was saying.

After the tour of Berlin, we were shown a film about venereal diseases. And boy, I've seen grown men faint watching this film. We were warned of the high rate of venereal disease in Berlin and told we had to be very careful. They said the German people blamed that on the Russians. The Russians were the first army into Berlin at the end of the war and raped young girls, grandmas', everybody. We were well protected as it was an offence to catch venereal disease. You could draw Durex from the guardroom when you went into town. On returning to camp, if you'd been with a woman, you signed a book then went to a wash-house and had a thorough wash.

I'd got friendly with a lad from South Wales who'd been in Berlin longer than me. He'd caught the disease and when he'd had a few drinks he used to get very depressed about it. He had a girl friend back home and had been told that any children they had could be affected by the disease. I don't know if that was the case or not because, I mean, we were only bits of lads and heard all sorts of tales.

We still had typical army food in Berlin and it was bloody rubbish. I wasn't a bit meat eater in those days and was very faddy about my food. Everybody used to like sitting next to me as they'd get all my meat because it was so gristly. No, I'm not a lover of army food as it was all crap in those days. But American food was good. We used to go on manoeuvres with the French and the Americans. These manoeuvres might last seven days and we were living in trenches half-full of water. Well, the Americans had the best of everything and we were living on what we could nick. So we used to try and get captured by the Americans as they had chicken and all sorts but they got wise to us and used to send us right back.

Our regiment was guarding Spandau prison in Berlin, doing a forty-eight hour guard. I think twenty-eight of us, plus four NCO's and an officer would go to the prison and we'd march from our barracks with our corps of drums playing. I suppose we were emphasising our English presence as the Cold War was at its height and the Russians might think of taking over. And the people of Berlin loved a military show and they loved us. We couldn't do any wrong because they were frightened to death of the Russians who surrounded them.

It's a massive place is Spandau prison, very austere, and we were on duty on wall towers like you see on television programmes. We had to climb up to these towers then pull the ladders up after us. So all we saw of the German prisoners was when they were in the courtyard.

There were seven of these prisoners in Spandau at the time and they'd come out into the courtyard in a morning for exercise and walk backwards and forwards. They walked in pairs except for Hesse who was on his own. None of the others spoke to him because he was classed as a traitor with flying over to England during the Second World War.

Being on guard in the wall towers, we didn't really get anywhere near the prisoners so obviously we couldn't speak to them. The Officers inside looking after them were very educated guys as they all had to speak English, Russian, French and German. It was very occasionally that we went inside the building. Once we had to escort painters around who were painting the interior. I remember Hesse's cell because he had an organ inside it which he used to play a lot.

At one time there was a lot in the English papers about supposed raids on Spandau to get the Nazi war criminals out. But, I mean, these prisoners were that decrepit, if we'd taken the bloody wires down they couldn't have walked out, they were so old.

There was still a black market in Germany. As my mother used to send me parcels, I used to ask her to put a jar of coffee in it and sell that on the black market. Also, we were allowed to buy two hundred cigarettes and as much rolling tobacco as we wanted from the NAAFI each week. The cigarettes were so cheap we used to sell them down the black market for beer money and roll our own cigarettes. Really, the only thing we spent our money on was beer. We used to like going to these corner cafes and a bar that was outside the camp. But always on a Saturday night if we weren't on duty we went by tram to a big NAAFI club. When you'd got off the tram and were walking across the green to this club there would be all these German prostitutes standing there. I couldn't repeat what they used to say to you but we'd answer, 'Oh bugger off, you dirty old cow.' 'Me not dirty, me clean,' they'd protest. That was because the Military Police used to pick them up regular away and they'd be given a medical and certificate to prove they were clean.

You used to get some wild lads in the Army. One lad who was in the same company as me, he was a bit of a wild man and shoved a bottle into a German taxi driver's face one night. He got eleven months detention for that. When he came back to the battalion after his eleven months, he still had to do eleven months extra service for the time he missed in prison.

Another lad, who was a mate of mine from South Wales, he was a bit of a boxer and had a fiery temper. He used to get put into the prison goal for seven days at a time. Now, a big lad from Swansea who had been made up to corporal and put into the Military Police used to give this mate of mine a hard time. This corporal eventually got broken back down and had to come back to our company. Well, my mate had gone into the barracks drunk one night and gave this ex-corporal a hiding. As I've said, these barracks were lovely buildings but the ex-corporal had been given such a hiding there was blood all over the place and my mate had him cleaning his blood up with a tooth brush. He got twenty-eight days for that and was still serving it when I came back to Aldershot. I was on guard one night and he said to me, 'I pleaded drunk but if I'd known I was going to get twenty-eight days, he'd have got a bigger bloody hiding.' But I felt sorry for some people in the Army because if they were a bit timid, it must have been very hard. I wouldn't say that I could physically take care of myself but I was lucky that I could rub along in company and get away with things.

'Jim, standing left, in ceremonial dress'

We'd been over in Germany about six months when the Battalion came home as the Coronation and Trooping of the colour were due to come off. We moved into Chelsea Barracks and it was a busy time. In the mornings we were practising for the Coronation and in the afternoons, for the Trooping of the Colour. We were really kept at it and your kit takes some cleaning. You've got your white belt to blanco, trousers to keep pressed, buttons to clean on your tunic and there's your bear skin. They did say that it took one and a half hours just for the bear skin alone. When you first get issued with one, it would feel all right but after you've been on parade for an hour and a half, it starts nipping around your head. That's why so many people faint wearing them. If you could just put your hand up and move it a bit but you can't because you'd get booked.

After we'd been practising all day, we used to hit the town at night. One of the lads with us, Richard's, was a right Londoner and he got a good skinful. The next day he was so bad (ill) that when he was marching shoulder to shoulder, two others on either side were literally holding him up. Because Richard's had been so ill and kept on his feet, he got a credit for that. What the officers hadn't realised was that it was a self-inflicted illness and he only kept his feet because he was being held up.

The biggest crowds I've ever seen were at the Coronation. For three days before, people were camping out on the streets just to grab a place. On Coronation morning, we left Chelsea Barracks at six o' clock and as it was raining we had our grey capes on. The regimental band was in front as we marched out and spread out on the Mall. There were millions of people there and when they saw us you could hear them saying, 'Oh, the Guards aren't much.' But about half-past-ten the weather cleared up and we got word to take our capes off. You could see right along the Mall all these red tunics coming into view and as soon as the crowds saw those they started cheering like mad.

The atmosphere with all the crowds was fantastic and there wasn't any thugs around then like there is today to spoil things. The Coronation procession formed up in front of us so we had a good view of everything. One of the highlights for the crowds was Queen Salote of Tonga driving past in an open carriage even though it started raining again. I remember seeing Princess Margaret who looked so tiny, just like a little doll, and thinking I could pick her up in my hand.

Our regiment had a haversack lunch in St James's Park. We only had twenty minutes out of line and you didn't really have time to eat the food. It seemed as though everybody was coming up to you, wanting to take a photograph of you holding their kiddies.

After the procession had ended we marched back to the barracks with our platoon right behind the band. An officer marches in the middle of the road and soldiers are spread out in fours behind him. Of each four, two soldiers of which I was one, were actually marching in the gutter on either side of the road. So there I was marching away and winking at girls as I passed. You could hear them saying, 'He winked at me, that Guard winked at me,' and I was thinking, 'I hope that bloody officer doesn't hear that.'

It was half-past-six at night when we got back to the barracks. Even though it had been a long day London was still heaving with people and we went out for the night. There was five of us together with three shillings and six pence between us. The four other guys said to me, 'Here Jimmy, you look after the money,' so off we wandered round London looking through the doors to see which pub we thought we might get treat in.

Behind the old Windmill Theatre we walked into a pub and I ordered five gills of beer. A bloke standing at the bar heard this and said to the barman, 'Make them pints for the lads' and paid for us. Before we got a swig out of our drinks he ordered us five more. The other guys went and sat down with some girls and I thought, 'I'm sticking close to this bloke, I'm getting free beer.' What happened was, this bloke's wife had come into some money and he was spending it for her. Every time he ran out of money he'd shout across to where she was sitting, 'Give us some more money.' My luck held as I even found a two bob piece in the sawdust. So when we eventually came out of the pub, I had the same money as I went in with plus twenty fags I'd bought with the two bob. After that we met up with some girls and it was six o'clock the next morning when we were walking back up to Chelsea Barracks.

After the Coronation and the Trooping of the Colour our regiment did public duties at Windsor Castle. You'd go as a squad, say thirty of you, marching from your barracks to the Castle. There you'd have a guardroom with beds where you could lie down or clean your uniform. We'd do two hours of duty and four hours off so it was pretty hard work. But as a young feller it was glamorous on duty and you thought, 'Bloody hell, I'm a big operator.' Of course you're not supposed to speak to the public on duty but you'd be amazed at how many dates you made out of the corner of your mouth.

The Prince of Wales is always colonel of the Welsh Guards. Years before it had been the old Prince of Wales who abdicated. In fact, he came to see us when we were in Berlin and inspected us. Now, we were all over six feet tall and he only came to about our belly buttons but he walked down the line and then turned to whoever he was with and said, 'Oh, the men in the Prince of Wales Company aren't very tall, now.' Just think, that little squirt saying we weren't very tall!

Anyway, as Prince Charles was still so young and hadn't been created Prince of Wales, the Duke of Edinburgh became Colonel of the Welsh Guards. By about September 1953 we were going to Egypt and I became the CO's orderly. So when the Duke of Edinburgh came to say cheerio to us at Windsor Castle, I had to march in front with my little pace stick, with our RSM behind and the Duke and all the commanding officers following him. And did the Duke speak to any of us? Did he buggery!

We sailed from Southampton on the troopship, *Empire Ken* and I enjoyed the journey. At Malta we put down and our drums beat the retreat at the quay side and then it was on to Algiers. For shore leave there, we were only allowed to change so much money but me and some mates thought we would be fly and changed some at a bank. Then we went into this cafe and started drinking wine which we weren't used to. The waiter kept trying to tell us to be careful but we all finished up with thick heads and were ill.

When we reached Port Said the Egyptians were up and swarming all over the boat before you knew where you were. Nothing was too hot for them to take away. Luckily our guns had been all locked up or they would have gone with them. From Port Said we went to El Bala which is midway between Port Said and Moascar and where we were stationed.

On camp we slept under canvas and one night the lads on guard shot at two intruders. They shot one intruder, just maiming him. When the guards reached this bloke, he was stark naked and had all his body greased so that you couldn't hold him. These two intruders had been through our tents and even though there were twenty of us to a tent, none of us had heard them.

EGYPT

Geography

When you think of Egypt, you automatically remember the River Nile, and to a great degree, the Nile is Egypt. The total area of Egypt is 363,000 square miles; it is about six times as big as England and Wales. Of this area 250,000 square miles is waterless desert; the remaining 13,000 square miles, watered by the Nile, supports 98 per cent. of the population. Egypt, more for convenience than anything else, has been divided into Upper Egypt, from the Sudan border north to Cairo, and Lower Egypt, comprising the Nile Delta—the triangle between Cairo, Alexandria and Damietta; an area sometimes known simply as the Delta. Another zone which has developed in recent years is the Canal Zone, owing its fertility to the Sweet Water Canal which is fed by the Nile, and stretches from Cairo to Ismailia, and then parallel to the Suez Canal. It is in the Canal Zone that you will be stationed.

Egypt is a predominantly agricultural country, although in the last forty years industry has expanded considerably. The backbone of Egypt's prosperity is still the "fellah," the peasant farmer. Because there is practically no rain in Egypt, and production is so small, the fellahin have evolved a technique of their own, by which they produce the maximum yield from their plots. Labour is plentiful and cheap—in the last hundred years it is estimated that the population has risen by 13,000,000 and the birth-rate is the second highest in the world—43 per 1,000 of the population. These facts explain too, the poverty of the Egyptian peasants; but the true fellah is simple, hard-working and frugal in his tastes, like the peasant population of many other lands; it is only when he moves to the towns that he loses these qualities. Cheap labour has also played its part in the development of the major industries of Egypt. Cotton accounts for four-fifths of her exports, and she is one of the foremost cotton-producing countries in the world. The rise of this industry has been due largely to the huge dams and barrages on the Upper Nile, erected under the supervision of British engineers, which have provided controlled irrigation all the year round, instead of the haphazard system which depended entirely on the flooding of the Nile. Other industries which have developed are those engaged in the production of tobacco, silk, cement, matches, furniture and clothing.

The Egyptian winter climate is delightful; dry, sunny and cool; in May the hot weather begins and does not cease until November. In April a hot, sand-laden wind, known as the "Khamsin," blows from the south and usually lasts for about three suffocating days at a time. During the hot weather troops wear khaki drill shorts and shirt-sleeves by day, and slacks at night; in winter battle-dress is worn.

'Excerpt from booklet, The Middle East given to troops going abroad'

It was the time that the troubles were on and the Egyptians wanted the British out of the country. So army vehicles that came along outside our camp had to stop at the road-block and wait until another vehicle came along as they had to travel in pairs. This was because the Egyptians would drive along side a lorry, jump onto the back and shoot the driver. We had to ride shotgun on the lorries with our gun and ammunition to protect the drivers. I suppose all this could have been frightening but we were very naive and when you're young you fear nothing. Often drivers were guys from a Mauritius regiment who were out there and as they didn't speak English we'd be sat all day in their cab without a word passing between us.

I was still the Commander's orderly and it was a real good job as you didn't do any work. Basically, what you did was go round all the companies each day delivering messages from the orderly room. Or the Regimental Sergeant Major would say, 'Go to the sergeants' mess and get me a pot of tea.' So off I'd go and as the RSM is THE boss man, I'd get him a pot of tea and one for myself. Even though I was still living in the Prince of Wales quarters, when our Company Sergeant Major came up and told us to scrub floors or whatever, I'd say 'I have to go over to the orderly room.' Often he'd tell me, 'No, you're not, you're staying here' but when you said, 'Well, I have to see the RSM,' that made our CSM scorch his underpants off. So I'd trot to the orderly room and sit there while the others did the work. Actually it was quite an honour to have this job as orderly because it was said you were the smartest guy in the battalion. But that's all you did, look pretty.

NAAFI/EFI

NAAFI operates the following services in the Middle East :

1. Canteens for Junior Other Ranks, both male and female, for units in camps and barracks.
2. Clubs for Officers, senior N.C.O.s, and O.R.s in Garrison towns and leave centres.
3. Leave Camps for families, single Officers, and O.R.s in Egypt and Cyprus.
4. Retail shops for Servicemen and their families in localities where families reside.
5. Bulk Issue Stores which supply messes with their requirements of food and drink.
6. Service and sports shops where sports gear and gifts of the widest possible range are available for sale to units and individuals.

'NAAFI'

'At Al Bala. Jim is standing on the left'

Socially, there was very little on camp besides the NAAFI. Our biggest entertainment was going swimming in the Suez Canal. There was a lot of emigration going on at that time and English people on the boats going home would throw apples and oranges down to us. Maybe on a Saturday we'd go up to Moascar which was a garrison town. There'd be a couple of trucks going and we'd be standing in the back of them. But you know what the Welsh are like, they're big singers. I know we went to one bar in Moascar and had hardly anything to drink, maybe two or three beers and all the Welsh blokes started singing. The bar was promptly closed down as they thought we were all drunk. But the Welsh are like that, they're not all good singers individually but sound real good when they're harmonising. And they will sing these songs, *Sospan fac* and *When you come home again to Wales*. It's just natural to them, they want to sing.

The worst thing about Egypt was when there was a sandstorm and boy, it's something. Sand gets everywhere. You had suitcases under your bed and when you opened them, they were full of sand. If a storm started in the night, you woke up and your eyes were full of sand. If it was on during the day, you had to wear goggles to keep the sand out. It didn't hurt but it was just that sand was blowing for about three days at a time.

The battalion was to do two years in Egypt but after six months my two National Service was up. Oh, we got the old bullshit. Our Adjutant said, 'You're one of the best platoons we've ever had,' which he told to everybody. Then there was, 'What do you think about staying on? If you want to stay on Mattinson, you can be a sergeant.' No way. I'd done my bit, I was on my bike.

I flew back from Fayid in a troop plane, an old York. We had to refuel at Malta during the night and then, because we had strong headwinds, refuel again at Marsailles. It was afternoon or early evening when we set off from Egypt and eleven o'clock the following morning when we arrived at Stanstead. From there, coaches took us up to London and we were pretty happy then because we'd done our time and were being demobbed.

We were demobbed very quickly. By that stage we were in huts at Perbright and there wasn't much for us to do and they let us go a few days earlier than we should have been. We kept all our uniform for going on Z Reserve but some that had worn out, we had to pay for and replace. I did two trainings with Z Reserve, one at Thetford in Norfolk and the other in Wales. These were quite good as you met up with your old mates again.

I should have joined the old comrades association because they have a branch at Liverpool but I hate paperwork so I just never bothered. Since doing National Service I've always worked at Gilbert, Gilkes and Gordon and altogether done about four million miles travelling for them. Often I was working in remote parts of the world where the natives had never seen a white man and the village headman used to beat messages out on a drum. At times like that I don't think I could have stuck it without having the discipline from my army days.

On the odd occasion working away I've bumped into lads from the regiment and they've looked at me and said, 'It's Matto, isn't it?' In fact, the other week the Duke of Edinburgh, our old Regimental Colonel visited Gilkes and I was introduced to him. Oddly enough he didn't remember me and ask, 'It's Matto, isn't it?'

SEVEN

'A bit of a rumpus'

Robert Jackson, *served in the REME, 1958-1960*

I left school and started an apprenticeship with a motor engineer at Kendal. Because I was working a six year apprenticeship and going to the Allen Technical Institute at nights, I was sent a deferment for National Service.

In 1958 when I was twenty one, I got a letter to go for a medical at the Fullwood Barracks on the outskirts of Preston. I'd never experienced anything like that medical. All these doctors looking in all the nooks and crannies. They gave you a full check-over and had the taps running so they would get a full sample out of you!

After the medical I was asked what regiment I'd like to join. Because I was a motor mechanic I thought the RAF would be better than anything else, so I put down the motor transport section in the RAF as my preferred job. But the next thing I knew, I got the papers to go down and join the REME at Honiton in Devon. You just had no choice in the matter, that was it.

I'd previously lived up at Borrowdale and Lorton, so I was a right country lad and hadn't much experience of travelling. Probably Blackpool was the furthest I'd been so it was a long journey to Honiton. As you went down on the train, there were other lads getting on but you didn't realise until you got to Exeter that you were all going to the same place.

When we got to Honiton there were lorries waiting to take us from the railway station to the camp. It would be night when we got there and we were put into wooden huts with pot bellied stoves, about thirty of us in each hut. The following morning the initiation into the Army started. It's a silly thing but it's the haircut that stands out in everybody's mind. You knew before you went in the Army you'd get a real short back and sides. I'd had one the week before, thinking 'Well, that's nice and short, I'll not need another one,' but I did have one. You're still in civvies and you go round the clothing department for your uniform. There's no measuring up, they just look at you, throw you the nearest clothes and then you're taken to a tailor who alters your two uniforms to fit.

When you first get your beret, it's all flat on top and you learn how to make it more stylish. To do that, you put your beret in boiling water and then plunge it into cold water a number of times. The material contracts which makes the beret much nicer and gives a tight fit. You can also shape the beret better while it's damp and find once it's contracted it's much more waterproof.

To try and get a good crease in your trousers, one of the old methods was to rub soap down the inside of the seam. Once pressed, the soap holds the material together. Unfortunately, I once listened to one of the lads who told me of another idea to get a good crease. As army trousers are made out of worsted material, which is thick and fluffy, he told me to take a razor and shave off all the fluff from the inside of the seam. Then when the trousers were pressed, with not having as much bulky material you got a sharper crease. I did this with one pair of trousers and did it too well. A few months later, the trousers split down the front because I'd shaved right into the material.

Now, if you go into a regiment like the Border's, you go in and do at least twelve weeks' training. REME is a bit different from other units because you only do six weeks' basic training. You get a very quick initiation then they want you for mechanical or electrical knowledge. I would have expected there to have been a lot more ex-apprentices in REME but there wasn't. They were from all walks of life and had been doing all sorts of jobs so I don't know how they got chosen.

The corporal in charge of our hut was all right. He was strict but fair and I wasn't in anyway frightened of him. The lads in the hut were from all over and we got on very well. However, I shouldn't say it but some of them, who were from the north of Scotland, spoke virtually Gaelic and we couldn't understand them which caused a bit of an upset at times.

I never found the food objectionable. I know a lot used to say it was terrible so I must have been lucky at the different camps I was at. There was plenty to eat and you did eat when you were in training as you were burning the calories off. You had choices of everything you wanted. You had a cooked breakfast, dinner and tea with a choice of three or four meats at meal times. The NAAFI used to come round mid-morning and in the afternoon and you could buy buns or whatever.

The first six weeks were basically to do your square bashing, learning how to shoot and have fitness tests at the end of it. I was quite well built when I first went into the Army but I lost stones of weight during basic training. I used to lie in a pool of sweat in that gym because of the rigours they put you through. It was all to get you fit and it really did get you fit.

'Robert, the young recruit passing through London'

We had all the different inoculations and I think one was for some sort of plague. After that one you were given forty-eight hours off but we were inoculated on a Friday when the weekend was supposed to be free, anyway. Once you'd had that jab your arm felt it was on fire and used to swell up with a big solid lump underneath it. Two or three lads were really ill in the middle of the night because of it and were carted off. We never saw them again but when they were fit they would return to a later course. However, for inoculations, that was the only time you tried to be at the front of the queue because the needle was sharper when it was first used. You see, they used the same needle for everybody.

After about five weeks at Honiton you were taken to another camp to do a test and see what your abilities were. Because I'd served my apprenticeship I passed the test all right and got a posting to a tank training unit. If I hadn't passed the test, I would have gone to one of the REME training camps where they would have taught me to become an engineer to their standards. That would have taken up to about six months more training before you got the qualifications and were passed on to a unit.

There were some lads who didn't want to progress any further and they were really swinging the lead. There were two who I remember who'd been at Honiton about six months. I think their idea was to serve their two years there because it was near home. The thing they had going when I was there was, they couldn't wear a beret as it gave them headaches. When we went on the firing ranges and squeezed the trigger to let off a burst of shots on machine guns, they used to just pull the trigger and fire off the lot. These two lads used to say they froze when they were firing.

After six weeks at Honiton and having no home leave, I was one of about half-a-dozen lads who were posted straight to Bordon in Hampshire. Lads from different camps were also coming into Bordon so there was a big influx. As we were coming in to specialise solely on tanks, we'd been filtered out from our camps and were coming in from different ways.

Even though I was older than most lads it was still a tremendous upheaval for me going from right in the country to army life and the dodges that some of the city lads pulled were out of this world. Because money was so short, one of the lads at Bordon organised a raffle. Everybody put in a couple of shillings, which between thirty and forty lads was a few pounds. The idea was, the lad who organised the raffle had a lot of papers and one had a cross on it. The one who drew the cross won the money. The organiser had secreted that one but said, 'Oh, will somebody draw out a paper for me,' which they did. That one went into his pocket and when everybody drew out their paper from the hat, he opened the one he had secreted and won the money. That trick works only once but those were the sort of things you had to learn about. Even one of the sergeants had a racket going. He used to take us out on exercise in one of the tanks to the local moors and have a couple of jerry cans with him. We used to dump one of the jerry cans filled with petrol and later that night he'd collect it, flog it or use it in his car.

One of the saddest things I witnessed was a lad who was dismissed from service because he'd done something wrong. The whole camp turned out while this lad's badges, beret epaulettes etc., were ripped off him right in the middle of the parade ground with the whole regiment lined up. I can't remember what he'd done wrong but it chokes me up today to think about it.

If anything, Bordon was a bit tougher than Honiton. You see there was a tremendous amount of equipment and sensitive stuff there. I don't know why but I found that worse as you didn't have time to think, with everything being more secret and stricter. As the Cold War was on we had a lot of secrecy and the camp was closely guarded. There were also Alsatian guard dogs which were kept in a compound. Vicious things they were, more like young donkeys.

I should have done a twelve week course at Bordon but before our course started, they had an intake of boy soldiers. These lads who'd joined the Army at sixteen or seventeen took priority. Our course was held back while they went through the process so I waited for two months kicking my heels while they did their course before ours could start.

I happened to be on guard duty on 5 November when we were told to be very, very careful because the IRA had made an attempt to get into an armoury two years before. With all the local fireworks banging off, they might try and come in under cover of all the noise. The IRA would have had a job getting into the armoury because it was like two buildings, one inside the other with these guard dogs in between. So if they broke through the first wall, they had these guard dogs to content with before they got into where the rifles and ammunition were. That was a real scary night because all we were issued with on guard duty was a pick-shaft. I remember walking around and guarding the armoury with my pick-shaft, fireworks banging off everywhere and expecting the IRA to turn up at any time.

After a few weeks at Bordon I got my first leave. When I stepped off the bus back home, Irene my girl friend was waiting for me. She hadn't seen me for nearly three months and just looked at me, saying, 'What the hell have they done to you?' as I'd lost a lot of weight.

You got two travel warrants a year but could go home most weekends. Because I had hardly any money I used to hitch-hike all the way up north on a Friday night. Two of us once got a lift with a pig wagon and it stunk to high heavan. Another time we were thumbing and a taxi stopped for us. We told the driver we couldn't pay but he said, 'I've already been paid and I'm going home to Birmingham.' He'd run somebody down south and was coming back empty. He was a really nice bloke and asked us to go and have a bit of a meal with him, then brought us to this end of Birmingham to pick up a lift.

In those days you could easily get a lift as long as you were in uniform. We'd leave camp at about four o'clock on a Friday afternoon and be home about dinner time on Saturday. We couldn't risk hitch-hiking back to camp as you had to be back at camp for eight o'clock on a Monday morning. So I used to catch the train on a Sunday night and when it arrived in London you had a quick scurry to where the train known as the Bordon Belle was. If the trains were late, you'd had it because you'd be reported as absent without leave and be on jankers.

Bordon was where I learnt to drive tanks and that qualified me to drive any track vehicle when I came out of the Army. Oh, it was great, driving a tank. Although they're big and lumbering, they're a real joy to drive. When learning to drive, we drove into a swampy area which was really muddy. You've got to drive in very slowly because if you don't you're nearly drowned in water. A bit of an experience was that.

At the end of the course we sat an exam on what we'd learnt about tanks. Then everybody was taken into another room and told, 'Right, you've all passed and these are the marks awarded.' A board was put up with all the vacancies from the different regiments and where they were based. If you got top marks, you got a choice, the pick of the postings. I did fairly well and chose a regiment simply because it was based at Catterick and I wanted to be near home. So I asked to join the 16/5 Lancers at Catterick.

It was about three or four days before Christmas when we were given movement papers and told, 'Right, that's it, away you go.' I arrived with another lad at Catterick and the camp was virtually closed down for Christmas. In those days they used to send everybody they could home and just have a skeleton staff. Now, that caused a problem as there was no bedding for us. The two of us were shown into this room, which wasn't heated and only had bed frames. We were so cold we literally lay in all our clothes including our great coats and hugged each other on a bed frame to keep warm. The following morning we went to the guardroom to find out what was happening and were told there was nothing they could do for us. Our paperwork hadn't been received because the camp had closed down and we might as well go home. So I was home for Christmas.

Back at Catterick I was still in the REME but we were what they called LAD, Light Aid Detachment, attached to the 16/5 Lancers. We were there to look after their machinery and I was on the tank side. Other REME lads looked after lorries, armoured cars or were electricians. It was quite a happy time because being a LAD, in our own little unit and having control of the transport area, everybody looked after you. A lot of lads had their own private little jobs they used to work on, such as the officers' cars. In the building that I was in, I know there was a motor cycle in bits that a lad was building up for himself and stuff was going right, left and centre out of the workshops. The downside were the winters. We were right up on the moors and it was so cold that if doors were left open even the sheep used to come in for warmth.

Provided I got a pass, which was reasonably easy to get, I could get home quite a lot. I used to come out of Catterick Camp, go up to Ripon and hitch it up the A1 to Scotch Corner then come over to Penrith and back down the A6. But that journey was dependant on Brough and Bowes not being blocked with snow in winter. Getting over Bowes in winter on a Friday night was the worst part.

Irene and I had been courting for a long, long time and were eventually going to get married. However, once I knew that the regiment was going to Germany we got married. Quite a lot of the lads got married before leaving Catterick because we didn't know exactly when we were going to Germany or when we were coming back. Getting married entailed having a talk with the Major and obtaining his permission because obviously it was going to cost the Army money. They would have to pay you two pounds odd marriage allowance. Big money! After obtaining permission from the Major I took a week's leave to get married and have a honeymoon.

We were given embarkation leave prior to going abroad and then the whole regiment had to meet up at Liverpool Street station. From there we went to Harwich and onto the boat for the Hook of Holland. That was a tremendous sight to see, all the troops boarding with all their kit. However, looking back, it was a frightening experience on the boat. We were on deck when we were leaving and then sent down below into the holds. By the next morning the air was foul as we'd been packed in like sardines. If anything had happened to that boat, we'd have been goners.

'Now in Germany'

At the Hook of Holland as you got off the boat you were given a coloured disc. The colour of the disc was the colour of the electric train you had to head for. Travelling through Holland, the scenery was very flat after the Lake District. At the German border you changed over to the old steam trains which were filthy. Once into Germany, the stuff some lads used to shout of the windows at the Germans was terrible. I suppose with it being just after the war, at the back of your mind you hated Germans. But one thing, the German railways were dead on time wherever you went. That was German efficiency.

After Catterick Camp, Osnabruck was a dream world. The camp was on a hillside overlooking a valley and it was absolutely beautiful with all sorts of flowers planted in the gardens. It was a modern camp, lovely to be in and the sheds for the tanks were all great big, new brick ones. The weather was marvellous and I had a really good impression of the place.

The food was fabulous. You'd go along for breakfast and there was all different cereals and bacon, eggs and sausage. At lunch time you'd have a choice of about six different meats – pork chops, steak and everything. On Sundays, especially in summer to ease the cooks' workload we'd have salads followed by fresh fruit. So it was rather nice on a hot summer's day having a salad followed by, maybe melons, bananas, oranges and apples. Actually, on the camp one of the lads was in charge of a herd of pigs. These pigs would eat up all the waste food and we always had fresh pork.

However, one of the cook's cut his finger and infected the whole camp. I went down to the MO one morning as I had a temperature of one hundred and three. Now, reporting sick in the Army was a nightmare as I had to leave my bed, pack up certain kit to take with me to the medical centre and from there I was sent in an open wagon to hospital. I think there were about thirty or forty of us, all with raging fever and sore throats, went into the local hospital. We were there for nearly a fortnight and had penicillin injections. One day I had a trainee who couldn't get the needle into my rear and it wasn't until about the sixth attempt he managed to jab the needle into me.

We were the lucky ones being in hospital because back at camp about a hundred other lads came down with the same condition. As the hospital was full, those lads were being treated by our own orderlies. The cause of this infection was traced back to the army cook who'd cut his finger, didn't dress it and then had his finger in the potato mixture. How it affected so many people, I'll never know.

The tanks were maintained all the time because we were usually on seventy-two hour standby in case war started, though sometimes it was dropped down to forty-eight hours. One day at the workshops a lad wanted a tank moving but there wasn't anybody around to do it for him. He wasn't trained but knew the basics of driving a tank so he jumped in to move it. Now, a tank has a low reverse for normal work and a high speed one for use in war time to reverse out of an awkward situation. Unfortunately, this lad put the tank in high reverse and went straight through the back of the workshop, bringing the wall down. That caused a bit of a rumpus.

On a typical day at camp we'd go and have breakfast and then report to the tank depot at eight o'clock. At ten o'clock you got a NAAFI break for about half an hour, then carried on working. Come dinner time you'd knock off, sometimes for a couple of hours and with it being such nice weather, sit outside and sunbathe. After that, you'd either carry on with maintenance or sometimes had sports just to break up the routine.

'Working at the weekend, Robert standing centre'
(Note the informal dress!)

We'd heard rumours there were army boxing championships going on and one day at the gym were told, 'We want to test out your boxing powers.' We were lined up according to height and as I was one of the taller ones, I was to go in the ring for the second bout. The first two lads went in the ring and they set about each other and really went to town. The lad who I was due in with next looked at me and we both shook our heads and said, 'No way.' When it was our turn in the ring, he tapped me and I tapped him and we both walked around until we were told, 'Out you come.' We were no good at all but the lads who were picked for training did all right. They got the best of everything and for a while didn't do guard duties only physical training.

Guard duty was two hours at a time, twice a night between six p.m. and six a.m. If you were doing bad ones, say eight o'clock to ten at night and then two in the morning until four o'clock, you couldn't leave the guard room until the guard changed at six a.m. After that, you'd have your breakfast and then be back on normal duty at eight o'clock. So that was a bit rough. In winter it was very cold. I mean, I've seen lads do guard duty wearing army issue pyjamas, full battledress, great coat, hat and gloves and still be perishing cold.

However, there was a comical side to guard duty. On camp there was a very friendly Alsatian. It used to sleep through the day but liked to come round with you on guard duty every night. The problem was we were still only issued with pick shafts and you'd hear this rustling in the bushes, wonder what was going on and then this damn Alsatian would leap out at you.

With the winters being so bitterly cold, although you had anti-freeze in the tanks, they could still freeze up as there was no heating in most of the garages. So, by the guard duty room was a bottle containing a weaker mixture of anti-freeze. The idea was, if the weather got so cold that the mixture started to crystallize, you knew you had to start up the tanks and warm them up. However, the tanks were maintained all the time because we were usually on seventy-two hour standby in case war started, though sometimes it was dropped down to forty-eight hours.

A lot of the time we were out on exercise on one of the nearby small training grounds. We would even go away for a month or six weeks to one of the bigger training grounds, maybe Luneburg Heath or Soltau. I was absolutely amazed on these big heaths as you'd be driving along and see all the ammunition and petrol that was stored out there. Millions and millions of gallons. You'd be in a fir forest and come across a stack of jerry cans as big as a house. Next there would be a huge ammunition dump just spread out.

It sounds a bit of an ego thing but I was a good mechanic, therefore I was put on the recovery tank. I was the driver and the mechanic; Mitch our corporal and a great lad was the commander; the other two were the electrician and the radio operator to keep us in touch with the other tanks. A main tank crew consists of five people and as ours was only four, we still got a five man ration so we were quite lucky. The thing we used to look out for was the water wagon because we had a problem getting enough liquid. The water wagon followed the tanks but you only saw it once a day or maybe once every two days. But everything else wasn't so bad

Our job was to follow the tanks wherever they went as the recovery tank is the breakdown vehicle. It didn't have a gun on, it had a winch with great big spades that let down at the back. Working on tanks we wore leather boots as wearing normal army boots with studs on there was a danger we could slip. On exercise, the bulk of the REME lads were in a base camp lived under canvas but we had a tent which fastened onto the side of the recovery tank. When the weather was nice, which it was a lot of the time, we slept out in the open and didn't bother with the tent. We used to get a bit of tarpaulin, knock four holes in it, tie it with rope like a hammock, sling it between two trees and sleep on that. It was wonderful. On the back deck of the tank is the engine compartment, which is massive. Other times, as the massive, twelve cylinder Rolls Royce engines of the tank were still warm, we'd put some camouflage netting down and lie on top of that. It was like sleeping in an oven. Lovely.

'One of the Centurian tanks'

The main battle tank that I trained on was the Centurion. It weighed forty-eight tons but with shells in, the weight went up to fifty tons. It was horrendous loading the tank onto a tranporter because sat in the cab, you couldn't see a thing. All you could hear were the instructions so you had to go very, very slow. On one occasion we went on an exercise by train and that was a nightmare loading the tanks on, one by one. But normally, going on an exercise, the transporters used to drive along the motorway. That was an impressive sight, solid armour for as far as you could see.

At night, driving a tank on the normal main roads, you just had two little side lights on. This was because, training for actual battle conditions, you weren't to use headlights. So you'd be driving down a road and see a car coming towards you. He'd suddenly spot you in his headlamps because you were taking up most of the road and he'd nearly land up in a ditch. There was no way he could move anywhere because you just had enough room to squeeze past him.

Normally when a night exercise was on, you'd have a mock battle with a tank and infantry regiment attacking another one. In our tank we'd be chasing around following these tanks and literally go for three nights without sleep. All night long the sky would be illuminated with flares going off and all these dummy bullets firing.

'Robert facing the camera at 'brew time. In the background is the tent fastened to the side of the recovery tank'

When we were out on exercise, although a lot of the land was big army areas, there were still a lot of farmers in certain ones. Sometimes if the food wagon didn't come and we were hungry, we used to nick potatoes from the side of the fields and cook them. At times when we were camped somewhere, farmers' kiddies would come and look at us. As we used to get sweets and bars of chocolates in our ration pack, we'd offer them to the children. They would never take any. We thought at the time it was inbred into them that they didn't have anything to do with the English. Or maybe it was like modern days when you don't offer children sweets. I really don't know the reason but it used to make me sad and I found it distressing when I had these sweets and chocolate and the children backed away from me.

It was over a period of time that you realised the possibility of a war. When you were out on exercise you had to watch what you were saying over the radio. One time we were exercising near the East German border and had a group of boy soldiers with us. As the regiment was over there for the first time and hadn't sussed out everywhere, they let these boy soldiers use the radios. One of them said something like, 'this is quite a good place for a tank to cross at section so and so.' He was reprimanded because the Russians would be listening in. They were also keeping an eye on us from their watch towers.

At the time it was like playing soldiers but we were actually preparing in case of war. Although all we seemed to do was maintenance, that was to ensure everything was ready at all times and in tip-top condition. If there was a war, each regiment had a predetermined position to go to and form a defence right across West Germany. It wasn't to attack, it was purely a form of defence. That's why we went without sleep for three days because that would actually happen in a real war. Let's say, you were partially prepared because nothing prepares you for the horrors of war but everything was in motion as there was the threat with the Cold War.

There was also the other side of the situation, when you didn't believe things you were told. It had been in all the papers and then we were told that the Russians had infra-red sights on their tanks which we didn't have. We were also told there was nothing to worry about as all we had to do was get a piece of string and tie a lot of cans to it. Once that was put across the road in front of us, the Russians could only pick out the metal of the cans and not us. I mean, it was absolutely ridiculous.

'On manoeuvres at Luneberg Heath'

I remember we had to do an atomic warfare exercise. We had to go around with our steel helmets on, nets over our faces, wearing full uniform and carrying our rifle at all times. If you were seen without a rifle you were on a charge. The latrines were a hole in the ground with a box over and sacking all round. So even going to the latrines you carried your gun and had all this netting over your face and you sat there thinking, 'If anybody sees me, what the hell will they think?'

To give us a real life picture of what went on in a war we were told, 'Right, today you're going to see battle casualties.' This had all been prepared for us on the parade ground. They'd got lots of lads to dress up as casualties and even taken ham bones and raw meat from the cookhouse and shoved them up their trouser legs. That was to make everything look realistic and it was horrible to see. These lads were supposed to have all sorts of injuries and disfigurements with this raw flesh from the cookhouse all over them. It was to prepare you for what you could come up against in a real war so it wouldn't be such a shock.

One day we were having gunnery practise on the range where they were firing armour piercing from the tank guns. Armour piercing doesn't explode, its job is to hit a tank and literally burn a hole through the metal. Well, one gunner got in a tank, set his sights too high and fired. We later heard that he'd hit a farm building six miles away. Although our recovery tank didn't have a main gun, we had a machine gun mounted on it, which our corporal used to fire on the ranges. As far as I can remember it fired six hundred rounds a minute. It was horrific to watch all these tanks firing away and imagining all the carnage they could create.

The armour piercing shells used on gunnery exercises had nylon round them to save the bore on the gun getting worn out when you fired. The nylon fell off as it left the barrel and as far as the Army was concerned, this nylon couldn't be used again and wasn't worth collecting. So a nearby factory had a contract to come and pick up the nylon bits and make nylon products with it. At the end of the day's firing, the workers would come and pick all the nylon up, take it away and use it. Again, that's German initiative.

I was one of the lucky ones in Germany and got leave for Christmas. I'd got married in March, gone abroad in June and hadn't seen Irene since. While I'd been in Germany she'd bought our first house and we had our first Christmas together in it. We had a carpet and a couch and that was about it. I don't know why we did it but we actually set to and decorated one of the bedrooms on New Year's Eve of my leave. We finished it about two o'clock in the morning and a few hours later I had to go back to Germany. I can remember I had a big brown suitcase and inside was a lot of food my mother had given me. I couldn't afford a taxi to the bus stop so I had to walk with this damn case. It was so heavy I put it down thinking, 'I'll never get to the bus in time,' because I had so much stuff to take back.

'Skiing party in the Hartz Mountains.
Robert is standing second left'

One of the highlights when I was in Germany was being chosen to go on a skiing course in the Hartz Mountains. There were four of us from our regiment along but with others from different regiments in Germany. We slept in a big old barn in a valley and every morning we'd get up and start the day with bacon and eggs. Then we went up into the mountains where the private skiing instructors would teach us how to ski. At lunch time they used to bring up to us a packed dinner with soup and buns. It was lovely being there with all the snow and deer about. At the end of the day we came back to the barn and had our supper. Because we couldn't go out anywhere we always had a film show in the barn, while we sat on the top bunks and watched. On the last night we were taken to a local tavern for a party.

At the end of the course we had a skiing race which I won. This was probably because I had learned to ski when I had lived at Selside some years before. Winning the race should have entitled me to go into the army skiing finals the following week. But because travel arrangements and accommodation had to be worked out well in advance, this wasn't possible.

I also went on a specialised course to Duisberg to train on the biggest tank in the Army. It was called the Conqueror and weighed well over seventy tons. Besides the sergeant lecturer, the other chap working on the tank was Hans, a German civilian. As the course only lasted ten days we didn't get out much but women used to hang about outside the camp propositioning lads and trying to get sweets and cigarettes out of them. One of the lads on the course did go to a local bar and took a lass out. He asked her in German how much she wanted paying and she said twenty marks. The lad thought this was a bit much and told her so. She asked, 'You English?' and when he said he was, she said, 'Oh, it's forty marks.' We told Hans about this and he roared with laughter for days afterwards about the woman putting her price up for Englishmen.

We'd had the usual films on VD and were shown pictures of what could happen if you caught it. Anyone who wanted to could get free contraceptives. They usually went to the medical and asked for them, which lads going home on leave used to do. One of the lads who I went over to Germany with, went out on the town and picked up VD. He was married and absolutely terrified of going home.

Towards the end of my time in Germany I was offered stripes if I stayed on but life had changed by then. I was married and didn't think the forces was a place for married people, especially as the regiment I was attached to moved every two years. This meant an upheaval for your wife and if you had children later on, it meant them moving school. You could put children into private schools but to me, that wasn't an ideal family life.

At that time, army pay was three pounds and seventeen shillings a week. I also got a marriage allowance and a clothing allowance, all of which totalled to six pounds and two pence. I then had to pay national insurance and send money home to Irene which left two pounds, fourteen shillings and seven pence for me to live off.

I had been out on exercise for a couple of weeks but knew that my demob was coming up. When I arrived back at camp one of the lads said, 'Hey, you get demobbed next week, don't you? You want to go and check-up to make sure everything is all right.' So I literally had one day to sort everything out and get all the paperwork together. I didn't even have time to tell anyone in England I was coming home.

Page 1
Army
Book
111

SURNAME AND INITIALS JACKSON, R. W.

ARMY NO. 23569659

GROUP NO. 58:12

Discharge from Whole-time and Entry upon Part-time Military Service of a National Service Soldier

Designation of HQ, AER, or TA Unit to which the soldier is posted for part-time service :—

49 MEDIUM WKSP REME (AER)
BROXHEAD HOUSE, BORDON
HANTS

Date due to report to TA Unit

CERTIFICATE OF DISCHARGE (*To be retained by the soldier*)

Page 2
Army
Book
111

Having completed whole-time service under the National Service Acts, 1948 to 1950, you are liable to further part-time service in the AER/TA unit to which you are posted until you have completed a total of five and a half years' service in all.

If this certificate is lost or mislaid no duplicate can be obtained.

Any unauthorized alterations of the particulars in this certificate may render the holder liable to prosecution under the Seamen's and Soldiers' False Characters Act, 1906.

ARMY NO. 23569659 RANK CFN

SURNAME (Block Capitals) JACKSON

CHRISTIAN OR FORE NAME(s) (Block Capitals) ROBERT. WILLIAM

UNIT, REGT. OF CORPS
for which enlisted REME
from which discharged 16th/5th The Queens Royal Lancers

Service began on 19-6-58 at 2nd Trg BN REME

Effective date of discharge from wholetime service 18-6-60

Total amount of full-time reckonable service 2YRS 24days

Reason for discharge N.S Release
QR 1955 para 503 (xxi)(d)

Description of Soldier on Completion of Whole-time Service

Date of birth 4-4-37 Height 5 ft. 10¾ ins.

Complexion Fresh Eyes GREY Hair BROWN

Marks and Scars (visible) FOREHEAD

Trade Qualifications

CIVILIAN TRADE Motor Mechanic

SERVICE TRADE Veh Mech A III

FINAL EMPLOYMENT " " "

Courses and Tests passed " " " P/o 301/17/12/58
6 T.B. Reme

'Robert's Discharge paper'

Back home I was on reserve for about five years. Though I never kept in touch with the regiment I learned what happened to it over a number of years. I know when I was demobbed, the regiment went to Hong Kong for two years. That's where I missed out – if you'd been single, that was a great life.

Although you had to do National Service, the Army's a great place for an individual. One of my biggest regrets is that I didn't learn German as the Army was running courses on it. I thought, 'What's the point in me learning German? I'm only here for twelve months.' But it's a good life once you settle into a regiment and you haven't a care in the world as to what's going to happen. You know you can be there for twenty years and you don't have to worry about expenses because everything is taken care of. It's a bit like being hospitalised as you've got everything done for you but it's not really the modern world. That said, I think I could have gone on and made something of it. After twenty years you would still be in your forties and retired with a pension. So it is something to consider.

I told you earlier that I'd been on a course at Duisberg. While I was there four of us were planning to go to the Nurburgring to watch some motor racing. As one of the lads was a regular soldier and had a car, this was a great opportunity for us. Unfortunately I was put on guard duty at the camp and couldn't go to Nurburgring. Many years later, after Irene and I moved into our present house, we had a new neighbour. I was talking to him one day and discovered he'd been in the REME. He'd also been at Duisberg at the same time as me AND he'd been responsible for the guard duty roster. So it was my next door neighbour who put me on guard duty and was responsible for me missing the motor racing!

EIGHT

'In deep jungle'

***Jack Irwin**, Served in the Royal Army Medical Corps 1952-1954*

I left school at fifteen and got an apprenticeship with the *Westmorland Gazette* at Kendal. As far as I remember posters appeared at various places in town, which said that the National Service Act required men who were born between such and such dates to register. Everybody had to register, regardless of whether they were deferred or not.

'Jack in RAMC'

I was in the sea cadets and you could apply to join the Royal Navy Volunteer Reserve. You did your two years at naval establishments then had to sign on for several years which I was quite prepared to do. John Shaw, the Commanding Officer of the local unit went to great lengths to arrange this on my behalf. Subsequently I went for a medical to Newcastle but failed because of a slight hearing impairment. I was told to see my own doctor in case there was just a minor problem and then go back to Newcastle. My doctor sent me to the Westmorland County Hospital where I was examined and it was confirmed that I had a slight hearing impairment. The chap who examined me said, 'Oh, you could probably get in the Navy as a sickbay-tiffy.' But I didn't want that, I wanted to be a stoker so I never applied back to Newcastle. I think that was one of the biggest disappointments I've had because I really would have liked to have joined the Navy as a stoker.

After that I went for a medical to the Majestic Building, Starch House Square at Preston. Not everybody passed their medical but they classed me A1. I said, 'I can't understand that because I've been rejected for the Navy. If I'm A1 for the Army, why can't I be that for the Navy?' So they downgraded me to Grade 2 and that was that.

After the medical, we were given a form to fill in, saying which regiment we wanted to go into. I put down the Lancashire Fusiliers, then the Royal Army Ordinance Corps as second choice and thirdly, the Border's. I finished up in the Royal Army Medical Corps, so it was ironic that I ended up doing the same job I could have done in the Navy.

I went into the Army on Thursday 7 February 1952. My calling up letter read, 'You will report to the depot and training establishment, Royal Army Medical Corps, Keogh Barracks, Ashvale, Aldershot, Hampshire.' And that's where I duly reported to.

I didn't travel by train on my own. Some more lads would get on at Lancaster, others at Preston and it went on like that until we got to Crewe and we more or less stabilised. I think there were a couple of lads beside myself going into RAMC but the rest were going into other regiments.

I can't tell you exactly how I felt but I do remember in some respects being quite excited about joining up. It's a wonderful world when you're eighteen and there was a certain amount of excitement wondering what was going to happen and if you were going to like the Army.

We changed trains at London and went on to Waterloo. From there you went to Ashvale. Anybody on that train would be bound for the RAMC and when we arrived at Ashvale, there was certainly a full coach of us and umpteen blokes got off that train. A sergeant was waiting for us and we went by bus to the barracks.

It was half-past-five or six o'clock at night when we arrived at the barracks and the first thing they did was give you a pint pot full of tea, a knife, fork and spoon. Then you went round the system being kitted out. After that you were allocated to whatever barrack-room you were going to and had to get your kit into some kind or reasonable order for parade the following day. There must have been about thirty of us in this barrack room and you had all this equipment to put away, start blancoing your webbing, cleaning your boots and all that carry-on. Then you could go and get supper if you wanted any. I'll remember that first supper for the remainder of my life. It was red cabbage, cheese and a rock bun, which was very aptly named. Later, I was to find that generally speaking, wherever you went in the Army, the meals weren't particularly delightful but they were acceptable.

At that stage I think it was a little bewildering because you never quite knew what you were supposed to do until you settled in. After travelling all day you were quite tired and when ten o'clock came, you had to go to bed. Now, there was one lad in our barracks who should never have been in the Army. He was quite all right physically but mentally, he wasn't. He had no idea about owt and I can never understand how doctors who were supposed to be professional people subjected that lad to the Army. Anyway, I had the misfortune to be the last one up along with that slow lad when the guard came round. So we got delegated to clean the blanco room where there was blanco on the ceiling, blanco on the walls and blanco all over. And I had to clean it and do everything myself because that lad was no help. I made sure that I was never the last one up ever again.

The next day it all started, the brutalisation that went on all the time we were in the Army. The idea of the military machine was to make you do something immediately. Regardless of anything, you automatically did it. Of course, it was just to make you not question anything. You did it and you didn't argue. The main thing was the barracking and messing about that the Army seemed so good at. But except for drill, being given the history of the Corps, you didn't do much other than keep the bloody place clean. Then you had these drill instructors, lance corporals who were like little gods. They could say anything they wanted and you had to do it. Depending on what kind of DI you got, depended what kind of a life you had.

Keogh Barracks would have been built probably just before the war, so in 1952 it was a relatively modern building. It was called B Reception Company and in the main, it was the reception company for blokes coming in to do National Service. You were there for a fortnight before you went to a training company at the depot area which was at Crookham.

We all went to E Company at Crookham and were split up into various training squads. We started learning basic things and had to take a St John's First Aid Certificate, then started with the basic introduction to nursing procedures. There was anatomy and physiology, which is the structure and working of the body. There was also such things as post-operative bed, the accident bed and all the other types of beds you had to know how to make. Also you were given a set of circumstances, such as you might get a bloke with a supposedly gaping wound or somebody with half their stomach hanging out and you had to deal with that. All these type of things you had to learn besides drill and that went on for about six weeks. We didn't go on the rifle range. RAMC, if you turn these letters round, make '**C**an't **M**anage **A** **R**ifle.' In the normal train of events, regiments got webbing and Bren gun pouches but the RAMC got brace attachments instead. After that, it was tests like taking a bicycle pump to bits and re-assembling it to see what kind of aptitude you had.

There was no hard feelings within the barrack set up. They were your pals and in the same blinking squad. If somebody wasn't up to scratch, you would try and pull them through one way or another because you didn't want to be backsquaded. You did your best to make things run smoothly and I was one of those people who tried to make themselves part of a crowd as I didn't want to get myself noticed.

At the end of all this we each had an interview with a bloke who I think was a major in the Royal Artillery. I went before him and said, 'To be honest and with respect, sir, I never wanted to come into the medical corps as I don't fancy nursing.' To a lad of eighteen this is something that lassies would do and it's effeminate isn't it? Well, this chap told me, 'You're good at reading and spelling so you could finish up as a clerk.' 'Well, that's isn't so bad' I thought. 'I'll accept that, finish my two years and come out.' Unfortunately, when we had the nursing written examinations, the first test you do in the RAMC, as luck would have it, I came about third from the top. So there was no way I could now escape nursing duties.

We were allowed into Crookham at night but one of the factors that controlled men, particularly privates, was the amount of bloody money you had. If you hadn't a lot you couldn't do so damn much. You see, a National Serviceman's basic pay was twenty-eight shillings a week and they used to take such things off you as barrack room damages. The low pay was one of the things that persuaded folk to sign on as a regular soldier because then you got three pounds a week, which was a lot better. With having very little money, the NAAFI was the best place to go.

After we'd done our basic training and passed the Commandant's parade with the whole shebang, you were available for posting. That meant you could be posted to any RAMC unit throughout the United Kingdom. You may have been able to apply to go somewhere specific but they really sent you wherever they wanted to.

What happened was, there was usually a gap of between two and three weeks between finishing the actual course and being posted. That's how it worked for us. In that period you would be working in the cookhouse or scrubbing out until you got your postings and given a home leave. For leave, there were what was called a PRI bus running up to Preston so for two pounds and ten shillings I came up on that, then home to Kendal.

When my posting came, it was 20 Company RAMC, which was the military hospital at Tidworth on Salisbury Plain. Tidworth was an old Victorian type of hospital but had open verandas and beautiful ornate ironwork and all that carry on. The story was that it was designed to be built in India but they got the bloody plans mixed up and built it on Salisbury Plain instead

When I arrived at Tidworth, I wandered round doing fatigues and decided I didn't care for the place. There was nothing there, just this garrison place with a lot off different regiments. To be honest, I never went on a ward, I finished up in the dining room serving out food. The next day the Sergeant Major came round and said, 'They're forming a draft for Malaya. I want some volunteers.' So for the first and only time I volunteered. I don't know if it was because I volunteered or because the other lads were fed-up as well but most of them who were in my lot volunteered. I didn't like Tidworth and couldn't envisage getting away from there, other than by draft. Also the fact that it was a month's voyage to Singapore really appealed to me. I never thought for one moment that I'd be killed in Malaya. Well, at eighteen, you don't.

We came home for a fortnight's privileged embarkation leave and then back to the depot at Crookham into what they called the holding and drafting company. We stayed there while they kitted us out with tropical gear and then we did training and route marching to keep us occupied.

A. LIFE ON BOARD A TROOPSHIP

It is idle to pretend that a voyage on a troopship is made under " luxury " conditions. Moreover, as a race, the British do not take kindly to cramped conditions unless the reason for them is plain and understandable. The following paragraphs, therefore, have been written to explain what may be expected and to indicate the ways by which time spent on board a troopship can be rendered not only passable but enjoyable. Conditions on a troopship are continually being improved—in many ships, for example, the number of passengers has been reduced, better sleeping and messing accommodation has been installed and additional recreation space provided. Unfortunately, owing to the many and conflicting demands on the ship-yards, and the acute shortage of shipping which has existed since the end of the war, improvements have not progressed as fast as planned, but it is true to say that the stories of discomfort experienced in the past are no longer strictly accurate and should not be accepted as necessarily your fate on board the particular ship in which you are ordered to travel.

Improved conditions are not everything, however. On board a troopship, as elsewhere, a great deal depends upon the individual himself, as to what sort of time he has. Is he content simply to carry out orders and do nothing more? Or is he prepared to join his pals in sports, such as tug-of-war or boxing ? Is he keen on games, such as tombola or whist ? Does he take an interest in the route the ship takes, the islands and places she passes ? Has he a hobby such as sketching ? Is he interested in some course of education ? Is he fond of reading ? Life on board a troopship depends a great deal on answers to these questions. It is fortunate if you happen to be travelling with your unit on the ship, as you will then already know some of your shipmates, both officers and other ranks. But it is more than likely these days, that you will be in a small draft, or even by yourself, and the others will be strangers. A trained soldier will not let this deter him. It should even put him on his mettle, and determine him not to let his unit or regiment down.

'Exerpt taken from Middle East Theatre booklet, Chapter One, Life on Board a Troopship'

We sailed on the *Empire Windrush* which was full of different regiments going over to Malaya. The troop decks were in what would be the hold and I was right down in the bottom of the ship. I thought, 'If anything happens to this bloody thing, I'll be drowned before I get up to the top.' The iron-framed bunks were in tiers of three and had canvas bases. Between you and me, this wasn't the best of arrangements. Some blokes would go to the canteen, get more ale than was good for them and then go to bed. The Irish bloke who was on our top bunk would come back from the canteen, turn over and be sick. The poor bugger underneath would get it all. That was the kind of thing you had to put up with. I wasn't seasick and I've watched the ship go up and down when the sea was rolling about. But I could never walk straight. It was as though I was drunk and staggering about because I never got my sea legs.

One thing that I found an irritation about the Army was the stupidity of the system. We left Southampton in shirt-sleeve order and by the time we got to the other side of the Bay of Biscay it was starting to get warm. Then it came on ship's orders that sergeants and above could change into tropical gear. But the yobs had to stay in shirt sleeves for another two or three days. Now, that is just class distinction as we sweat just the same as the other buggers and the change would have been just as good for us as it was for them. It was things like that used to get up my nose.

We sailed to Port Said, went through the Suez Canal and into the Great Bitter Lakes. From there into the Red Sea to Aden, Colombo and on to Singapore. You came down the Malacca Straights and saw the shore line of Malaya and it was quite impressive. It's a beautiful country.

It was on the ship going out that we got our postings and it was Penang where I was being posted to. Penang, that was wonderful and I couldn't have hoped to be posted to a better place. When we came off the ship at Singapore, our batch of fifteen of us were transferred to a transit camp for the day. There we got a cup of tea and a meal and as we were tired, we went to sleep in some tents.

There was a single-track railway system in Malaya which we went on that night and were given a pack of sandwiches and a water bottle. We arrived at Kuala Lumpar early the next day, went to another transit camp and then on another train journey. Now, bearing in mind we thought we were going to Penang, a bloke gets on the train and says,

'19 Field Ambulance?' We answered 'Yes,' and he told us to get off the train as we were being taken to Taiping.

There were military bases at Kuala Lumpar, Taiping and Penang and from there the infantry regiments patrolled the various aspects of territory they were responsible for. To my knowledge, during the time I was in Malaya, there was only 16 and 19 Field Ambulance and I was serving with the 19 at Taiping.

When you arrived at your station you were given rifle training on the ranges, did drill and then went on a part-time course to the British Military Hospital, Kamunting where you were taken under the jurisdiction of the sister tutor. She was responsible for training her own staff and RAMC personnel. Oh, she was very professional there's no doubt about it. She took pride in her job and didn't want any idiots sent to her and she wasn't going to have them. If you didn't come up to the standards she wanted, or she thought you were swinging the lead, you got a report sent to the CO at the field ambulance. But it was for your own benefit because you had to know what you were doing.

When we were being trained by the sister tutor, we had to sit an examination to be a nursing orderly class (NO3). But to get paid ten bob a week for that, you also had to take your army certificate of education as well. I'm not the brightest of individuals, never-the-less, I took the certificate of education along with a pal of mine. After we'd finished this examination, we were called into the inner sanctum by a sergeant. He said that one of us had copied from the other as we had the same answers. I can say before God that I hadn't copied and my mate said he hadn't, so whether it just happened to be a coincidence, I don't know. Anyway, this sergeant told us that our examination was being disregarded but we still had to sit the NO3. What he was saying was, one of us had fiddled the papers but we could still pass the nursing examination, be sent out as a medical orderly but wouldn't get paid extra for doing it.

Now, ten bob is a lot of money when you're only on twenty-eight bob a week. So I told the sergeant, 'Yes, I'll do the NO3 exam but I'm not going to pass the bloody thing if you're going to do me out of my ten bob.' You've got to pick the people you say that kind of thing to and I knew he was a reasonable sort of bloke. So away he went for a while and when he came back, told us, 'Look, I've decided to let your results stand,' so I had passed the certificate of education examination. Mind you, if I'd not passed the NO3 exam, they would have given me a hell of a life in the field ambulance. They say you can beat the system but you can't, they get you in the finish.

After that I got posted to a Gurkha regiment at a place called Kuala Kangsar. Their officers were English and Gurkha, known as Queen's Gurkha Officers. The Gurkha camps and set up were run the same way as the rest only they wouldn't eat beef under any circumstances because of their religion. I liked the Gurkhas and thought they were a very nice people.

'In Malaya, Jack standing left'

I was at Kuala Kangsar for about three months when the medical officer said there were a lot of men at C Company, Taiping, who were suffering from jungle sores as a result of continual patrolling. Off I went to Taiping but since, in general, the company used the garrison centre I was duly returned to the 19 Field Ambulance. From there I was sent as duty medical orderly to the leave centre at Sandy Croft, Penang for a fortnight.

Now, Penang is a beautiful place but there could be social problems to navigate there, particularly with women. You see, if you were stationed at Penang where there were dance halls, you wouldn't have to look for women, they would find you. You wouldn't have any trouble finding a partner, no problem at all and this was a distinct danger for the troops.

If any of the troops were going to become involved with women, they'd have to come to the prolific ablution centre where I worked and medication was handed out to them. Soldiers had to put their name in a little black book to say that they'd received medication. Later on, if these blokes became infected and hadn't got their name in this book, they were for the high jump as it meant they hadn't taken the precautions they were supposed to.

One of the incidents that happened to me was, that I had swamp fever and was sent to hospital. I was put in the same ward with these blokes who had diseases from women. Some had the misfortune to get gonorrhoea but that wasn't so bad as it could be cured. The ones who got gonorrhoea and syphilis together had quite a harrowing time. Now, just being in the same ward as these blokes was quite an eye opener to me. It made me think twice and be wary.

After a fortnight at Penang I went back to field ambulance. From there I was posted to the First (Battalion) West Yorkshires and went as a medical orderly to Ipoh. This was down country from Taiping where the Battalion Headquarters were.

Now, in the normal course of events in a war, you had a front line. Wounded personnel would be transferred from there to a regimental aid post, then a casualty clearing station and on to field ambulance, which would be a bit behind the front line. Due to the fact you didn't have that kind of situation in Malaya, invariably what happened was, RAMC personnel would be either on the wards in hospitals or detached from a field ambulance as a medical orderly, as I was.

From the field ambulance, you usually went to an infantry regiment and were an infantry man. The only difference was, that we carried an medical pack and tried to do our best for soldiers' individual concerns. Many a time you were the first contact between the casualty and further medical assistance. I always felt it was quite wrong that field ambulance staff were the poor relations of the RAMC. The cream of personnel were in the hospitals and on field ambulance you weren't in the same category. That's the impression I got. And really, what happened to the poor sod you were dealing with depended on how you did your job in the field ambulance. You see, in Malaya, if you have just a scratch it goes septic in next to no time.

From Ipoh we used to go out on patrol. A patrol was usually three platoons of about seventy to eighty men who make up the company. Usually you'd go to a specific area which none of us, except the bloke in charge of the patrol, would know anything about. The system used to be, you were taken to a milestone on the side of the road. From there you would go through the rubber estates and into primary jungle and then into secondary jungle.

Primary jungle isn't very thick and is more or less a step beyond the where rubber plantations are cultivated. After the primary comes the secondary jungle, which is usually quite damp or swampy. Because of the height and foliage of the trees it's unlikely you'd get very much light and it could be semi-dark all day. You'd go through the jungle to where you made base camp. For tents, two blokes would share a ground sheet on the ground and the other ground-sheet would be over the top of them on a bamboo pole. If you were going to stay at base camp for a length of time, you might thatch the side of the this tent with banana leaves to make it as comfortable as you could. Granted, they weren't very comfortable but you tried to keep the water out. Then you'd go from your base to wherever you were going to conduct an ambush.

These patrols into the jungle would be initiated by some form of intelligence from the hierarchy somewhere. They would be told there was going to be some communists coming along a particular track at a certain time and we would set an ambush on that track. On each side of the track there might be eight rifles camouflaged so they couldn't be seen. They weren't directly opposite each other, because you could injure your own men. At both the top and bottom of the track would be a Bren gun pointing onto the track. If there was information that communists were coming from a certain area, the bloke on one Bren gun would stay to one side out of the line of fire. Then it was just a question of whether the communist patrol came.

I went on a few of these patrols and never saw a communist yet. They were not silly, they were very clever people you were up against. I know we once went into the jungle, climbed up hill and stopped for a break by a magnificent waterfall. I just happened to look down and you could see the track down at the roadside which we'd come up. Therefore, if there had been terrorists and had a sentry posted by the waterfall, they would have seen us coming and just disappeared.

We did have radio contact and trackers with us. The trackers we had were Ebans from Sarawak and they could tell just by looking at a track if it had been used. We'd come across places where there were still warm ashes from the fires left by the communists but we never saw them. You also came across patches of ground that had been worked and cultivated by nomadic tribes that wandered around the area.

The first operation that I went on with the West Yorkshire's was about four days. I went on about four operations all together, the longest one was about a month. That was a bloody long time, believe me, right in deep jungle. It isn't the jungle that's frightening, it's the unknown because you don't know what you're going to walk into. There was always the night and dawn chorus, with crickets, flying foxes and other things making a noise about you. You got used to it but there was always that little bit of wondering what we were going to get into. That feeling was always there.

Usually I was the only medical man on patrol. Everybody carried field dressings and I'd also carry vials of morphia, penicillin powder for jungle sores and different ointments. If you got a gun-shot wound, you had problems. The patient would be suffering a lot from shock and the condition of his flesh would go septic. There was nothing you could do except put a field dressing on the wound and get the lad out of the jungle quickly.

One lad dropped his Sten gun and shot himself through the ribs. The bullet went in the bottom rib and out the top. How it missed his heart, I don't know. When I examined this lad I said to the Company Commander, 'We've got to get this bloke out of here and he's got to be out fast.' There was no way he could walk and we couldn't carry him. So what they did, the lads in that company worked all night. They cut trees down with machetes, built a platform on the side of the hill where a helicopter could come in and land and take the lad out by air.

If you were going out on patrol for up to five days, you'd carry your own food. Each day you had what was called a twenty-four hour ration pack. These usually consisted of concentrated cheese, hard tack biscuits, maybe tins of liver and beans, some rice pudding, a tube of condensed milk, tea sugar, maybe a Mars bar or a tube of wine gums and some fags.

On the patrol I did for one month, you were supplied by drops. They dropped you socks, underwear, everything. You see, the only clothes you had were what you were wearing. You might shove them in a river and try and clean them but you couldn't wear them very long as they'd drop off your back. They also used to drop fags by air and you got a tot of rum every night, just a little nip and I used to put mine in a cup of tea. The sergeant who was in charge of the rum ration never let it out of his sight. I think he was three parts cut most of the bloody time.

Obviously you had to keep quiet in the jungle. The idea was you didn't try and advertise yourself. Some regiments were more efficient than others at keeping quiet but I don't think many would be as quiet as the Gurkhas. They were very, very good soldiers, there's no doubt about it. But there were some good British regiments out there at the time. Manchesters were there, the Green Howards, the Royal West Kents and the Suffolks were as good as any of them.

Coming out of the jungle, you got maybe a week or a fortnight's rest to recuperate. Really speaking, there wasn't a lot you could do unless you were stationed at somewhere like Taiping where you could go down into town. So you were either in the jungle or in camp, where you had a canteen or NAAFI. But I don't bore easily. I can do nothing and it doesn't bore me at all. However, you'd have your ordinary regimental duties to do. You didn't sit about, they always had something arranged.

I remained with the West Yorkshire regiment till about the middle of November 1953 and then I was called back to field ambulance as I was due to be demobbed. I should have been called back earlier but there was a shortage of trained medical orderlies at the time. And being left on detachment with the West Yorkshires until the last possible moment meant I was deprived of local leave. Then I was stood down where you just sort of slonked around and passed time away until it was time to catch the troopship back home.

I came back to Southampton on the *Dilwara* and then on to our depot at Crookham for about a week. Then our kit was taken off us and it was home. I came back to my job at the *Westmorland Gazette* but still had to do part-time territorial service. I was posted to 166 Border Field Dressing Station RAMC, Carlisle, which was at the Castle. All you had to do was report there and eventually, you'd be sent a letter telling you to go down to the drill hall at Kendal. From there you'd be picked up and then on to these weekend camps.

Weekend camps covered a bank holiday Monday so you'd have three days with the territorials. We'd meet at Kendal drill hall, go up to Windermere drill hall and stay there overnight. We tended to use the coppermines at Coniston for handling stretchers and lowering them over crag ends and all that carry-on. We also did two fortnight camps in the Catterick area. One was at a place called Gandale, under canvas. That was in 1954, a particularly wet summer and we were in a hell of a state. The following year we went to Richmond but that wasn't too bad as we were in hutted camps (spiders). As National Service was coming to an end, I did a couple of years with the territorials instead of three.

I didn't want to do army National Service, I wanted to join the Navy. But with the Navy I would never have seen Malaya and I quite enjoyed that. In fact I went back there last year with a party of 'vets' as it was the fiftieth anniversary of the King's Own Yorkshire Light Infantry being posted there. Oh, it's all very different now from the Malaya I knew. They've made vast progress and it's a nice country. I hope to go there again next year.

Perhaps I'd have been as well stopping in the Army rather than coming out if only I'd had the sense to see that at the time. There was the opportunity to learn a good trade but I couldn't wait to get out quick enough. That's how I've come to look at it in later years. But as one of my colleagues said, 'You don't really know. You might have gone to Kenya, Aden or Northern Ireland and could have been killed.' So you don't really know whether you took the right option, do you?

NINE

'Forty rifles trained on his head'

Adam Kirkbride*. Served in the 1st Battalion, Border Regiment, 1955 – 1957*

I'd been working at Mossbay Steel Works at the mill making rails since I was fourteen. Once you got to eighteen, this letter about National Service arrived, telling you to go to Carlisle Castle for a medical. You got a rail warrant to go and outside Carlisle railway station there was a military lorry waiting. A sergeant would tell you to get in it and you were taken away to the Castle. There you'd been seen by about half a dozen doctors. One to look at your eyes, one for your ears and so on. Then you'd be told, 'Turn round and touch your toes.' That was to see if you were a queer. After that you were asked what regiment you would like to be in. You were given about three choices and I wanted to go into the Medical Corps but was shoved into the Border Regiment. Then it was just a matter of waiting until the Army sent for you. About a fortnight later you would be sent for. The Army never forgot about you.

That was the start of ten weeks' training, where everything was knocked into you. Most of us lads had never been outside of Workington or wherever we lived and you were about shiting yourself. When you get into the Castle, they said, 'Right, in a line,' and you got kitted out with everything you were going to use for two years. Then this horrible larl sergeant come in and gives you a right dressing down. 'My name is Sergeant Smith. They spell it B-A-S-T-A-R-D and don't forget it.' You were split up into two groups of forty lads, then lined up facing each other. This is the first night and you've never been away before and never left your mam. And you look across at these other lads standing there and think, 'Jesus Christ, he's a funny looking bugger' or 'Look at that skinny little sod.'

By the time the following day comes, you've knitted together and you all stick together and you all help each other. And in them days you got these borstal lads, or from Doctor Banardo's homes or ones from broken homes. Some of them were thick, they couldn't write or owt like that and you had to show them what to do. You had to show them because when you were on parade and there's thirty-nine of you doing everything right and one doing everything wrong, you were all kept in and not allowed out. So every morning before parade, you'd dress them properly or show them what to do until eventually they got to know what they were doing.

Now I'd always kept my hair short and had it cut at the City Hairdressers in Workington the day before I went to Carlisle. But once at the Castle, it was, 'Get in a line, you're all going to the barbers.' Everybody had D.A. haircuts in them days or Elvis Presley cuts and once at the barbers, it was 'How would you like it cut, sir?' and the answer was, 'Oh, just trim it.' But that bloke went right over the top of your head and took the bloody lot off. So I came back to camp and stood in line for the inspection and there was a dig in my back with a stick. It was the Sergeant, 'I sent you for a bloody haircut and I'm hurting you because I'm standing on your bloody hair. Now, go and get a haircut.' Back I went to the barber who says, 'You've just been in here, haven't you son?' He gives me another scalping and back I go to stand in line. The Sergeant took a look and said, 'I thought I bloody well told you to get your hair cut. Go and get another one.' So back I went to the barber and told him, 'Cut the bloody lot off, marra.' I don't think my hair ever grew again.

Now, when you had been given your uniform, you were given a big pair of boots. Mine were size twelve. If you look at a pair of work boots, they've all got pimples on them and we had to get these pimples off. There was only one way, you used a hot iron and ironed them. Once these pimples were out, you dipped a duster into a tin of black shoe polish and started polishing by going round and round the surface of these boots in little circles. Hour after hour, hour after hour till your boots were like a mirror. You didn't want to put them on because you'd done so much work on them. Same with your uniform, you ironed and smartened it up. A lot of lads burnt or singed their shirts and had to buy another one.

We got twenty-one shillings a week, which worked out at three shillings a day. But everybody had to send seven shillings a week home to their mothers' who spent it because they were hard up. That should have left you with fourteen shillings but you didn't get that because the sergeant major would want some money for barrack room damages and we'd ask, 'What barrack room damages?' and the answer would be, 'Somebody broke a window.' The Army always made sure they got their whack and you were left with seven shillings and a tanner. As soon as I got this money, I used to buy a hundred fags which cost five shillings so I had half-a-crown to last me a week.

The food was crap but it was wonderful. I mean, if you're hungry, you'll eat owt. You know the background I come from, you either ate food or you didn't and you got nowt else. I used to sit beside these well-to-do lads who had money and it was, 'Oh, I don't want that,' so I'd say, 'Well, shove it on my plate,' and I'd eat their's. We'd never had kippers for breakfast at home or dehydrated stuff but you learnt to eat it all.

After about three weeks, they've knocked all this marching into you, taught you how to salute and things like that, they take you out to the green at Carlisle Castle. In all that time you've never been outside the wall and here's forty tripods with .303 rifles on them. The Sergeant says, 'Never, ever point a weapon at anybody in case it goes off.' And then he deliberately walks away because he knows what's going to happen. When he turns around, there's forty rifles trained on his head and what a telling off he gives you. He knows it's harmless because there's no bullets in the guns but that's the start of learning how to hold a rifle and fire one.

Now, you had to learn how to fire for your pay. The better you got, the more stars you got and the more stars, the more money. So it was onto the range and some lads couldn't even look through the sights of their rifle. Now, there was about twenty-four targets in the butts and these targets all moved up and down. If you were put in the butts working these targets, the Officer would shout, 'Put them up,' for the lads to fire at. Well, I'd get on the field telephone and say, 'It's me, Big Adam. Who's on number ten target?' When you realised it was a lad who couldn't shoot, you'd say, 'Right, put ten rounds into the grass banking.' Then you'd get a pencil and dig it through the target score. Once the firing was over, the Officer wanting the score would shout at me, 'Number ten target?' and I'd shout back, 'Two magpies, one inner, two bulls and an outer,' which were the marks on the target. And that was the chap passed his firing test. Otherwise if we hadn't fixed it for him, he wouldn't pass and get his firing money.

After all that firing, our dinner would be brought onto the range in big cans. Over you'd go with your two mess tins, one for your drink of tea and the other for the meal. Maybe it was dehydrated taties you were having and that would be just splattered all over your plate. Then whoever was serving you would have the cheek to say, 'Where would you like your cabbage?' Well, everything was just mixed up on your plate.

At about this stage you had to pass a third class written examination. As I say, there was some lads who weren't very bright and I wasn't too bloody clever myself. So I used to write things down on my hand or on a larl bit of paper to jog my memory. Nearly everybody passed these exams but some failed them deliberately. You see, if they failed, they had what was called, 'early nights' when they were taken off guard duty, given extra milk to drink and made sure they got their sleep for re-sitting the exam the next day. You got the same ones skiving all the time.

We learnt all about the Border Regiment and towards the end of our training had F.F.I. That was Free From Infections talk, about keeping away from women, venereal diseases and things like that. Then we were shown pictures on the subject. Well, we'd never seen owt like that and you were just about spewing your innards up looking at it. But by that stage of your training, somebody would say, 'Hey, I've never had a hard-on,' and somebody else would reply, 'No, I haven't either.' And there's eighty of you and none of you have and it was, 'I wonder why?' Bromide had been put in your tea. Nobody knew that they're doing it and suddenly, everything was all right with us. They'd stopped putting the bromide in the tea and that's when you're training's finished.

At the end of training we were told, 'Right, you can all go for a drink, now.' So you'd go into the bar at the Castle and after a couple of hours you were stoned out of your head because none of you were used to drink. The following day it was the passing out parade and you're going to get your postings. In them days there were all sorts of places you could be sent. Hong Kong, Singapore, Korea, Christmas Island, Malaya, Egypt, Kenya, Kuwait, Germany, Cyprus, Northern Ireland, or British Guyana. And that was just some of the postings.

My mother and one of my sisters came to watch the passing-out parade. Everything's smart and the band's playing. It's like a scene from that film, *An Officer and a Gentleman*. The Sergeant comes along and he's saying, 'Get those shoulders back, Kirkbride. Smart lad, smart lad.' By this time there's tears in his eyes and there's tears in your eyes. And at the end of the parade, when we're getting into the truck, he says, 'I want you all to behave yourselves because I'll hear about it if you don't.' We know he won't and as by this time we're going off in the truck, we all shout back, 'Oh, piss off.'

You have a larl bit of leave at home, then you report back to the Castle and they march you down to the railway station in uniform. We were going to Germany and had to get the train to London. That took ten to twelve hours in them days as it was all steam trains. From London we went to Harwich where you got the night train across the Channel to the Hook of Holland. Over there you got fed and watered and then boarded a train. There were loads of trains. Yellow trains, blue trains and green trains which took you all over Germany to where you were stationed. It used to take you three full days from home to your camp in Germany.

'View of Gottingen Camp, Germany'

Oh, in Germany you thought you were on another planet. Gottingen where we were stationed was a university town and it was a fantastic place, beautiful and spotlessly clean. None of us had been out of our village or town and now we were in another country and nearly up to our necks in snow. Windows had shutters on them to keep the snow out and when you were on guard with the temperature twenty degrees below zero, you borrowed as many clothes as you bloody well could. You were only allowed to stop out for half an hour because it was that cold. And during that time you used to prowl round the camp, ducking and diving, looking for warm spots.

There was no Berlin Wall in Germany at that time. We used to do what we called border patrol with a Bren gun each and were only as far as from here to the house next door from the East Germans and the Russians. The distance between us was all ploughed field which was mined and had bloody big wired fences and wooden towers to stop anybody getting over. Anybody trying to get over would have no chance as if they got over the mines and wire fences, the other side would still have shot them. Later, when other Border lads went to Germany, we used to say, 'There was no wall in Germany when we were there. It was only when you useless buggers got there that they put the wall up.'

'Football team at Gottingen'
Standing left, Basil Telford (Carlisle), 3rd left ? McGuiness (Liverpool), 3rd right Sandy Carey (Workington)
Kneeling, left, Adam, 2nd left Corporal 'Buster' Hartley, centre, Jim Casson (Parton)

On a typical day you woke up at reveille, at half past six. The first thing you did was get washed and shaved. You made your bed space and then everybody had their own larl jobs. One would be in charge of the toilets, another in charge on the bathroom, somebody else would be in charge of the floors. When everybody had done their jobs it was eight o'clock, breakfast time and you dashed down to the canteen. Once you'd had breakfast, you dashed back to the billet, got tidied up and there'd be bugle call, on parade.

Now, each night lists were posted up on the wall giving details of the following day's duty. So after being on parade, maybe it was gym and you had to be ready in your PT gear to be marched to the gymnasium. After that it could be rifle range and you jumped in a lorry and off to the range for a couple of hours. Then it was coffee time at the NAFFI. What next?, church parade with RC's to the right, Protestants on the left and other denominations just piss off. But there wasn't any other denominations in them days, you were either RC or Protestant. You'd all be sitting having a fag when an officer would walk in, so everybody would jump to their feet. 'Stand easy, men. Carry on smoking.' Well, the officer would give you a lot of religious crap and when he finished, the bugle would sound so you'd go for your dinner. In the afternoon it might be bayonet practice until four o'clock when another bugle sounded. That was the end of the day and you could please yourself what you were going to do unless you were on guard.

The first time I was ever on guard, I worked with a lad called Jackie Sandham and he says, 'Here you are,' and gives me a pick-axe handle. When I asked what it was for, Jackie said, 'If there's any trouble in this pub, just bray them with it.' That was in case any of the British lads caused trouble but nine times out of ten they behaved themselves.

There was A,B,C,D and HQ companies and they all took turns in doing guard duty. If it was your company's turn to do guard duty, you did it all week. Otherwise you just went to the pictures or for a drink. If you had ten shillings to spare, you went and bought two hundred fags on the camp. In them days there were twelve German marks to the pound so a mark was worth one shilling and eight pence. So we used to sell Germans twenty fags for einer mark (one mark) and from our ten shillings we made six shillings and eight pence profit. We did this so we could get into a pub because we had very little money. But we didn't go off the camp much as there was everything you needed on site. Besides the NAAFI, all camps had what was called ABC cinemas and we used to get the latest pictures. And we had three or four outside swimming pools for when the weather was good. Also, there was the gymnasium where you could do fencing and basketball or whatever you wanted.

'Having a drink in the NAAFI'
1st left, Wimm Vickers, 2nd left, Les Thompson (Maryport), 5th left, Jim Casson, (Parton).
Standing behind is Harry Hodgson, (Cleator Moor), centre Sandy Carey (Workington)
and 3rd right, holding his glass is Adam.

I'll tell you what else we used to get, ENSA. These were shows that were put on for servicemen and they were spot on. Can you remember Eddie Calvert, the trumpet player? He came and put on a show for us and they were absolutely spot on because we'd never seen owt like them before. I think it cost about two shillings to get into one of these shows but a lot of lads didn't have the money to go. There were very few dances on camp. In fact I'd only been in Germany a couple of nights when they had one and I went to it. My God, there were lots of ugly women there. Well, I didn't know who was who and I was dancing with this larl fat thing who turned out to be a major's wife.

They were all German staff who worked in the canteens. I never complained about the food on the camp, ever. I used to shovel it onto my plate because I was that pleased to get it. When you got well in with these German women they'd put an extra slice of bread on your plate and things like that. There was never owt left for the pigs when we finished because we used to clean the bloody lot up.

It was in the NAAFI that I got into trouble. Me and a lad called Jimmy Fitzpatrick were made up to lance corporals. When you had stripes of any kind you ate in separate messes to the lads in the NAAFI. One evening I'd been on athletics training and was hungry. As I had one shilling and nine pence to my name, I went into the NAAFI and bought a pork chop. I was sitting eating it when a stick crashed across the table. I looked up and it was one of the regimental police who'd bashed his stick in front of me and Jimmy was with him. As I shouldn't have been in the NAAFI this policeman shouted at me to get out. In my own way I told him where to go so he ordered Jimmy to throw me out. Well, Jimmy just said, 'I'm not throwing him out, you'd better do it.' So off went the policeman to find somebody who'd throw me out. At that Jimmy said he thought it would be a good idea if I left so off I went to the barracks. I was just getting into bed when the door crashed open and the military policeman was standing there. Unfortunately I told him to shut the door before I knocked him through it and up popped a sergeant major who was standing behind him. So I was thrown in goal for the night.

At nine o'clock the next morning, I was marched in front of the Major. The charge was that I had refused to leave the NAAFI and all this crap. Now, the Major was in charge of the athletics team and knew how good I was at athletics. Also, the military policeman who was making the charge used to compete against me in the high jump and I always beat him. So the Major just said, 'Case admonished.' I didn't even know what admonished meant and when I asked, this policeman screamed at me, 'You bloody bag of bones, turn left, turn left,' and marched me outside. Once outside, all he could do was shout, 'Admonished, admonished,' at me and that was the case closed.

There used to be these 'ladies of the night' hanging outside the camp. In fact, the day I arrived at Germany there was an identity parade as this German lass had been raped. Or was supposed to have been. You see, they used to come to the perimeter wire and offer their services to the lads. Anyway, we were all put on this identity parade and this lass comes along and she stops. There she is standing in front of me and staring at me. I'm standing there nearly shiting myself and I suddenly thought, 'It isn't me. I've only arrived and was crossing the bloody English Channel when all this was supposed to happen.' The woman couldn't find the bloke who was supposed to be responsible and that was the end of the story.

But there was one, a lady of the night, who came to the camp and they called her Kipper Feet. Even now, I could say to thousands of lads who did National Service forty odd years ago, 'Who's Kipper Feet?' and they'd say, 'That lass who was on the main gate.' Anyway, they used to smuggle her into camp. Now, the Regimental Sergeant Major was Tiny Shaw who was even bigger than me and every morning the corporal from each company would go on parade and tell him the strength of their company. So the RSM would shout, 'A Company,' and Jackie Sandham, our Corporal would shout, 'One major, one captain, two second lieutenants, three warrant officers, forty men, one sick and two leave, otherwise all present and correct, sir.' Then the RSM would come to B Company and when their corporal eventually got to 'All present and correct, sir,' Tiny Shaw would shout at him, 'Get that bloody Kipper Feet out of the bloody lockers.' 'Yes sir,' B Company corporal would answer. So Kipper Feet would be scopped out of there and the following morning she'd be in bloody Charlie Company or somewhere else till she'd done the rounds.

We used to do training exercises with the tanks and one day the major in charge of them turned to our Major and said, 'Your lads have done well. Give them the day off. They can go to one of two places, either to see Belsen or the Rhur Dam where the Dam Busters went over.' So off we went, half the lads in one lorry and the others in the second one. I was in the one which ended up at Belsen.

There we were in full battle dress carrying our Bren guns with two hundred rounds of .303 ammunition going into Belsen. We saw what the Jews were told were showers for them to go into but were really the gas ovens. Then our Major says, 'How many prisoners do you think were in that cell?' Now, this cell we were looking at was only about six feet long and three feet wide and somebody says, 'Six prisoners.' One of the lads replies, 'Don't talk so bloody daft. How can you get six people in there?' And then the Major said, 'It could hold ten prisoners.' When you thought about how thin the prisoners were, they were just skeletons to manage to get ten of them in the cells.

When we went inside Belsen itself, nobody speaks. There's not a bird chirping or a cricket. Just silence. It's as if God says, 'Nobody speaks in here.' There are big earth mounds with the words, 'Two thousand buried here,' or 'Fifteen hundred buried here,' wrote on top and it went on like that. Then you looked to the right and there was a big marble stand. It was so big it looked like a cinemascope screen. And written on the marble in three languages, English, German and Hebrew, are the words, 'Here lie forty thousand Jews murdered by the murderous Nazi. Israel and the World shall never forget them.' It was exactly ten years after the war and I remember those words most vividly.

My mam used to get the *Sunday Post* and in one issue in 1962, somebody who'd been in the Argyll and Sutherland Regiment wrote in about how he felt when he went to Belsen. On reading it, I realised he must have thought the same as I was thinking at the time. I still carry that newspaper clipping with me, it's in my pocket now.

'On manouvres'
Photo left. Adam is sitting left, on tank.
Photo right. Adam standing left, with Private McGuiness (Liverpool)

'Still on manoeurves.
Adam is standing centre with the Bren Gun'

'This time it's night manoeuvers'
From left, Basil Telford (Carlisle), Jim Casson, (Parton),
John Cunningham (Parton), Ian Howson (Carlisle)
Adam and Mike Chester

I mentioned about doing training with tanks. We used to do planned war games with these three bloody great tanks. I'll tell you the names of them, Choo, Chin and Chow. The idea was that these tanks would take you into the attack and then the infantry would carry on the attack. One and Two sections would climb up the front of the tank, as the tank tracks were just like ladders, and hang onto the netting that's used as camouflage. Our sections would give firing cover to Three and Four sections on the ground behind us. Mind, your arse would get sore sitting there on these tanks as they used to be red hot. Well, me and Billy Fulton were on the tank and for some reason, the tank commander was given the command to reverse instead of going forward. We were thrown to the ground and these tank tracks were reversing on top of us. I managed to get my belt off, with all my kit attached to it and the tank mangled that and then my rifle. We managed to get to one side and out of the way but there was such a hullabaloo. The officer came running up saying, 'Kirkbride, Fulton are you both all right?' I was shaking.

Now, I never wrote home very often and I could never understand Ma's writing when she wrote to me. She used to set off by telling me so-and-so had died and you never could make out who'd died as she went on about something else. When a letter came from Ma, I just used to see if there were any postal orders with it. But word had got back to Salterbeck about the tank accident. One of the local lads in the regiment was writing to a lass who lived next door to one of my sisters. In his letter he wrote that Big Adam had been run over by a tank. So of course, I got this garbled letter wanting to know which hospital I was in. I was thinking, 'What the hell are you on about?' It took me ages to sort all that out.

During National Service I got two home leaves. The first one was about nine months after going to Germany and the second, nine months after that. Going home on leave was brutal as it took three days. You travelled all the way up through Germany and Holland by train then met up with other service trains at the Hook of Holland. You got on the troopship at night and while you're asleep, it crossed the Channel and you wake up in England. Then the bloody RSM lets the others off the ship first and by the time you've disembarked, you've missed the train north.

So there I was in London for the first time on my own. At the railway station I joined the enquiry queue to find out about the next train to Carlisle. There was a larl air force lad in front of me and I heard him ask about trains to Carlisle and he was told there was one later that day. So I asked him if I could knock around with him until the train came. We put all our gear into the station lockers and this lad asked, 'Have you had owt to eat?' I'd never had owt for two days as I had been caught at customs with six hundred fags I was taking home. It cost me three quid to pay duty and all I had left was two bob. Fortunately this lad knew a Salvation Army place and though they'd finished making breakfasts, they took pity on us and cooked us bacon, eggs and tomato dip. That meal only cost one shilling and nine pence but I was standing there with my hand out for my three pence change.

Eventually, we got the train home and I slept until we arrived into Carlisle. This lad I was with was waving to a bloke on the station. He said, 'It's my dad come to pick me up in his car.' 'That's champion,' I told him, 'You'll be home before long. What part of Carlisle are you from?' The lad answered, 'Oh, I'm not from Carlisle. I come from a spot called Workington.' It was amazing, we'd knocked about together for a day and we didn't know each other's names or that we were from the same town. Anyway, this lad and his dad gave me a lift to the street where I lived. By that time it was two o'clock in the morning. I knocked on our front door and the auld lad (Father) came down stairs in his long johns to let me in. He hadn't seen me for nearly a year and the first thing he said was, 'What a bloody time to wake a feller,' and I got a right telling off. But as soon as Dad seen the fags I brought him, it was 'Oh, you're a grand lad.'

I went to bed and later that morning when I got up, PC Varty, the local policeman came and knocked on the door. When I opened the door he said, 'Eh, young man, thou's in the forces?' 'Yes officer' I answered. 'Well, I've come to see about thy young brother. He was knocking out all the gas lights on the street last night.' 'Oh, he can't have, officer,' I told him, 'Joe was at the pictures with me last might.' 'Was he? I must have been wrong then.' said Varty and off he went. So I got Joe off the hook over that as the auld man would have killed him if he'd found out.

After you'd been home a couple of days, there was nowt to do. Your marras were back at camp and the others who were home were all courting. Mind you, even if you did go out, you still had to be in the house for half past ten at night. When leave was finished, I found out that a lad from Cleator Moor was going back to Germany and we arranged to meet on the railway station. But we got on different trains and his went via Carlisle and mine, via Barrow. Now, the Carlisle route was quicker and the Barrow one took twelve hours. So I sat on my own for twelve hours until the train arrived back at London, then it was another two days back to camp at Germany. You always arrived back at camp at midnight and all the lads knew when you were due back, so your bed was made. All you had to do was get your gear ready for duty the next day.

ORDER OF CEREMONY

AT THE

UNVEILING OF

THE CASSINO MEMORIAL

TO OFFICERS AND MEN OF THE
ARMIES OF THE COMMONWEALTH

BY

FIELD MARSHAL THE RIGHT HONOURABLE
THE EARL ALEXANDER OF TUNIS
K.G., G.C.B., G.C.M.G., C.S.I., D.S.O., M.C.

SUNDAY, 30TH SEPTEMBER, 1956, AT 12.00 NOON

'Cover of the programme at the Unveiling of The Cassino Memorial'

THE CASSINO MEMORIAL has been built by the Imperial War Graves Commission.

On the columns of the Memorial 4,068 names are carved on marble panels. On the walls of the stairways leading from the road to the entrance of the War Cemetery are inscribed, in English and Italian, these words :—

1939–1945

WITHIN THIS CEMETERY STAND MONUMENTS
WHICH BEAR THE NAMES OF SOLDIERS
OF THE BRITISH COMMONWEALTH AND EMPIRE
WHO FELL IN THE ASSAULTS UPON THE SHORES
OF SICILY AND ITALY OR IN LATER BATTLES
TO FREE ITALIAN SOIL AND TO WHOM THE FORTUNE
OF WAR DENIED A KNOWN AND HONOURED GRAVE

AROUND THEM ARE THE GRAVES OF THEIR COMRADES
WHO DIED FIGHTING IN THESE PARTS TO
OPEN THE WAY TO ROME AND THE NORTH

The land on which the Cemetery and Memorial at Cassino stand has been generously given by the Italian people.

Relatives and other guests invited to the Unveiling Ceremony will be welcomed at any of the following special services which have been arranged in Rome on Monday, 1st October :—

CHURCH OF ENGLAND

8 a.m. *All Saints' Church, via Babuino.*
Celebration of the Holy Communion with Special Memorial Prayers. Celebrant : The Reverend Canon V. J. Pike, C.B., C.B.E., D.D., Chaplain to the Queen, Chaplain-General to the Forces.

CHURCH OF SCOTLAND AND THE FREE CHURCHES

8 a.m. *St. Andrew's Church of Scotland, via XX Settembre.*
Service of Holy Communion with Special Memorial Prayers. Officiating Chaplain : The Reverend Norman Maclean, M.B.E., Chaplain to the Forces, Church of Scotland Chaplain.

ROMAN CATHOLIC CHURCH

8 a.m. *The Crypt of St. Peter's Cathedral.*
Commemorative Low Mass celebrated by the Right Reverend Monsignor J. M. Clarke, C.B.E., Senior Roman Catholic Chaplain, Italy, 1943–1945.

JEWISH SERVICES

Prayers for the fallen were recited in the Synagogues of Rome during the Sabbath Services held on Saturday, 29th September.

'Part of the programme at the Unveiling of The Cassino Memorial'

While I was in Germany, it was coming up to ten years since the Battle of Monte Cassino and the Border Regiment was chosen to take part in the ceremony marking the event. As we travelled on the Rome Express, we weren't allowed to take our weapons with us as we were going through different frontiers so the Canadians flew our rifles and bayonets over to Italy for us.

When we were put on the Rome Express we were given haversack rations, which were four big doorstep sandwiches. There were two of cheese and two of sardine which stank to high heaven. Not realising how long we would be on the train, we hoyed these sandwiches out of the windows. After eight hours, the cry was, 'Where's the food, sir?' and we were told, 'You've got it, you've got haversack rations.' Well, we had nowt to eat and were on that train for two days. Eventually, as we were going through Rome, this chap came along and said the dining car was open. One sergeant could speak Italian and I asked him to find out how much a meal cost. It cost a thousand liras, which was next to nowt. I had three pounds and ten shillings with me, which I changed into liras and went for a meal. It was a beautiful meal. I never used to eat spaghetti or owt like that but I was so hungry, I ate the lot. With my other two thousand liras, I went with a lady of ill repute.

Oh, it was a big ceremony at Monte Cassino with Alexander of Tunis there and the cemetery was beautiful with lily ponds and marble memorials. Most of the allied nations were there. The ceremony lasted a day and it was red hot. We all wore khaki uniform in them days but the Australians, Canadians and New Zealanders were in shorts. We were sweating cobs and a couple of the lads passed out. The Borders had eight wreath bearers so there we were, all dressed up with these five foot wreaths to hand over during the ceremony.

Guests had been invited to the ceremony and when it was over, a lady said to me, 'Will you take a photograph of the cenotaph for me?' I asked her if there was any name inscribed on the cenotaph that was wanted me to get into focus. She just said, 'The top one.' I looked down and saw she had two young lads with her, about ten and twelve years old who were wearing miniature ribbons on military medals pinned to their chests. I took the lady's camera and looking through the lens to the top name on the cenotaph saw it was of a major who had fallen at the battle of Monte Cassino. It was obviously his two sons who were wearing his military medals.

When I was home on my next leave, my uncle Tom came to the house and we got talking about this ceremony as he'd been with the Borders at the battle of Monte Casino during the war. 'Wait till I show you those,' I said, getting out some photographs that I had of the ceremony. Well, uncle Tom looked at them and started to cry. He told me that Alexander of Tunis had been the best of the lot. When the lads were digging in at Monte Cassino to make gun emplacements, they were digging into solid rock. They were chipping and chipping away and it was red hot so they were stripped down to the waist. When any of the top brass were there, it was 'Get dressed,' but not with Alexander. He was the one who brought cigarettes and chocolate for the lads.

When it was nearly the end of your time in National Service, you were asked if you wanted to join the Army as a regular. But all you wanted to do was get out and go home. And whoever was due for demob had to sign forms and blokes handing out these forms used to act the goat. They'd put a signing-on form underneath all the others which you didn't read and just signed. Then you'd be told, 'You've just signed on for another three years.'

Now, you did two years National Service but if you'd been in goal whatever amount of time you'd spent there was added onto your service. You see, you signed on to serve the Queen and you weren't serving her in prison so that time wasn't counted. One lad that I knew rebelled against everything and in total did six months in goal. So when his group of eighty lads were due to be demobbed, seventy nine of them went home and he had to stay another six months to make up his time.

When you arrived back at Carlisle Castle for demob, you were there for the best part of a day. One or two lads would be cheeky to the sergeants and they were given jobs to do. At the end of the day you just went and handed your kit in, signed for it and were given a rail pass back home and that was it. Once home you automatically got your old job back. It was up to you when you started work but everybody wanted to start work as soon as possible. You see, in most jobs in them days, you had to work for two years before you were entitled to a holiday.

With National Service, most lads did it and couldn't wait to come home. You didn't realise how good you could have made it. You could have learnt various languages but I didn't bother. After two years all I knew was, 'zwei bitte,' 'danke shon,' 'kommen sie hier,' and 'mein liebling.' If you had qualifications and things like that, it would have been easier for you but a lot of lads were like me, thick as a crisp.

The Border Regiment automatically keeps in touch with you and I've just been to a reunion do. At the reunion was Bob Hodges (Major General Hodges C.B., O.B.E.), who had been our Lieutenant, then went up through the ranks until he became Colonel. Anyway, Bob gave his after-dinner speech and was reminding us of funny incidents from years back. Later that night, I said, 'Can I have a word with you, sir?' He says, 'Bob's the name, Adam.' Oh, that was champion and I showed him old photographs of the lads in the regiment. Do you know, he remembered everyone from forty years ago. Looking back to my National Service, I had a wonderful time.

TEN

'Corporal Cod'

ဢ

***John Pickering**, served in 1st Battalion,*
Lancashire Fusiliers 1949 – 1951

I left school at fourteen and went to serve my time as a brushmaker in Kendal. I was eighteen when I went to Preston for my National Service medical. I wanted to be A1 because I wanted to be an infantryman. But everybody wanted to be A1, even if they didn't want to be a National Serviceman. You didn't want them to find anything wrong with you and lads that this happened to were very disappointed.

'At Warminster. Middle row, left, Horace Wells (Kendal) and John on the right'

A few weeks after you passed your medical, you were sent up to the Army. I was sent up to Hadrian's Camp with the Border Regiment at Carlisle. All your kit was given to you. Some of it was the wrong size and you had to get it changed and everything sorted out. Maybe a cap was too big for you or boots were too small. One of the first things was getting a haircut. Not only were you scalped but everybody could see your big ears when you lost your hair.

Looking back, the first thing you remember is feeling homesick that first night. You see, it was frightening when you first went to Carlisle and you were definitely homesick. I've seen lads go to the canteen for their first meal and they would be sitting there with the meal in front of them and they couldn't eat it. You knew what was wrong with them, they were homesick.

Our billets were in spiders, rooms which lead off from one big room. There wasn't anybody else from Kendal in my barracks but I knew two or three local lads who were already on the camp and had more or less done their basic training. One of the new lads would say, 'They've given us these boots to bull up,' and a Kendal lad would fetch his and show you how it was done. Then he would lend you his iron to take the dimples out of the boots. Many a night you spent hours sitting on the edge of your bed just bulling these boots up because you had nothing else to do.

At one stage of your training, you were given a chair and told to clean it down and make it look respectable. Of course you would say, 'What do I use to clean it?' and be told, 'You'll have to find something.' So you went back to these Kendal lads and ask them how you did it. 'Get a piece of glass,' was the answer. So you got a piece of glass, broke it up and used that to scrape the chair clean.

I come from an army family. I've four older brothers who'd been in the regular army and in the war, so to some extent I knew what to expect with National Service. Now, our corporal was a good 'un but corporals tried to frighten you and I knew what was coming. I'd heard it before off other people. When a corporal said silly things like, 'Am I hurting you? I should be because I'm standing on your hair' or 'You broke your mother's heart but you won't break mine,' I knew they were trying to frighten you, that's all.

But some lads did get picked on. We had one lad and in PT he couldn't even do a forward roll. It was pathetic how he was doing it. You felt sorry for him but everybody took it out on him. Then there was another lad who was a bit scruffy and couldn't keep himself or his equipment clean. When we had a CO's inspection where everything had to be spotless, the Officer would say, 'Sergeant, get him out of here. We don't want him in here, get him out.' And they would chuck this lad into another room until the inspection was over.

Even though you'd passed your medical to do National Service, you still had to pass other tests. In a lot of respects, you were still at school because you had to pass Education One, Two and then Three. If you passed these tests you got more money. You also had to do silly elementary tests like putting a pump or lamp together. There were some people who couldn't do that and didn't pass their tests. The Army also learnt you the ways of the Regiment, telling you what the Regiment did, its history and battle honours. Then we all had to go and see the doctors again, maybe for chest X-rays and other things we didn't have at our first medical. Some lads didn't pass these medical tests and were discharged. So even though you were doing basic training, you could actually be thrown out and the ones that were, were very disappointed. But like elsewhere, there were duffers, wide boys and trouble makers.

We had injections or tabs as we called them while we were at Hadrian's Camp and people were really frightened of them. That's true, because some people actually did faint or were really poorly and in bed for a few days afterwards. Often if you'd had a tab you would be made to go and do something like shovelling coke to keep your muscles going.

Officially, on Sunday mornings we were allowed out of camp to go into Carlisle. Unofficially, I'd go into Carlisle and catch the bus or train to Kendal, have a meal at home then go back. If the Army had wanted me, I would have been in trouble because you weren't supposed to leave Carlisle. Looking back, if I had missed the bus back to Carlisle and not been there for roll-call the next morning, I would have been absent without leave.

When you'd finished your basic training at Hadrian's Camp, you had your passing out parade, then moved to another part of the camp. You see, it was a big camp and lads were going there every week. When we finished our basic training, we were kitted out to go to Mogadishu in East Africa to meet the Border Regiment out there. So we were given embarkation leave and I came home telling everybody I was going to Mogadishu. But when we got back to camp, we were told we weren't going there, we were going down to a place called Warminster at Salisbury and being put into the Lancashire Fusiliers.

'Still at Warminster. John and Horace Wells'

Down near Salisbury Plain there was a village called Imba. Nearly every soldier who's been in the area did their training there because it was like a small battle ground. Imba was absolutely knocked about for that sort of thing. That's where we did our infantry demonstrations for our top brass and officers, and others from all over the world.

For these demonstrations we just went out on dawn or night attacks. There was just the odd casualties because you used what was called a fixed line. That was when the machine gun or Bren gun would fire bullets to a certain place all the time. The fixed line had so many ordinary bullets and than a tracer to show lads where the bullets were going. It didn't fire at people. Sometimes, to make a sound effect, they would shoot down a rabbit hole. We dressed up as Germans and all sorts and fought these mock battles between ourselves. Many a time I was a German.

There was a big NAAFI on the site where you could spend your spare time. We went into Salisbury but most of the time went to Warminster which was nearer the camp. I think our wage was about twenty-one bob a week and I sent some money home to my mother and saved some for when I eventually came home. Money was also taken off us for barrack room damages and if you lost any equipment, they would take that off your wage as well. Some people were always in the red because they seemed to be losing things left, right and centre. Out of the money we had, some of it went on soap, boot polish and toothpaste so you didn't have much left but you got used to what you had.

One lad was careless and never put anything away so it was always stolen. That meant he was always in the red in his pay book to pay for the stuff he had lost. I think the lad was picked on because he was a duffer. That's what they would do if you didn't turn on them. A feller once pinched my cup. I pinched it back and we nearly got into a fight over it. Like nearly everybody else, I kept my hands to myself and looked after my stuff but anybody who was careless would loose theirs. The saying was, 'If anybody pinches your stuff, go and bloody well pinch theirs.'

We lived in spiders at Salisbury and one corporal would come into ours when he wanted something doing. He was probably given his stripe because he was a regular but he was a bit of a goon and hadn't a bloody clue. I had a mate in another spider and once went to talk to him. This mate was a good artist and drew a fish, a cod with big eyes. Now, this corporal did have big eyes so my mate wrote underneath his drawing, 'Corporal Cod.' Well, of course, the Corporal came in and saw the drawing so he had it in for us after that.

I suppose I couldn't keep my mouth shut over certain things and one day in the pay cheque, Corporal Cod shouted at me to stop talking.

This annoyed me because I hadn't been talking and instead of keeping my trap shut I argued with him. So I had to spend the night in the nick and was on company orders in the morning. Anyway, we had a good sergeant major who spoke up for me, said I was a good soldier, played football and did running for the company, so the charge was dropped.

Company officers all had their fads about different things. With one it might be about your cap not being straight. Another one might be looking at studs on your boots. One was always looking out for people with dirty nails. I remember we'd been cleaning our Bren guns and rifles after a demo, one time. Well, there's nothing worse than getting oil in your finger nails with doing that. So when we went on guard duty, the stupid guard commander put us on company orders because we had dirty finger nails. After a while you began to take notice of who was on duty and somebody would say, 'So and so's guard commander.' Then you'd know what he'd be looking for. If he had a fad about clean shoes, you'd make sure yours' were bulled up to hell and then you'd be OK.

We were down at Salisbury for six months. In that time we had one leave home and a coach brought us all the way up here. It dropped everybody off at different places like, Lancaster, Penrith and Carlisle. It picked us up after our leave to take up back down to Salisbury. At the end of six months the whole battalion was being sent out to Egypt and our place at Salisbury was taken over by the Northumberland Fusiliers. We got embarkation leave then sailed from Southampton with the *Empire Fowey* on her maiden voyage. We only stopped at Malta and reached Egypt about seven or eight days after leaving England.

We'd been given a talk about Egypt and it being so hot. We were told that every so often we'd be taking our uniform tops off. To start with, we'd have our shirts off until dinner time, then put them back on again. That was to get you acclimatised and eventually, you finished up doing everything bare from the waist up. A lad with red hair in our company was excused taking his shirt off. Permission was given to red-headed lads who had pale skin to keep their shirts on as generally, they burnt easily with the sun.

On reaching Port Said it was the smell that hit you. It stank like hell. At Port Said we got on a train and went to a place called Fayid where there was a big army camp. The camp was placed out of town on a desolate road with other camps off it. Instead of barracks, we were in tents with mosquito nets over our beds but that was mostly to keep flies off, not mosquitoes.

Further on from the camp was a picture house on the roadside and an Egyptian cafe where you could get a meal of egg and chips which was our main diet at nights. Then there was the Church of England and Church of Scotland buildings which also laid on meals and soft drinks. After that was a little village with a bazaar and past the village was the lido and beach where you went for a swim.

At the time the Suez crisis was only just starting. We were there when King Farouk was in power and when he got dethroned by Nasser. There was always little bits of skirmishes at different times in Egypt because they didn't like us. They didn't like us at all and made it obvious but we had no trouble at our camp. There were various places you were told to keep out of, restricted or dead-end areas where you could have gone down and never come back. It wasn't until later when I was back home that the serious riots started. On the newsreels at the Roxy Cinema in Kendal I saw our Regiment in the fighting.

Out-of-Bounds Areas

There is always a very good reason for these and it is always for your good. Maybe the native population in the area is hostile to troops. More often than not an area is " Out of Bounds " for moral reasons. Some areas are out of bounds altcgether, others may be driven through in a vehicle, W.D. or civilian.

C.R.M.P. and S.I.B. patrols arrest a large number of free-lance prostitutes per month in Port Said, Ismailia, and Suez. A very large number of these girls have V.D.; and it is almost certain that you will be infected if you visit a brothel area.

Public health authorities in Egypt do not provide a free cure for V.D. This prevents many girls from obtaining treatment—even if they desire it.

'Excerpt from 'The Middle East' brochure'

Actually, we didn't do a lot of work in Egypt, usually guard duty and fatigues. We guarded other camps and at one, the wogs as we called them, tried to come over the perimeter wire at night to pinch stuff. That was at Tel El Kebir, an ordnance camp, where there was a couple of you on duty at different intervals all round the perimeter. We heard tales of these wogs coming over the wire and being shot. Mind, I never shot anybody. In fact, one night, me and this other bloke were on guard and thought we'd have a sleep. I said to him, 'I'll have a sleep first, then you wake me and you can have a sleep.' Well, I went to sleep and then he fell asleep. It could have been drastic if the wogs had come over as we might have had our throats cut.

Another thing we did was manoeuvres in the desert. You used to go marching and have your rifle with you and one man in the platoon always carried a Bren gun. If the person who was carrying the Bren gun got tired, the rest of us took turns in carrying it and the only thing we thought about and wanted was water. You'd climb little hills and with the soft sand you were taking one step forward and two steps back. At night we'd dig a trench to sleep in for protection and sometimes we were digging in soft sand. As you shovelled it to dig a hole, more sand was running back in. When the trench was eventually dug, we'd be lying there looking at the stars and saying to each other, 'I wonder if they can see that star at Kendal.'

In the desert you relied on your officer to read the map and compass because you could soon get lost if they didn't know what they were doing. Once we did get lost. All our equipment and kit such as pullovers were on lorries and we were marching along to meet them in our shirt sleeves and the officer got us lost. We had to sleep overnight and we were freezing as there was a heavy dew and you're wet through in the morning. Anyway, the next morning we found the lorries – only a couple of hundred yards from us.

You weren't warned so much about Egyptian women but the fellers. They were the ones you had to worry about. Our officer gave us a talk one day. 'Right' he says, 'these fellers are queer fellers, so if anybody approaches you and tries to tap you up, just give them a bloody good belting and you won't get into any trouble from us.' He was right.

We had an Egyptian barber and that's where I learnt Arabic. I would ask him how to say various things, so eventually I could say quite a bit. I can still tell you how to get lost in various ways, ask for things, say 'thank you' and all the naughty words. But that barber was a queer bugger an' all as he used to stroke the back of our necks when he was cutting our hair.

The drink was quite cheap out there but it was deadly stuff. It was a local drink called Stella beer and it was powerful. As there were hardened drinkers among the regulars who went into the NAAFI every night, there were always fights in camp. Time and time again, there were fights. Even when we were going out to Egypt on the boats there were lads who were put in the nick. Then when they got to Egypt, they were put in the Regimental Police because they were tough guys and would knock you about. There were people who were scared stiff of them and if you were put on jankers, they didn't half put you through it.

You see, there were the Military Police, red caps as they were called. They were like ordinary policemen but could charge you any time and lock you up. You could be in town somewhere, walking along with your hat stuck in your lapel and they'd come up to you and say, 'Get that hat on, sonny.' They would just keep you in order.

It was the Regimental Police who were the police on the camp and for your regiment. They'd look after things and do prison duty if anybody went in the nick. Oh, they were terrors and you got some bad 'uns. You never said a wrong word to them, you kept quiet. If there was a skirmish coming out of the NAAFI, the Regimental Police would be called. They fetched a 1500 cwt truck and just whipped whoever was causing the trouble into the back of it. And I've seen the police jump into the back and give them a good hiding.

When we were on guard, you went into the guardroom, then see that the prisoners were all right in the nick and take them something to eat. Many a time I've seen these police in there giving the prisoner a good belting. They knocked hell out of some of the prisoners. You knew this was wrong and you didn't like it but the Regimental Police would thump you as soon as look at you.

I remember one night I was asleep in our tent when I woke up to find two fellers standing over me with their fists raised. One bloke looked at me and said to his mate, 'That's not him.' His mate asked, 'Where's Duffy?' 'He's lying over there,' I told them and over they went to where Duffy was lying. The next thing I knew, Duffy was running down the road bare buff with these two blokes after him. He'd been giving them a bit of lip in the NAAFI. It was dangerous, it was. Some blokes would think nothing of knocking hell out of you if you weren't careful.

What we used to do when we finished work was ask somebody what dinner was like. If they said, 'Oh, don't bother,' we would go straight to the lido, have a swim, then get egg, chips and tea and after that a nice, ice cold drink. Then finally, stop at the open air picture house. We couldn't go far but once we found out two Kendal lads, Walter Johnstone and Thomas Wilson were up at Suez and we travelled by truck along the Suez Canal to see them and have a night out. Then they came down to Fayid to visit us.

I'd been in Egypt about a year when we left for Jordan and the 'Loyals' from Preston area took over from us. We were taken by plane over the Sinai Desert to Jordan in one of those old planes with propellers. The advance part who go first and get things ready, they went by sea.

The camp we were sent to was at Aqaba up the Gulf of Aqaba near Eilat. However Eilat was over the border in Israel or Palestine as it was called then. It was a huge camp we were at, spread over different areas. The Battalion was split into four or five different companies and you had different jobs to do. We were just guarding, always guarding places. You know them look-out posts on a stand? We used to climb up one of them and just keep observing what was happening on the Jewish side. Noting everything down, that's all we did. We had binoculars and watched the Jews, noting if a plane landed or a car was moving. I think a lot of it would be a load of silliness but we still had to write it down. It was a boring job and I was glad to be off that.

At one part of the camp there was a road block. All we did there was watch wagons carrying these big melons going down to the Gulf of Aqaba. We'd stop and search them to make sure that was all they were carrying. Our camp was on the side of the road block and there was an Arab legion tent just up the road. Maybe it was because we had to live together and work together but I found them great. We used to go and just call on them and they'd give us a little cup of tea with sugar but no milk. Then we'd start asking them questions and learn about different things. We used to spend many an hour talking to them.

It was at the road block camp where we had an old tin for burning rubbish. In a morning when the tin was cold, this little lad passed with his goats and he'd be scrimmaging in it for something to eat. Many a time we'd take a loaf out to him. He'd put the bread in his hankie and away he'd go with his goats. Then late at night, back he'd come home with them.

There weren't many places to go as, though the people weren't hostile, Jordan was a very poor country. We'd just go down the road to where the boats came in and have a swim or go further round the coast and that was beautiful. Mind, at one time some army lads were allowed to go to Cyprus but that was only the regular soldiers. That was a bit of a sickener until we found out that they'd all come back with a dose of you-know-what and were all going to the MO.

Both in Egypt and Jordan we still did a lot of sports. In fact we played against other regiments and went round to different camps playing football. You played on all sorts of pitches. One of our pitches was about six inches of soft sand so you can imagine what that was like. Once a naval ship, the *Mauritius* was anchored off the coast and all the sailors came ashore for a sports day. It was a fabulous day. It was out of this world because we beat them easy. Mind, thinking about it, with being sailors on board ship, they wouldn't have been able to do the training we did.

My mother used to send me a *Westmorland Gazette* and a book or magazine. These took a long time arriving. Sometimes two or three weeks and sometimes you got everything all at once. One of my brothers used to write to me and wherever I'd been stationed, he'd been there. So he'd write to me and say, 'Where are you now?' When I answered his letter and told him, he'd know all about the area with being there himself.

Towards the end of my service we flew back to Egypt. We went to the Moascar Garrison, which was all stone buildings. Further down the road was the town of Ismailia and that's where we went for a bit of recreation as the lido was there. Ismailia is also where the Sweet Water Canal is. If you mention the Sweet Water Canal to anybody who's been in the Army at Egypt, they'll know where it is. The wogs used to swim in it, wash in it and they did A LOT in it!! You would be walking down the road and see a woman bending down washing in the water. Then you'd see a larl lad peeing in it and somebody further down would be washing utensils in it. Folk reckoned that if you tumbled in there you would need inoculations.

Now, I actually went to do my National Service for eighteen months. But we were more or less ready for coming home when the Government put another six months onto your time so I did two years' service. Did it sicken me? It bloody well did I tell you. Some lads who had only another two or three weeks to do had to stay on but others with the same time left managed to get demobbed.

Back in England we came up to Bury just to put all our stuff there, came home for some leave, then back to Bury and got demobbed. After that we went up to Carlisle and had to do three and a half years in the TA. So even though you were back at your own job, the Army kept calling you back in for a bit of training. During that time we went on basic training for three weeks and had weekends away. Once we went down to Salisbury and twice to Wales. In fact one of my brothers who's just older than me, he got called up to go to one of these camps with me.

I've never bothered keeping in touch with my regiment. I had to do my National Service, I accepted it and went along with it. I more or less did everything I was asked to and kept my nose clean. There was some good times and some bad times.

In Jordan I saw a place that people now pay money to go and see. That was the Red Rose City, Petra. You go down a narrow gorge to it and there's beautiful buildings built out of solid rock. It was a marvellous place and I was really chuffed to see it. And where we used to go swimming, now I believe the shore line is full of hotels. But then it was only a nice beach with a lovely, clear blue sea and nothing else. It was beautiful when I was there and some day I hope to visit and see the changes that have been made.

ELEVEN

'A lovely racket going on'

***Geoff Trusler**, Served in the Royal Navy 1949 – 1951*

I was born at Keswick but as my father was a police officer, we moved to Penrith and then Appleby. We were in Appleby all through the war until 1946 when we came to Kendal and I joined the sea cadets as there wasn't a unit at Appleby.

'Geoff in the Kendal Sea Cadets'

After leaving Kendal Grammar School at sixteen, I worked as a junior at the Provincial Insurance Company. Once you were eighteen you had to register for National Service and it was in July 1949 that I went to Preston for a medical examination. There were about fifty of us from all over South Westmorland and the Lancashire area, right on the top floor of this building at Preston, which had a glass roof. It was a red hot day and we all felt dreadful. I remember thinking, 'God, I feel rotten, I'll never pass A1.' but I did.

'Kendal Sea Cadets marching through Kendal town centre. Geoff is on the far left'

We had our medicals in the morning and I opted to join the Navy. Because I'd done that, I had to sit an examination the same afternoon. You also had to put down a second choice in case you failed to get in the Navy. I couldn't ride a motorbike and hadn't even a driving licence but my second choice was despatch driver in the Army. Anyhow, out of the fifty odd lads, I was the only one who joined the Navy.

In the November I was called up and a travel warrant came for me to travel to Plymouth. I'd been away on courses for three week periods with the sea cadets but leaving home permanently was quite a wrench. Oh, the train journey was dreadful going to Plymouth. Later, when I had been home on leave and going back again, I'd leave Kendal about half past six at night. The train would get to Crewe at midnight and then you had to wait until about two in the morning for the Manchester train. Normally that was already packed so you just kipped in the corridor or wherever you could. Then it was all the way down through Bridgnorth, Pontypool, Bristol, Taunton and Exeter. Eventually, you'd reach Plymouth about eleven o'clock in the morning, so it was over a fourteen hour journey.

At Plymouth we were put in wooden buildings, sort of spider blocks. In charge of us was a petty officer and we had lectures, personal hygiene talks and haircuts. The food wasn't too bad and we were well fed. I remember breakfasts were bacon and tinned tomatoes which everybody called 'train smashes' for obvious reasons.

I can't really remember how I came to be a Jack Dusty (stores assistant). I think it was a question that the navy required certain vacancies filled. We were all writers (clerical), stewards or store assistants. There were two categories of store assistants. SAS(S), which was to do with nuts and bolts or SA(V) and that was victualling, i.e. clothes, food, drink and cigarettes and I was SA(V). So after we'd had all our lectures and were kitted out, we came up to *HMS Ceres* for basic training.

HMS Ceres was at York Road on the outskirts of Wetherby, right opposite the race track. We were a month there, doing square bashing, rifle drill, lots of PE and that type of thing. The disciple was pretty hard and I remember one PE session where the PTI spotted this lad from Liverpool who's ankles were dirty. He chased the lad off to get himself scrubbed and told him never to appear like that again. Two or three weeks later, the PTI spotted this lad, again with dirty ankles. Four of us were ordered to take him to the heads, as they called the washrooms. There he was put into a bath of cold water and the PTI stood over us while we had to lay into the lad. We had to scrub him from head to toe with old fashioned scrubbing brushes. His skin was red-raw but he was never dirty again. You see, when you got onto small ships, hygiene was essential because there were so many of you living in such combined space. If anybody wasn't hygienic it caused problems for everybody else.

At night we used to go out to Boston Spa, Leeds or York. But the officers were very strict about appearance and before you were allowed ashore, our Officer-in-Charge inspected our clothes, shoes and all the rest. Many a time he turned people away for the most petty things and if you missed the liberty boat, you had to wait an hour before you could go again. Yet this Officer was one of the scruffiest devils I've ever come across. His shoes were down at heel and had never seen polish for weeks.

I recollect we also had church parade and you were divided into groups of Catholics, Church of England or Methodists. Some of the blokes said they were Church of Turkey to try and get out of going to church but it didn't work.

From *HMS Ceres* we went to a place called Moorlands in Wetherby itself. I believe Moorlands at one time had been a holiday camp before it was taken over by the Navy. There we did our specialist training and all the paperwork that was involved. The majority of blokes were regulars who had joined the Navy as a career. We enjoyed ourselves at Moorlands as there was a load of WRENS, about three to every one man. We had a whale of a time and, as you can imagine, there was a well worn track between the billets.

It was at Moorlands that I learned never to volunteer for anything. We were all lined up one day and a chief petty officer or whoever was in charge said, 'Who's got a driving licence?' Two lads stepped forward and were told, 'Right, you two, go and get a wheel-barrow and sweep that road outside.' I was lucky because I had a very cushy number in the guard room. Every lesson lasted an hour and at the end of each one, I used the Tannoy system to pipe that the hour was up. I did the same when the lads were going ashore.

The Navy issued us with cigarettes which were four and a half pence old money for twenty. But we couldn't really afford much on four bob a day. We were paid fortnightly, less two shillings and sixpence which was taken off for our stamp. It was at Moorlands that I met a lad called Walter Hart from Edinburgh. In order to try and make some money, we set up a dobie wallah situation. We'd wash other people's shirts for three pence a time and that helped to eke out the money.

For leave the ship's company was split into two parts. You were either on first or second leave so that the ship was manned at all times.

I came home for Christmas in 1949 and after eight weeks at Moorlands I was posted to *HMS Drake* at Plymouth. *Drake* was what they called a stone frigate because it was an onshore depot. There I worked in the MVO, which was the main victualling office and my job was solely to do with RUM!!

In the old days, everybody got neat rum. But what a lot of sailors did, they saved their rum up for maybe a fortnight or longer then drank it all at once and were incapable for doing their jobs. So, in order to stop that, the Navy introduced two parts of water to one part of rum (grog). And by rum it wasn't this rubbish you buy in pubs, it was real good stuff. The funny thing about it was, you could put one tot of rum in a glass with two tots of water, leave it for an hour and it would be OK but after that it went off. The idea was to get the sailors to drink the grog straight away instead of saving it up.

In the dockyard there were about three thousand men. They were divided into three categories, G men, T men or UA's. G men were grog men who were entitled to a tot of rum a day. T men were tea-total, didn't drink and got three pence a day from Aggie West in lieu of grog. Aggie West was a benevolent person who'd set up retreats for sailors which were spread around the country. She hadn't approved of drink so if you were tea-total you got three pence a day from Aggie's benevolent fund. The UA's were under age and not entitled to grog.

Every day the mess caterers would come to me with all their figures so you had to rely on these to be accurate. So many G s, so many T s and so many UA s and then I had to work out from these figures how much rum each mess was entitled to. The funny part of it was, one gallon of rum and two gallons of water and you didn't get three gallons of liquid because it used to shrink.

As you knew by half past eight in the morning that you'd need at least nine gallons of rum for that day, it saved time to pump the rum into a beaker (copper barrel) then, instead of waiting until eleven o'clock. You had a copper pump to prime the rum from the big barrels into the beaker. When we eventually withdrew the plunger from the pump, the pump was still full of rum and of course, it was ours.

At eleven o'clock you went down to the drill shed. All the mess caterers were there with what they called their fannies, which were buckets similar in shape to the ones charwomen used. The mess caterers used to line up and the officer of the day would stand there while you issued the rum in big brass measures.

In order to compensate for shrinkage and spillage of grog, we used to flood all the copper measures and strictly speaking what was left when everybody had been served was thrown over the side. But the officer of the day knew the score, we'd trained him well and fixed him up with neat rum before we started serving. Our mess was always the last to be served and the officer would say, 'Just before I sign, anybody else to be served?' When he was told there was just our mess to be served, he'd sign the book and off he went. Well, what was left in the beaker was ours. Our mess had maybe twenty ratings and sometimes we could have up to three gallons of rum left, so we used to have a pretty good time.

While ordinary sailors got grog, petty and chief officers were allowed to have neat rum. Once they got above officer rank, they were gin and tonic men. Most of these 'wingers' had worked their way up through the ranks, been brought up on rum and didn't get it any more. One warrant officer in particular, I've turned to at half past eight in the morning and said, 'Do you want a glass, sir?' He'd see off half a tumbler of neat rum, then produce a flat bottle from his back pocket and say, 'Can you fill that up for me?'

As you can imagine, a lot of ratings were hardened drinkers. One that I can remember was what was called a three badge FA. He had a lot of service in so wherever he went in the Navy, he was the senior man. But instead of being a leading hand or petty officer, he kept being demoted through getting into trouble because of drink. This chap was just a stores assistant and couldn't even hold a paper to read. He would have to put the paper on the table and lean over it because of the shakes.

As there was always the chance of people or ships coming to the depot at night, there had to be somebody on duty all night. I never did a duty watch as I always had a bottle of 'neaters' in my locker. The old hands used to like their rum so when it was my turn for duty watch, I always used to say, 'Does anybody want a tot of neaters?' A mate would always do your eight or ten hour stint at night for some rum.

I had a lovely racket going with rum, cigarettes and ration cards. See, in those days, there were still ration cards and WRENS didn't get duty free cigarettes. I was very friendly with the chief petty officer in charge of the cigarette store. He liked his rum so I used to swap him cigarettes for rum. The leading WREN in charge of the ration card office was from Aspatria. I'd give her cigarettes and she'd give me ration cards. I've seen me come home on leave with maybe ten ration cards, give them to my mother who'd say, 'Well, I can't go to Wildman Street Co-op with these because I've already been there. And I can't go to so-and-so as I've been there as well.' I think half the time my mother never got them spent because there was no other shops for her to go with coupons, she'd already been to them all.

'Geoff, whose job was soley to do with rum!'

There used to be special leave trains that left Devonport because of the number of men going on leave. I know at Exeter there was always a mad scramble to get something to eat from the tea trolleys on the platform. Then at Crewe it was a long wait for the train up to Manchester and the north. One occasion at Crewe I met up with this sick berth attendant who was from Carnforth. We had about two and a half hours to wait for the next train so we went into town. The first pub we came to was a railway men's club. As we were both pretty good on the dart board, we were playing the railway men for pints and had four or five pints in no time. We went back to the station and when the train came in it was pretty full so we finished up with the guard in the guard's van. I had a pint of rum with me and between the three of us we drank it before we reached Carnforth.

The last I saw of the sick berth attendant, he'd got out of the carriage on the wrong side of Carnforth and as the train pulled away, he was being pursued by a railway policeman. I often wonder if he managed to get away. When my father met me at Kendal railway station, he was wearing a trilby hat. I'd never seen him wearing one of those before and was so inebriated I didn't recognise him. My father didn't want my mother to see me in that state so he walked me round town for an hour and a half trying to sober me up.

You met all sorts of chaps in the Navy including homosexuals which were quite rare in those days. I can remember one that I was standing along-side when I was shaving in the heads one night. He told me he was going to get a flat ashore and I wondered how he could afford to do that. Then we found out. When one or two ships came in, their captains would ring up this chap. He was obviously a friend of theirs and obviously well paid.

I think the Navy was more relaxed than the other services but discipline was still fairly strict. We used to have rounds every night at nine o'clock when the officer-of-the-day used to come round with the chief petty officer for inspection. The officer wore gloves and he would run his hands along the tops of the lockers and other places to make sure that everything was clean. Again, it's the hygiene aspect, everything had to be clean and if they weren't, you were in trouble.

For nights out there used to be a bus from the dockyard gate into Plymouth. Mind, even with our rackets, I've seen us absolutely skint and pay-day a few days away. In our particular mess, we used to have an old leather armchair, which we'd tip up and if you found half-a-crown that had slipped down the side of the chair, that was a night out. In those days it was a penny-half penny for the bus fare into

Plymouth, three pints of scrumpy at nine pence a pint and a penny-half penny for the bus back to the depot.

You could have a night out on half-a-crown but ordinary local girls didn't want anything to do with you because you were a sailor. The Victory Ballroom was just across the road at Devonport. It was sixpence to get in and if you took a bird, she got in for nothing but once she found out you were a sailor, that was it.

It was said that on Union Street in Plymouth there were sixty-eight pubs. That street was the recognised beat for the pro's. You were well kitted out after you'd been paid and walking down that street, you'd be propositioned left, right and centre. The amazing thing was with these pro's, they all knew which depot or ship you were from. They could even tell you the movement of the ships and when they were due in. This was especially true of the movements of the Yanks as compared to us, the Yanks were well paid.

Talking of runs ashore, Walter Hart and I used to go to a pub called The Admiral McBride, which was in the Barbican area of Plymouth. I sometimes used to sit down and play the piano there and people used to pay me for playing. But Walter and I spent most of our time on the dartboard. I was good at scoring twenties and Walter was good on nineteens. Now, The Admiral McBride was a sailors' pub and if we went there in the early evening, we'd mess around on the dartboard. Sailors would come in, watch us play and then say, 'We'll take you on for a pint.' Then we'd play properly and won many a pint there.

The thing I remember most about Plymouth was the devastation. Remember, it was 1949 when I went there and the city centre was virtually non-existent with the bombing from the war. But coming into Plymouth on a regular basis, you could see the huge steel and concrete structures going up as there was a lot of reconstruction going on.

One of the big features of Plymouth was the King's Birthday Parade. A few days before-hand, we had this dress rehearsal. We sailed down from the dockyard in a MFV (motor fishing vessel) to Millbay Docks. From there we marched through Plymouth to the Hoe. Across the Hoe was a very wide road where we all lined up in ranks, Army, Navy, Air Force, WRENS, and WRAF'S, all six thousand of us. A huge wooden tower had been built with a wooden platform on top where there was a seaman with a rifle. It was an ingenious idea because wherever you were on parade, you could see this seaman on the tower. The officer of the day would say, 'Slope arms.' You'd see the seaman with his rifle slope arms and then when the chief petty officer dropped his flag, everybody sloped arms. It must have been magic to watch from afar because suddenly everybody sloped arms, presented arms or whatever. And they did the Fuer De Joie, which is spectacular. There's three ranks and three times you fire a volley down the line and back up again.

I was in the sailing club at Plymouth. Oh, it was great. I loved sailing, the slap of the waves and the fresh air. You started off on whalers, the big boats. Then they got down to cutters and eventually two man dinghies as you got more proficient. I can remember one occasion there were enough men to crew two whalers and five of us were left over. The officer-in-charge said, 'Oh, as there's only five of you, take a cutter.' So off we sailed down the Tamar and sailed round Plymouth Sound most of the afternoon until it was time to head back up the Tamar. Well, the tide was coming out so fast that we couldn't get up the river. It wasn't etiquette to row and have sails up at the same time so we tacked past Drake's Island, then down with sails and out with oars. As there were only five of us instead of eight in the cutter, we'd make about two hundred yards against this current and be knackered. Our hands were getting blistered and so it was ship the oars and up the sails. By this time we were back where we started but even boats who were full manned couldn't make it either. Eventually one of the aircraft carriers sent out two motor cutters to tow us all back.

I progressed to two-man dinghies and I took this WREN out for a sail one day. We were coming back to the catamaran which is the landing stage at Devonport dockyard and I said to her, 'Right, steering in towards the catamaran. When I shout 'jump', you jump.' This was for her to jump onto the catamaran and tie the boat up for me. As the silly girl tried to jump, she pushed the dinghy with her foot to get some leverage. Well, when she did that, she pushed the dinghy away and into the water she went. Fortunately I managed to get her back onboard. By the way, the WRENS quarters were named, *HMS Impregnable* but they weren't!!

The dockyard and depot used to have Navy Days when they were thrown open for the weekend and the public came to view the ships and all the rest. In the drill shed there was a huge model of *HMS Hood* in a glass case and a beautiful thing it was. At one Navy Day, as usual the public were coming into the shed and admiring the model. As they went past the show case, two sailors were telling them this model was being raffled and selling them raffle tickets. The sailors were caught eventually and in serious trouble. I don't know what happened to them but they were showing a bit of initiative.

After Plymouth I was drafted to a minesweeper base, *HMS Lochinvar*, at Port Edgar, South Queensferry. That base was virtually underneath the Forth Bridge and our job was to supply all these wooden minesweepers with bedding, clothes and other supplies. It was a dangerous job on minesweepers just after the war as at that time there were still a lot of mines to be disposed. The divers, the minesweeper chaps were absolutely barmy. All they got for doing their job was an extra three pence a day danger money.

Every-so-often in my job I had to go across to *HMS Cochrane* at Rosyth dockyard, which was the main supply base. We'd go by MFV's across the Forth and because the fog often used to come down, we had some hair-raising trips. But you thought nothing of it in those days.

I used to go into Edinburgh nearly every night and you could stay at a place called The Sailors' Rest, which was in East Register Street at the top of Princes Street. It cost a shilling a night to stay at The Sailors' Rest where rows of beds were cubicled off with wire netting over the top. I'd stay there and at six o'clock in the morning they'd give me a knock to catch the first bus back to *Lochinvar*.

Initially National Service was just eighteen months but the Korean War broke out so we were kept on for two years. I'd be up at *Lochinvar* for about three or four months until the November of '51 and went back to Plymouth to be demobbed. You were then put on what was called Z Reserve, which meant in the event of any emergency you were one of the first to be called back. On being demobbed, you were allowed to bring home just about everything except your hammock and great-coat.

Now, the uniform you had been issued with was a sort of serge material that was horrible so most of us bought our uniform at Gieves. They were the navy tailors and all the officers bought their suits there. Gieves made what we called our doeskin suits out of lovely material which we paid for at so much a week. So obviously when I left the Navy, my doeskin suit came home with me.

Once home, I went back to work at the Provincial Insurance Company which I hated so I joined the police. On joining the police I was told, 'You can forget about Z Reserve, now that you joined the police, it doesn't apply to you.' Consequently I took all the badges off this nice doeskin jacket. Then I cut off the navy blue buttons, sewed brass ones on and made it into a blazer. My naval peaked cap I gave to the little boy next door and that was that.

Three years later, through the post I received a letter saying I was called up and to go to *HMS Implacable* an aircraft carrier at Plymouth. So I thought, 'Oh, I'll report this to the police and that'll be it.' But it wasn't. I had to go to Plymouth. So off came all the brass buttons from the doeskin jacket and on went the navy-blue ones and the badges. I had to retrieve my cap from the little lad next door, who fortunately had kept it as a souvenir. My only pair of black shoes had toe caps on, which you weren't allowed to wear in the Navy but I wasn't going to buy any new ones just to go down to Plymouth for three weeks.

The first night we had ashore at Plymouth, we were all lined up for the inspection by the Officer-on-the-Watch. Now, the naval salute is different from the police salute and I gave the Officer the wrong one. This immediately drew his attention to me and the toe caps on my shoes. He went mad. I explained the situation and he said, 'I'll allow you to go out on this occasion but don't let me catch you in those shoes again.' Fortunately he was never Officer-of-the-Watch again.

I was down at Plymouth for twenty days and what a waste of time. A goods train was pulled along-side the dry dock and we spent the best part of the week unloading it. We stored all the provisions into the bowels of the ship and into various store rooms. Then we spent the next week getting it all out again and putting it back onto the goods train. It was a sheer waste of time but I made the most of it. You could buy clothes dirt cheap. For instance, a pair of shoes were about three shillings and six pence and officers silk pyjamas were about five bob. I was earning good money in the police force at that time compared to other lads, so I'd gone down to Plymouth with a big suitcase and I had it full when it was time to come home.

I'm a strong advocator of National Service and think a lot of trouble today wouldn't happen if lads got a bit of discipline. I enjoyed my National Service as I had a cushy number and rackets going. I've always said that if I hadn't settled back in civvy life or even the police I would have gone back into the Navy. Looking back, I learned more in those two years than I would have in ten years at Kendal.

TWELVE

'Brilliant times'

***Tony Johnstone**, served in the RAF 1957-1962*

I hadn't done very well at school. I wasn't very bright and would rather play rugby than study. Really, I wanted to be an engineer so I went to the Labour Exchange and had the chance of going in the Navy as an apprentice up on *HMS Caladonian* at Rosyth. But my father said, 'No, you're too young to go away from home. I'll get you a job.' So he got me a job as a trainee manager at Montague Burton's, the men's tailors at Workington. I used to have to get dressed up in a suit, wear a white shirt with detached collars that were sent to the laundry to get starched. Learning how to use collar studs and everything at sixteen was quite a feat. Actually, I quite enjoyed the job and I was there for about twelve months. Then my father died suddenly and I went and helped my mother in the family business.

The family business was a pet shop in King Street at Whitehaven. My father had left the police to buy this shop. He used to buy all sorts of pets and we never knew what he was going to come home with next. We had a baby alligator at one stage which we kept in the bath. It was only about two feet long but it was enough to frighten the hell out of everybody. I can't remember whether he got shot of it or it died. Then my father tried to breed tropical fish. He once bought a dozen of the old square acid battery jars from a scrap yard. These were filled with water, a gold fish put in each one and were lined up on a shelf in our back yard. However, we got up one morning in winter and these bloody jars and the fish in them were frozen solid.

Anyway, I was working at the pet shop when I got a letter about being available for National Service. Then I had to go to the Whitehaven Job Centre or Dole Office as they used to be called and sign a form saying that I was available for National Service. My mother rang Bob Bracken for his advice about National Service. Bob had been a policemen with my father at Workington and they'd been very good friends. He was my godfather and during the war went into the RAF. Now when you're five or six years old, you look for a hero and here was my godfather, uncle Bob, who used to come home in his RAF uniform. At the end of the war he went back into the civilian police but didn't stay long and returned to the RAF police. So when my mother rang Bob for advice he said, 'Get him into the RAF where he'll learn something. In the Army he'll just be a foot slogger.' So that was it, I said, 'I want to be in the RAF. I want to be like my uncle Bob.'

The next thing I knew, I got another letter saying I had to go for a medical to Carlisle Castle. So I arrived at the Castle and from then on, you were chaperoned the whole time. First of all they did your medical and the doctor noticed that three toes on one foot and two on the other have skin across them like webbed feet. He asked, 'Is that a hindrance to you, boy?' Trying to be friendly I said, 'Oh no sir, it's bloody grand. I can swim twice as fast as anybody else.' He wasn't amused by all that but I passed the medical as I was reasonably fit.

After the medical you had an interview with people from the three services. I was offered the Army but told them I only wanted to go into the RAF. But the only way into the Air Force was to sign on for an extra year. I think it was a con that I fell for because later I came across people in the RAF doing their National Service.

I didn't sign-on at the Castle. I had to go to the RAF recruiting office at The Crescent in Carlisle one morning to do that. At the recruiting office there were about half-a-dozen of us lads from Cumberland, Westmorland and the Dumfries area of Scotland. The same day we were given our travel warrants and sent away for training. We were told what time the trains ran from Carlisle and to make our way down to Bedford Railway Station where we'd be picked up and taken to RAF Cardington.

Away we went and it was an adventure as I'd never been away on my own before. But I was apprehensive as I'd never slept even away from home and didn't know what to expect. At London we changed trains for Bedford and when we got off the train there, two old Bedford trucks were waiting for us and a big sergeant shouting, 'Everybody get into a truck, into a truck, into a truck.' One or two lads went up to him, saying 'Are these trucks going to Cardington?' and got a load of swear words in reply before he told them, 'Of course they're going to Cardington.'

Introducing the Royal Air Force

to the

National Service Entrant

1. Since 1949 all National Servicemen have had a compulsory Statutory liability which requires them to complete 5½ years Regular or Reserve service with the Navy, Army or Air Force and under the National Service Act 1950, the period of 5½ years is completed by means of 2 years whole-time service followed by a further period of 3½ years **unpaid** Reserve service. Until recently the shortest regular engagement in the Royal Air Force has been for 5 years Regular service followed by 4 years Reserve service and the longest engagement has been for 12 years Regular service, these being the only engagements open for National Servicemen enlisting for Regular service with the Royal Air Force. It was decided this year to introduce two new short regular engagements (open to National Servicemen only) and the engagements are for 3 years Regular service followed by 2½ years **paid** Reserve service or for 4 years Regular service followed by 1½ years **paid** Reserve service. National Servicemen enlisting on these engagements will have no further liability under the National Service Acts as they will have completed the required 5½ years Regular or Reserve service. The added attractions of Regular engagements over National Service are set out in detail overleaf and may be summarised as follows :—

(a) For every man who undertakes a Regular engagement there will be a choice of trades.

(b) They will become eligible for the higher regular rate of pay from commencement of service whereas the National Serviceman is not granted this privilege until he has completed 18 months service.

(c) They will be granted the Regular airman's clothing allowance from commencement of service.

(d) They will be granted the Regular airman's leave and free travel warrant entitlement from commencement of service.

(e) They will be issued with a complete outfit of civilian clothes and granted the full regular terminal leave on completion of engagement.

(f) Their Reserve service will be paid.

Admission to the Amalgamated Engineering Union. (A.M.O. A59/50)

1 (a) **FULLY SKILLED TRADES.**

An airman who has been trained and mustered into one of the undermentioned trades is eligible for entry into one of the fully-skilled sections of the union, provided he has had not less than five years experience in that trade :—

Fitter I.
Fitter II.
Fitter II (Airframes)
Fitter II (Engine)
Fitter Armourer
Fitter General
Fitter Marine
Fitter M.T.
Metal Worker
Blacksmith and Welder
Machine Toolsetter & Operator
Draughtsman (Engineering)
Coppersmith & Sheet Metal Worker
Carpenter I.
Carpenter II.
Carpenter (Boat builder)
Instrument Maker
Instrument Repairer I.
Electrician I.
Moulder
Air Radio Fitter
Ground Radio Fitter
Radar Fitter (Air)
Radar Fitter (Ground)
Wireless Fitter
Grinder
Miller
Turner
Welder
Blacksmith

(b) **SEMI-SKILLED TRADES.**

An airman who has been trained, and mustered into one of the undermentioned trades, is eligible for entry into one of the semi-skilled sections of the union, provided he has not less than three years experience in the trade :—

Armourer (Bombs)
Armourer (Guns)
Armourer (Turrets)
Armourer Mechanic
Aircraft Finisher
Electrician II.
Electrical Mechanic
Flight Mechanic (Airframes)
Flight Mechanic (Engine)
Instrument Mechanic
Instrument Repairer II.
M.T. Mechanic
Ground Radar Mechanic
Air Radar Mechanic
Air Wireless Mechanic
Ground Wireless Mechanic
Airframe Mechanic
Engine Mechanic

Admission to the Electrical Trades Union. (A.M.O. A59/50)

1. Airmen mustered in fully-skilled electrical trades. A Regular airman who has completed his training and has been mustered into one of the undermentioned trades, is eligible to enter the Auxiliary Section of the Electrical Trades Union during his service, and, provided that at the time of discharge he has completed not less than 26 weeks in that section, he will be eligible to transfer to the fully skilled section of the union :—

Electrician Grade I.
Air Radio Fitter
Ground Radio
Radar Fitter (Air)
Radar Fitter (Ground)
Wireless Fitter

2. Airmen mustered in semi-skilled electrical trades. A Regular airman who has completed his training and has been mustered into one of the undermentioned trades, is eligible to join the Auxiliary Section of the Electrical Trades Union. This is the section of the union which qualifies for semi-skilled rates of pay in industrial employment. He will not be eligible to apply for transfer to the fully-skilled section on the same terms as those quoted in para. 1., above. In certain circumstances, however, the union may consider the experience and qualifications of a member who has served not less than five years in a semi-skilled trade may justify transfer to the fully-skilled section :—

Electrician, Grade II.
Ground Radar Mechanic
Ground Wireless Mechanic
Air Radar Mechanic
Air Wireless Mechanic

Recognition by Trades Unions—Dental Mechanics. (A.M.O. A314/50)

1. Agreements have been reached with the Associated Dental Technicians' Section of :—
   (a) The Society of Goldsmiths, Jewellers and Kindred Trades,
   (b) The Union of Shop, Distributive and Allied Workers.

whereby dental mechanics of the Royal Air Force are recognised as being eligible for membership of the unions for the purpose of employment in the British Isles provided that they have
   (a) passed the prescribed course of training in the Royal Air Force,
   (b) obtained a classification not lower than leading aircraftman ; and
   (c) a minimum of five years experience in the craft.

Agreement with the National Society of Painters. (A.M.O. A452/50)

1. Agreement has now been reached with the National Society of Painters, whereby Regular airmen who have attained the classification of leading aircraftman in the trade of Aircraft Finisher, Group B, will be recognised as eligible for direct admission as tradesmen into the society, on completing their R.A F. engagements.

Agreement with the Constructional Engineering Union. (A.M.O A482/50)

1. Agreement has now been reached with the Constructional Engineering Union, whereby Regular airmen who have at least three years experience in the trade of Aerial Erector, Group B, will be recognised as eligible for direct transmission as tradesmen into the union, upon completion of their R.A.F. engagements.

Negotiations are proceeding with other Trade Unions to obtain recognition of further R.A.F. Trades.

When we arrived at camp we were marshalled into a room, told which billet we were in, given a set of blankets and sheets for our beds, then it was off to the mess for a meal. Actually, the meal wasn't as bad as I thought it was going to be. I thought they'd be horrendous, I really did. There were a lot of people who complained about the food but you wondered what the hell they had to eat at home because, over-all, the meals were not bad and some were very good.

I can't remember if I ever saw the lads I travelled down to Cardington with again because it was so awe-inspiring to see two or three hundred people all together. There were a lot of lads from London, Birmingham, Glasgow and the North East. I was very nervous and shy and tended to think of myself as a country hill-billy. If a Cockney came up and spoke to me I would believe everything he said as I thought he was the fount of all knowledge. I remember the first night as there was a coloured guy in the billet. It was the first time I'd come across anybody at close quarters who was coloured and he was a nice lad. But there were these lads from Tyne and Wear and they started on him, calling him a black enamelled bastard and told him to get out and into another billet. The colour prejudice was unbelievable. I'd never even heard language like they were using and for them to be using it against somebody else, it really flummoxed me. And the coloured guy, he just seemed to take it. He would answer back at times but on the whole, he just seemed to soak it up because that's what most coloured people did in those days.

So that was the first night and oh Christ, the bed was cold and damp. The only heating was from one of those pot-bellied stoves in the middle of the room. If you were at the far end of the room, you got none of the heat from it. And if you were right next to it, you roasted. They used to put coke into this stove until the chimney was glowing almost white hot for two or three foot up.

I had a friend from Workington who was already in the RAF. When I told him I was going to RAF Cardington, he said, 'Oh, look up my mate there. He'll look after you and see you all right.' I did look up his mate, who was a little Welshman, always fighting and always in trouble. Now, being a raw recruit you weren't allowed out of camp but this chap, being stationed there, knew all the holes in the camp perimeter. So he sneaked me, still in my civvies, out of camp and into the local pub.

At that time I was one of those Northerners who thought they were the world's greatest drinkers and drank John Peel Golden Bitter. Well, of course, this Welshman got into trouble with the locals over a girl. I stepped between him and the other feller and I was the one who got a lovely shiner.

The next day we had our photographs taken so I was one of the few, if not the only one who had a black eye on his ID photograph. I explained that away by saying I'd fallen but there was a lot of fighting going on within the camp. Street-wise people were trying to prove themselves against others who were also trying to prove themselves and so there was friction. You'd get Sunderland lads saying they were better than Newcastle lads and that would lead to a fight. As far as I was concerned we were all English or British. There was a lot of Welshmen with us who were rather clannish and stuck to themselves. But they took me under their wing and as, where-ever I go I end up talking the lingo, I started talking like these Welsh lads.

RAF Cardington was a huge place as it used to be the aerodrome for the airships, the R101 and everything. By the time we were there it was purely an RAF reception centre for trade selection tests and that was about it. For trade selection, you were given fifty questions on electricity and general knowledge and had twenty minutes to answer them. Afterwards you were called into a room for an interview by a sergeant or officer who had your results. Beside him was a board with a list of jobs and these were graded into groups. What jumped out at me when I looked at the board was the one job I wanted to have from the word go – RAF police. And when I said that's what I wanted, I was asked incredulously, 'You want to be a policeman? You want to work shifts?'

We were at Cardington for six weeks and then got our postings to where we were going for square bashing. There were only two camps you could go to: RAF Bridgnorth near Wolverhampton and RAF Wilmslow near Manchester. I got RAF Wilmslow and there must have been a fair old number of us going because it was a troop train we went on and it didn't stop between Bedford and Wilmslow. When we got off the train there was about ten trucks for everybody to pile into with their luggage.

At the camp you were divided up into different flights with a corporal in charge, then given a billet. Now was the time we got our uniform. We went round this hanger and it was like a conveyor belt.

There were all these storemen in the hanger asking, 'What size chest?', 'What size waist?', 'What size shoes?', 'What size hat?'. Well, I'd never worn a hat since I'd left school and had to say that I didn't know. Then it was, 'Oh, you'll be about seven and one eighth.' You'd get this hat which would be resting on your ears and the sergeant standing by would be shouting, 'That's no bloody good. Get it changed.' Eventually you were laden down with all your uniform.

Back at the billet there was a photograph on the door of the proper layout for a kit inspection. You'd go to your bed and lay all your kit out, which all had to be folded in a certain way. Then you had to make a bed pack with your blankets, sheets and pillows and make sure the pillowcase was on top. Nobody knew why they did this. Years later I asked why and was told, 'In case anybody wet the bed.' It was a tradition which went back God knows how many years so that when there was an inspection, they could see if the mattress was wet.

Our corporal had his own room at the end of the billet. Corporal Rogan, he was like God. In a morning somebody was detailed to make him a cup of tea and give him a knock at six o'clock. We thought Rogan was a bastard but he wasn't really, he was all right. You just built up this love-hate relationship with him.

It was at Wilmslow that you started to gel as a team and work together. Except for that one incident at Cardington with the coloured guy I never came across any other bullying. Maybe somebody would get picked on but it didn't last very long because somebody else would say, 'Hey, if you don't leave that guy alone, I'm gonna plant you one.' I never came across bullying from the corporals or sergeants either. They would shout and gollar at us all but nobody in particular was singled out.

Being in uniform is a great leveller. At Cardington we'd all been in civvies and you had the smart fellers with the money. The rest of you were the poor buggers with nothing and it showed by what you wore. But once everybody was in uniform at Wilmslow it was a wonderful feeling. I think that was the greatest thing I've ever learnt was that levelling and the friendship which seemed to last for ever and ever.

If I had ten shillings and you had nothing, we had ten shillings. That's what it was like. A guy would come and say, 'Hey, I'm going out with a WRAF tonight. I've only got one shilling and six pence and I need another three shillings, have you got some money?' Somebody would say, 'I've got two bob', and somebody else would say, 'I've got a shilling.' That would be it, everybody would muck in and laddo could take his WRAF out. There was an awful lot of that.

There was very little stealing. It was dealt with very severely, if it got as far as going before an officer. Usually it was dealt with at local level. If you caught somebody pinching, he'd get a bloody good thumping and wouldn't steal again. That was a good thing because you had to have that feeling of trust in everybody. The idea was, if you had trust, you could trust your life in their hands. That's what the forces wanted because if some military situation arose, you shouldn't have to look at a bloke and think, 'Christ, if I can't trust him with my wallet, how can I trust him with my life?'

Looking back we laugh now at things that happened then more that we did at the time. Maybe it was because we were totally knackered by half past nine or ten o'clock at night and getting into bed. You were up at six in the morning, got dressed, washed and shaved. Then there was breakfast, come back and made your bed-pack before going out on parade. After that it could be PE, route marches, fire-arms, RAF history or drill. If we got the format to any sort of parade wrong, there was an extra session at night which we all had to attend.

One day used to be taken up with injections and you always used to have drill after them to keep your circulation going. It was all very primitive doing injections with one basin of vaccine. I don't think anybody would get away with it now under the hygiene regulations. First of all you walked between parallel bars similar to those in a gymnasium. Your arms were on the bars so you could be injected from both sides and you had umpteen injections that morning. There was a combination injection, the TABT it was called and that used to hurt like hell. After having that your muscle would swell up to the size of a tennis ball and was rock hard. Then you'd have a test where a curved needle was used to inject just under the skin of both arms. That test would leave a red mark and if it didn't, you had to have the injections again so everybody hoped and prayed it went OK.

Another day you'd go to the gas chamber where you'd be taught how to use a gas mask. They'd put you in this chamber with tear gas and you're all walking round with a gas mask on, holding the man in front. You're walking round and everything's fine as you can see with the mask on. But when you had to take it off and still march around, you could feel the gas burning into your lungs. Everybody was coughing and spluttering with their eyes watering. Then the door of the chamber would be opened and you had to run outside into the wind to get the gas off you.

I think I got twenty-eight shillings a week at the square bashing. In those days there was a lot of emphasis put on sending money home to your parents. It was expected but it wasn't forced on you. We all opened a post office account and that was great. Money was taken from our wages for that and you never missed it. Every now and then I'd think, 'I wonder how much I've got in my account?' So I'd go to the post office, get five pounds out which was a lot of money in them days and blow it. Oh, it was marvellous.

You had one twenty-four hour pass and a forty-eight hour one while you were at Wilmslow. With my twenty-four hour one I went to my auntie's at Bury and with the forty-eight one, I came home. That was the first time I'd seen my mother since I'd joined the RAF. Of course you had to wear uniform to come home and I felt ten feet tall and really proud. As there was a long wait at Carlisle for the Workington train my mother came in our car to meet me. When she saw me wearing my uniform, she cried her eyes out.

Towards the end of our course we had to go away for a two-day Reliability and Incentive course. We went out into the Peak District with tents and did map reading, cooked our own meals and broke ice in a stream for a morning shave. On the last night of the course, there was a night exercise and our poor corporal slipped and broke his ankle. As we had only two weeks to go to our passing-out parade, we got another corporal.

You had all the rehearsals for the passing-out parade. You'd also be pressing your uniform, polishing the brasses, bulling up your shoes and you'd rehearse and rehearse until you got your marching right. But we had a tick-tocker in our billet. A lad called Mellor was our tick-tocker. He was a lovely, quiet, country lad who you could imagine walking behind cows. But get him on parade and as he put his left foot forward, his left arm went forward. Now, on parade you're told, 'Keep your head up high and watch the man's arms in front of you because from his arms you know what his feet are doing.' Well, you'd get behind Mellor and you'd see his right arm swing back and you'd think, 'Christ, I'm out of step.' You'd change step so that your arms were swinging with his arms but your feet weren't in step with his feet. So when it came to the passing- out parade, we actually stuck Mellor on point duty as a marker on a corner of the parade ground so that he didn't have to march.

There were usually three flights at a time for the passing-out parade. You'd all be on a side road lined up together and then the band would march around the corner and stop. The Parade Commander would shout, 'Parade, shun. Parade will march on in column of route. RAF Central Band leading. Right turn.' All you heard was this one bang and that was a hundred feet all clamping down on the ground at the same time. Then it was 'By the centre, quick march.' There was the boom, boom, boom of the band and believe me, you can walk a million miles behind a band. You'd march onto that parade ground behind this band swinging your arms shoulder high and you're that proud.

A group captain would be the reviewing officer. Now, the highest rank you'd probably seen in the whole time that you've been in the RAF was maybe a squadron leader. A wing commander, they're pretty rare. A group captain, they're like rocking horse shit as there's only one on every camp. You start thinking of all the greats, Leonard Cheshire, Peter Townsend and all the other group captains. You see, with us, the Battle of Britain was still fresh in everybody's mind. People like a group captain would have been in the RAF during the war and most of them had medals on. And on the passing out parade, you're all standing there at attention when the Group Captain walked by, looking you up and down. Then he comes out with a few words, 'Well gentlemen, you're all very smart … wonderful parade … well turned out … you're a credit to your sergeants … keep up the good work, we need people like you'. All the old spiel to get you going.

At the end of the parade, it was 'Parade will march off, Central band leading.' Off you all marched with parents, civil dignitaries and everyone who was invited to the ceremony clapping. Then, it's funny as the corporals come around and shake your hands, saying 'Well done, lads. You've done us really proud.' The day before we'd been a load of shit and they were shouting, 'God Almighty, get those arms right. You'll never pass out at this rate.'

We'd been told a couple of weeks before our passing-out parade which camps we would be going to next. I had to go to RAF Netheravon, which is just outside Salisbury and thought, 'Christ, I've never been that far south in my life.' The camp was way out in the wilds with just a little village and a pub on top of a nearby hill. I arrived at Netheravon for my twelve weeks at the beginning of October and it was bitterly cold. It was then at eighteen years old that I really appreciated the Lake District. Salisbury Plain is so flat you just looked and saw nothing. There were no mountains or fells and to me, it was lifeless.

There would be about three hundred trainees at a time at Netheravon all at various stages of training. We'd done our basic training and were now basic trainees who the permanent staff treat like shit. It really was strict discipline but everybody was treated the same. Everybody who was there wanted to be a policeman, they all wanted to learn and they all stuck in and helped each other. Actually, it was like school in as much as you had different subjects and different instructors. I can't remember much about the NAAFI because you seemed to be spending so much time on the work plus keeping your uniform spotless.

Breakfast was from half-past six until quarter-past seven so the catering staff could never serve us all fast enough. There was a corporal cook who used to stand by the mess door and as soon as it was quarter-past seven he used to shut the door. Those of us who hadn't squeezed into the mess were locked out and got no breakfast. He took great delight in that.

After breakfast we had to be out on parade at half-past seven. This was in the days of the 'hairy Mary's,' the old battle dress and trousers. They really were uncomfortable bloody things and when you were first issued with them, they used to itch your legs and crutch. We were taught how to wear white gaiters, white belt with cross sash, white pistol holster and white canvas cover over your cap. These all had to be blancoed except for the brasses on the belt and cross strap which had to be shining like anything.

Being winter, we used to get awfully foggy, damp mornings and you'd be standing on parade, absolutely freezing. You could see the moisture gathering on your trousers that you'd spent all night pressing and within an hour the creases had dropped out because of the damp. Then your brasses were starting to go green and if the rain came on, all the blanco used to run off your hat onto your uniform. It was absolutely horrendous.

As part of our uniform, we had to bend our trousers down over the top of the gaiters so that you only saw half the gaiter. You tried like hell to get that right and never could, yet the permanent staff were spot on with theirs. Then we found out how they did it. They all had tiny chains in the bottoms of their trousers and the weight of these used to pull the trouser down to hang properly. Well, we did that but if it wasn't done right, you'd be on parade and when the command 'Halt' was given, you'd stamp your foot down and the chain used to drop out.

At Nertheravon we learnt all about military law and civilian law because we had the same powers of arrest as civilian policemen. We practised point duty on camp with military vehicles. Then about two or three weeks later we were siphoned off into different areas, either P1 or P2. P1's were the station police who manned a station barrier and guardroom for people coming in and out of camp. P2's, which I was in was the investigation side and later on in your service you could do plain clothes and undercover work but at this stage everybody was in uniform.

I'd just been moved to the P2 when I was told, 'You're going to have to do some police driving,' and went down to the police driving school at Hendon for a week. There was living accommodation for the police cadets and people who worked there so it was very much like an army camp with lots of courses going on. I'll always remember they had this huge skid pan and lovely shiny, black cars to do your driving in. I was only eighteen, a boy racer and thought I knew everything. But that was knocked out of me until I knew nothing, then I was built up properly. I learnt an awful lot at Hendon and that really has paid dividends for me.

It's said that where you ask to be posted, you'll be sent somewhere completely different. I had been told that but it doesn't work out like that, I can assure you. I wanted to be posted to either Bridlington or Hornchurch where my pal from Workington was stationed and was told, 'Ask for Northern Ireland.' I put down Northern Ireland and that's where I was sent to, the one place I didn't want to go. When our course finished at Netheravon on a Friday, there was no passing-out parade. You just got everything together and onto waiting buses. Four of us travelling to Ireland had to go into Salisbury, then catch a train to Lancaster and on to Heysham for the ferry. I remember thinking, 'Christ, I'm only about sixty miles from home. Why can't I go there for a few hours.

We sailed from Heysham to Belfast. In those days you had to travel in uniform but the troubles at that time were nothing like the recent ones and a cease fire had just been declared. We landed at Belfast and had to report to a trooping centre there before catching the Londonderry train. We got off at Limavady where a minibus was waiting to take us to the camp. Our journey had taken nearly twenty-four hours and as you arrived at the camp at a weekend, it was shut down. They had to get a duty officer out and put us up in a transit billet until the Monday. Come Monday and the station opened, we were processed, given our gear and a proper police billet, where they'd be eight or ten to a room. I think there would be about forty-nine policemen including dog handlers at Limavady, which was a coastal command from where Shackleton aircraft flew.

As station police we were each armed with a Webley .38 revolver and a Sten gun. Our duties were to man the guardrooms and barriers at the main entrance of the camp and onto the airfield. We also had two out-stations to guard. One, a square brick building, was a Cathode Ray Direction Finder (CRDF) Unit at Magilligan Point. This CRDF unit had sandbags all around it and big orange sodium lights facing outwards. The only trouble was, when you had to change over the guard, you virtually walked through those sodium lights and were a sitting target for anyone wanting to take a shot at you. The threat of someone attacking or taking a shot at us wasn't to be scoffed at. One man at a time guarded the CDFR unit, the rest of the men were in the guard room two hundred yards away.

Right opposite this out-station was an army camp which the TA used. We had to guard it during the hours of darkness, doing two hours on and two hours off. One weekend the TA officers who were using the camp decided to attack the CDRF unit for a joke. I was there that night as guard commander and the lad on duty at the CDRF unit rang the guardroom I was in and said, 'I think we're being attacked, corporal. I can see some people climbing the hill towards me.' I went outside and put up a white flare and sure enough, in its light, saw some fellers moving towards the unit. We didn't know who they were but as soon as I saw them I put up a red flare, which was the signal for the police and troops at Limavady to attend. Before they arrived we managed to round the fellers up and take their old Lee Enfield 303 rifles off them, so it was a bit exciting and our adrenaline was going.

I had the blokes spread-eagled against a fence searching them when I felt something nudge me. I half turned and there was a bloke we'd missed rounding up and he was nudging me with a rifle. I was petrified and thought, 'He's going to shoot me.' Then out of the corner of my eye I saw one of our lads creep up behind this bloke and knock him out cold. By that time re-enforcements had arrived which consisted of the station guard with fifteen men, the RUC and the B Specials who were like our special constables. The six blokes we'd captured were taken off to Ballykelly and we had to carry on with our shift as though nothing had happened.

The next morning when we arrived back at camp our Warrant Officer told me, 'The gentlemen you arrested are in the officers' mess. They're officers from the TA but they're under close arrest. Have your breakfast now as you've got to see the Group Captain in an hour's time.' When I saw the Group Captain who was also the Station Commander, he said, 'I would like to congratulate you on your alertness last night. It could have turned out really nasty if the proper rules of engagement hadn't been gone through and some people might have been killed. There's a gentleman in the other office who would like to say a few words to you.' In came an army colonel who offered his apologies on behalf of the Army for the TA officers who'd decided to try and attack us the previous night. So for a few days I was the hero and it was, 'Oh, we caught the Pongos (TA) out.' But really it hadn't gone all right because I'd missed rounding-up one feller and if he had been a terrorist, he would have shot me.

I don't know if it was because of that incident but within a fortnight I became a substantive corporal. Now, if you're an acting corporal, it's a position on the station where you're serving and if you're transferred, they can take that rank away from you. However, once you become a substantive corporal, it's a permanent position even if you're transferred and you receive a corporal's wage. So I received my ranking very quickly as there were a lot of people who'd been in the force longer than me and were still acting corporals unpaid.

The second out-station we used to guard was a transmitting station at Bernault. This was an aerial farm and a lot bigger site than Magilligan Point with barbed wire fencing all the way round it.One incident at Bernault proved very embarrassing for me. We'd had a card school going on and playing with us was the dog handler. I'd been playing in the billet with his Alsatian called Simba and it was an absolutely brilliant dog. When it was time for me and another lad to patrol outside we took the dog with us and left its handler playing cards.

Outside the camp perimeter there was an aerial about fifty yards away that had to be checked every hour. As it was my turn to check it, I told the lad with me not to bother going for the keys to unlock the gates, as I'd just climb over. So I climbed over the gate while Simba sat and watched me. I checked the aerial and came back with the dog still sitting watching me. 'Hello Simba' I said, 'I'm back again. That's a good boy. I'm coming over the gate now.' I climbed over the gate and managed to get one foot on the ground when the next thing I heard was a growling and barking. The dog went for me and bit my bum actually drawing blood.

Well, I got into the guard room with my britches arse hanging out and blood everywhere. Somebody had to put sticking plasters on my bum and when we went down to camp the next morning in the mini bus I could only sit on one cheek. And during the journey the dog was sitting opposite me, looking right into my eyes, and growling all the time. The dog handler kept saying to me, 'Oh, it's all right Tony lad, it just likes the taste of you.' It was really embarrassing as I had to go and get a tetanus injection and of course, daren't say that the dog had been out loose without its handler.

I was young, single and daft at that time. Along with other mates I used to go to Muff, just over the border from Londonderry to a big dance hall there and some of the smaller village dances. It was at a dance that I met my first serious girl-friend. She was a Catholic who lived in a very nationalistic area of Dungiven and used to say, 'Oh beJesus, if me father knew I was going out with a serviceman, he'd kill me. If he knew I was going out with a Protestant, he'd kill me twice.' So we used to meet in Coleraine or Limavady then later I'd take her back to Dungiven, and drop her on the outskirts so nobody would see us together.

I'd been brought up in a mixed religion family with both Catholics and Protestants and there'd been no animosity so I couldn't understand the bitterness in Northern Ireland. Anyway, just before Orangeman's Day on 12th July, I was going for a walk down a lane at Limavady with this girl-friend. We were passing little cottages which all had Union Jack flags and pictures of the Queen in their windows. I just happened to say that it was nice seeing all the photographs in the windows and my girl-friend answered, 'Oh, beGod, if the Queen walked down the street, I wouldn't get up from the tea-table to see her.' Well, I'm a bit of a monarchist and that really upset me so I turned round and said, 'Ah, but if the Pope came, you'd be there kissing his ring.' That rather good phrase was the end of the romance.

We did have a member of royalty visit Ireland as Lord Mountbatten fly into Balleykelly and inspected *HMS Sea Eagle* which was the naval base in Londonderry. He came back to a reception in our officers' mess before going on to Belfast. For the journey to Belfast I had to act as his guard and sit in the front of the limousine with the driver, while Lord Mountbatten sat with his ADC in the back. When the limousine set off I was sitting to attention with my revolver and Sten gun over my knee and Lord Mountbatten leant across and tapped me on the shoulder saying, 'Relax son, we've a long way to go.'

During the journey Lord Mountbatten would have a conversation now and again with his ADC. Then there would be periods of silence when he was reading papers but when he got sick of that he would put them down and start talking to me. I didn't ask him any questions and only replied when spoken to but I felt very honoured indeed. Lord Mountbatten asked me about my family and what part of the country I lived in and he seemed very knowledgeable about all sorts of things. When I told him I was from Workington he mentioned that the coal mining industry there was in decline but we still had the steel works. Then mentioned that he knew about the Lake District and had gone sailing on Windermere. I was only young and for somebody so high up, a member of royalty to be actually speaking to me was marvellous.

I'd been in Northern Ireland about a year when I was sent on a detachment to Nicosia in Cyprus as the troubles were on over there. All three services were in Cyprus and while the RAF were busy on the stations it was felt that everybody had to do their bit and go out on patrol. So we'd be doing these patrols and walking down streets when the locals threw chamber pots out of the windows at us. If you've never heard one of those hit the ground from ten or twenty feet up, it sounds just like a bomb going off.

Again, we had CRDF units to guard in Cyprus. Like Ireland, these units were out in the fields, away from the airfields. One we went to check on, the chap inside was fine and everything peaceful with Cypriots working away in the fields. When we went back four hours later he'd been hacked to death with scythes and there was no bloody sign of the people who'd been cutting the harvest.

Another time I got a call-out to go to a house where a WRVS woman lived. She'd answered a knock on her door and been shot at point blank range. I didn't like Cyprus and I don't like talking about it. I had friends killed there and others maimed out there. I came back home on leave from that detachment and remember walking along Pow Street at Workington and walking close to the shop windows. After every three or four yards I was looking behind to see if anybody was sneaking up on me with a knife. No, I didn't enjoy Cyprus at all.

After Cyprus I went back to Ballykelly where everything continued as before. Wednesday afternoon was sports' afternoon and we had rugby and football teams. I used to play rugby for the station and thoroughly enjoyed it. However, a boxing competition had been arranged with our station to fight some boxing club from Belfast. I had never boxed in my life but was persuaded by the PTI to box at light heavyweight. So I went training and running with the other boxers and thought, 'Oh, this is great.'

On the night of the boxing match a few of us were sitting in the changing room all ready for our matches. Two big fellers from the opposing club were sat near me and as they looked identical weight I thought their light heavy weight hadn't turned up. When I was called to the ring one of these fellers was my opponent and he had a build like a gorilla. I was knocked down three times in the first round and three times in the second round. The fight was stopped in the third round because I couldn't see where the other bloke was. What a state I was in. I had my nose broken, a couple of teeth knocked out and my eyes were shut. I actually got a runner-up medal for that fight but I always say it was my bravery medal for getting up every time I was knocked down. Later I was told, 'You should have stayed down when you were hit.' 'Well' I said, 'That bloke hit me so bloody hard, I bounced back up again.'

Believe it or not, I was enjoying life so much that towards the end of my three years service I decided to sign on for another two years. Unfortunately, a short time later I found out that my mother was terminally ill with cancer. I put in for a compassionate posting and was posted to RAF Ouston which is on the old military road about twelve miles this side of Newcastle. This was the nearest RAF station to home that had RAF policeman on site. There was 14 MU at Carlisle but that was manned by MOD police.

RAF Ouston was a flying training station and also 11 Group Fighter Command Headquarters. It was a really small station and the Station Adjutant was Pilot Officer Tulley, a grand feller who was from Carlisle. I went there as as NCO i/c police section and I was the only regular policeman there, the rest were National Servicemen. Ouston was a very easy camp to work at. You were virtually just booking people in and out of the station and doing security patrols. There was no trouble there what-so-ever. I never charged anybody and from my point of view it was a very, very easy posting and a very nice station.

Again, I was playing rugby for the station and once again the PTI came and asked 'Hey, have you boxed before?' I told him what had happened to me at Ballykelly and said, 'I'm not boxing again.' The PTI replied, 'Nobody from the other team has entered for the light heavyweight match. If we put your name down, you're going to get a walk-over and that means we'll get the points and the medal. So I agreed to fight and on the night of the fight I was sitting in the changing room when a bloke from the opposing team asked, 'Is anybody boxing at light heavyweight?' When I told him I was, he said, 'Oh bloody hell. I was told it was going to be a walk-over.' Well, as I'd been told the same, I suggested we go into the ring and just spa for three rounds. The bloke was more than willing to do this because he told me he'd never boxed before or done any training.

When we got called into the ring, our PTI said to me, 'That's a dirty trick the other team have played, putting somebody in the ring with you. That bloke has boxed before and was conning you that he hasn't.' I thought, 'What a dirty trick to play on me.' As soon as the bell went to start the first round I ran across that ring and hit the bloke such a bloody smack, I knocked him out straight away. Back in the changing room when the bloke came round, he wanted to know, 'Why did you hit me like that when you knew I hadn't boxed?' I turned to our PTI who said to me, 'Oh, I knew he hadn't boxed before but told that story just to get you mad so you'd win.' I felt really sorry for that lad. I'd belted him because I'd thought, 'If I don't hit him first he's going to knock the shit out of me.' But once again I got a medal for boxing.

By this time my mother had died and in 1962 I got a posting to go out to Christmas Island. I flew out via Singapore and at Singapore it was discovered I had an ear infection so I wasn't allowed to fly on in case my ear drum burst. However I was fit enough to do duty at Singapore and worked with the RAF police at Changi.

I loved Singapore, I really loved it. The people were so friendly and everything was so cheap. At that time we had our tropical kit or KD (khaki drill) as it was called. That was made of really rough material which used to come nearly down to your calves. But in Singapore there were all these little tailors where you could go and get measured for a pair of shorts or shirts. You'd be measured one day and the new shorts would be ready the next day but they were made of maybe garberdine or cotton, altogether different from the stuff we were getting issued with. You could also get shoes made and a feller would draw around your foot, take a couple of measurements and in a couple of days these lovely shoes were ready that fit like a glove.

Our work from Changi covered doing town patrol because there were a lot of prostitutes who used to walk the streets. The actual brothels were close together and in out-of-bounds areas that we used patrol. But having said that we used to go into the out-of-bound areas ourselves off duty. But work-wise there was very little for us to do and hardly any crime.

There was only one flight a month to Christmas Island from Singapore and it was two months later when I flew there. Christmas Island was supposed to be a hardship posting and you got extra pay for being there and in those days it was good money. But it wasn't a hardship posting, it was Paradise. We fished, we swam, we did small-bore shooting and we sun bathed. We had a football league, a cricket league and a sailing club so there was plenty to do. There was also a swimming pool dug out of the coral which had an inlet so the sea could come in and out. Over the inlet to the pool there was re-enforcing mesh to keep the sharks out but the number of small sharks, two to three feet long, that could get through the mesh was unbelievable.You'd be swimming away in the pool and somebody would shout, 'Shark' and everybody was out of that water like nobody's business.

There was no Army or Navy police on the island, only four of us RAF police including a sergeant. The sergeant did the day shift while the three of us worked from four in the afternoon until eight the next morning. We did one night on duty and two nights off. And workwise, there was very little to do. There wasn't a single report of theft because we all had to muck in together and trust each other.

We did have somebody break into the NAAFI stores, which were big warehouses made of corrugated iron frames. A feller had undone some of the nuts on the framework, pulled one of the sheets back, went in and got paralytic drunk. The NAAFI manager found him there, still drunk, the next morning. We went to pick the bloke up and he was put in the cells as the nearest jail we had was at RAF Changi in Singapore. That would have meant flying the prisoner down to Fiji, on to Darwin and then up to Singapore. As there was only one flight a month it wasn't worth it. So the bloke did his time in the RAF guardroom. You see, even when the bloke got drunk, he'd stayed where he was because there was nowhere for him to go.

'Tony sitting 2nd left on bench
'Weight lifting on Christmas Island'
'Tony standing centre'

There were only a few hundred British servicemen on the island, some American servicemen and natives from what used to be called the Gilbert and Ellice Islands. The natives used to come with their families and work for so many years at a time on the coconut plantations on Christmas Island. They had their own villlage, shops, school, three native policemen and district commissioner who was the link man between them and the RAF. The native village were out of bounds to servicemen as this was the only place on the island where there were women. When I first arrived, the native women were all bare breasted but because of all the men around, their district commissioner thought they should cover themselves up. So the women wore string vests which were twice as sexy as it became 'who can spot a boob' type of thing.

I had only once incident with a native. I was on duty in the guard room when I got a phone call to say a 'Gilbo' had been drinking. This wasn't allowed but the native had been working on the camp and some of the army lads had given him drink. I found the native, put him in a Land Rover and took him back to his village. As soon as I pulled up outside the native police station, he leaped out of the Land Rover and started to run away. Those were my fitness days so I ran after him and rugby tackled him. I'd got him by the legs and was unable to defend myself when he sat up, knocking hell out of me with his fists. Suddenly I heard a thud and then silence. I looked up and there was a native policeman who'd knocked the bloke unconscious. The policeman said, 'I kicked him on head'. Now, we had to wear shoes because the coral would have cut our feet to ribbons. But the natives, including their police, were always bare footed even when they were playing football. The soles of their feet must have been half an inch thick so the policeman had just kicked this bloke with his size fourteen foot and knocked him out.

With being a policeman I was very fortunate as I could go to the native villages on patrols. I got very friendly with a native policeman and he invited me to his house for supper. However, to go to his house I had to get permission from the station commander and the district commissioner. I was allowed to go but it wasn't a straight, 'Yes, you can.' It was worded as 'If you're on duty that night and are patrolling in the village, yes we'll understand you going to his house.' The reason for this was, if I'd been allowed to go to the village, they would have had to allow everybody else permission who wanted to go.

Anyway, the native policeman took me to his home, which was a bamboo hut on stilts. Pride of place in the hut was a photograph of himself at his passing-out parade at Hendon Police Training College dressed in his traditional costume of navy blue top, brown skirt, brown socks and big boots. That photograph was his prize possession to prove that he'd been to a police college in England and he'd even seen the Queen. All the natives were so monarchist and pro-British it was unbelievable. They were lovely people.

Atomic tests were still being carried out on Christmas Island. Prior to any testing, scientists and other civilians would fly in and we had to sort things out. We used to do security patrols and guard any secret equipment. Also, we had to make sure that the natives were all in their community centre so no-one would get hurt. Really, the centre just had a wooden floor, no walls and coconut trees holding the roof up. We didn't know anything about atomic energy in those days. To show you how silly it was, you could go fishing on one end of the island and eat the fish you caught but not from the other end of the island for fear of contamination. Well, let's face it, fish are bound to swim around an island.

When an atomic test was to take place, it would be very early in the morning and still pitch black. Even though it was dark, you'd be issued with dark goggles and could go and sit on the football field. We had to sit with our back to the direction of the bomb. Now, with these goggles on, they were so dark you couldn't even see the sun when it rose. But the flash from the bomb would still blind you, even though you were sitting with your back to it. First of all you would hear a rumble and then feel the rushing of the wind even though we were about forty miles away from the testing. The wind was so strong, we be moved about six inches along the ground with the blast of it. All the hot air would be rushing past you as you moved along the ground. Then the 'all clear' would go and you'd just carry on with your normal business.

Christmas Island is built of three pillars of coral from the ocean bed and no-one knew if the atomic blasts would affect it or cause the island to sink under the water. So on the jetty we always had landing craft similar to the ones used on D Day in case there was a need for an emergency evacuation. You were all given a number which was your safeguard to get off the island and if the warning went off, you all had to run to your embarkation barge.

All our supplies for Christmas Island came from Hickham airbase in Honolulu. As we had a small RAF detachment there I went to Honolulu a few times in an old Hastings aircraft. It was about a seven hour flight and there was no comfort what-so-ever in those Hastings, which only had a few rough and ready seats at the front of the plane and the rest was the cargo hold. These planes would go to Hawaii twice a week, coming back two days later. It was surprising the number of times something went wrong with the planes on the way to Hawaii but never on the way back. So when the plane landed in Hawaii, it would be unserviceable for three or four days while the engineers tried to find what was wrong with it.

The Americans said there would never be another Pear Harbour episode and they always had two aircraft circling the Hawaiian Islands twenty-four hours a day watching their airspace. If any plane came into that airspace it was challenged until the pilot gave identification. Well, we were up in the air one day and got their challenge but our pilot ignored it and carried on. Within a few minutes we had a jet on each of our wing-tips looking to see who the hell we were. They kept calling for us to identify ourselves but our pilot just kept looking at these planes and shrugging his shoulders, pretending that his radio wasn't working. When we landed at Hickham airbase, our equipment had to be thoroughly tested. Even though everything was found to be working, bigger tests had to be done in case of intermittent faults. Of course, all this meant more days in Hawaii for us.

At Hawaii we stayed at Hickham airforce base or the rest and recuperation camp called Fort Derussy in Honalulu itself. The Americans are brilliant as they have these places where servicemen can go and stay at very little cost. You'd go into the mess hall and while you paid for everything it was at a greatly reduced rate. We might be paying twenty-five cents for a beer whereas if you went into one of the bars in Honalulu you'd pay about one dollar, fifty cents.

As the Americans had a small contingent of their military police on Christmas Island for a month or two at a time before returning to Honalulu, you'd get to know them. So we'd take our leave in Hawaii, get in touch with them and they'd take us on the town to all the places we weren't supposed to go to. We used to have some brilliant times. I remember sitting on the beach at Waikiki and pinching myself as I couldn't believe I was there. You see, when I went into the forces, we didn't even have a television at home and I thought, 'I've seen this beach on films and I'm actually here.' Then looking round and seeing the typical American cabs and realising I was on the far side of the world, in Paradise, with dollars in my pocket and being paid for being there. Unbelievable.

Now, back on Christmas Island the British servicemen used to get football, cricket or hockey teams together to play up at Hawaii. I just loved my rugby and wasn't any good at these other sports so I went to the Station Commander and said, 'If I can get a rugby team together, can we go up to Hawaii for a few days?' I was told that if I could get a team together and if we were any good and could get a fixture to play in Hawaii, we could go. So we got a team organised and got in touch with the liaison officer at Hickham base asking if he could get us a fixture. A few days later we got a signal back that they'd got us a fixture against the Mormon College of Hawaii.

As we were getting off the aircraft, the RAF Liaison Officer approached me, saying, 'Ah Corporal, the French fleet are in Pearl Harbour and want to know if you fancy a game of rugby today?' That was fine by us and we were told the match would be played at the Mormon College. The French team rolled up and we played our match and beat them. As you know Mormons don't drink tea, coffee or alcohol so we were given milk or fruit juice after the match. The Mormons were very polite and looked after us but when the French and ourselves got onto the coach, it was, 'Let's look for a bar.' We'd been told there was a great Japanese bar called the Club Kinsa so we went there. It was six o'clock the next morning when we all came out of the club absolutely pie-eyed. We were covered in lipstick, we were covered in make-up, we had strippers all over us. We'd had one whale of a time.

Unfortunately we had to play the match against the Mormon College that same day and everybody was hung-over. We went to the college, got changed and ready for the match and I told everybody, 'We beat the French and they know how to play rugby. We're gonna play the Americans who don't know anything, so we can really knock up a fine score. Right?' Well, we ran onto the field and the Mormon team ran out. I don't think there was a single American playing for that team. There were Fijians, Samoans, Maoris and Aussies and they were all built like Jonah Lomu. All that happened in that match was, we kicked off, they got the ball and scored tries. All our full back did was be sick, pick up the ball, kick it up to the kick off again and be sick again. We were beaten fifty-nine points to nil. That night we went back to the Club Kinza to drown our sorrows.

The American Air Force have what is called MATS, which is their Military Air Transport Service. They also had a wonderful system that if there were any empty seats on these planes going somewhere, their forces could have them. When I was at Hickham for three days, an American MP I knew said, 'How do you fancy a trip off somewhere?' So we went to MATS and got two spare seats on a flight to Tokyo that evening. When we arrived at Tokyo, the American went to the MATS there and asked, 'Do you have an aircraft going back to Honolulu in the next three days?' We were told, 'We've got one going back in half-an-hour, then we've nothing for a week.' As I only had three days leave we had to fly back on the aircraft we'd just flown in. All I saw of Tokyo was the runway and the terminal and that was it. All the way back I was saying, 'You silly bugger, you should have checked the flights back before we set off.'

That American was Jim Derusi, a New Yorker, a really street-wise guy who'd go for the main chance every time. He was the same with girls. He'd notice two girls and say, 'There's two over there. Let's go over'. His opening line to the girls was, 'Can I introduce my English friend?' Of course that was a great let in for us both as I wouldn't have had the courage to introduce myself. Then in an aside, he'd turn to me and whisper, 'I don't think much of yours.' All girls looked all right to me as I'd been on Christmas Island for months.

Going to Hawaii on duty was more of a jolly as we didn't do very much. You used to work with the American Air Force and MP's, doing town patrols, station duties like guardroom duties and looking after things if there were any crimes. If servicemen got drunk or tried to wreck a bar, the owners would ring the civvie police up. Then the civvie police would ring the military and say, 'Get a shore patrol. Your lads are causing havoc and we're going there.' We only had a small detachment of British servicemen working in Hawaii so we had no real crime, just drunk and disorderlies, a bit of fighting, that sort of thing. But we had no jurisdiction over the Americans, it was just working with them. However, when President Kennedy visited Honolulu, he came off Air Force One and all the American Air Force Police were there as a guard of honour and there was me tagged on the end. The carpet was out for the President and he walked straight down it while we all stood to attention. Things like that you don't forget.

'At RAF Leuchars 1996. Tony is sitting centre with the Cumbria & North Lancashire wing of the Air Cadets'

Unfortunately in 1963 I left the Air Force after five years and returned to West Cumberland. In 1978 I read in the local paper that the Workington ATC Squadron could close due to lack of adult support and I thought that would be a shame. Even though I'd had no involvement with air cadets and had only seen them on airforce bases, myself and another chap, Ron Elder said we'd help. The chap in charge of the ATC was Squadron Leader Ron Leathers, an ex-RAF regular who'd stepped into the breach when the CO had left. Initially, Ron Elder and myself were Pilot Officers and then Flying Officers. Then I became Flight Lieutenant and commanded the Squadron from 1978 to 1984. After that I was promoted onto what is called Wing Staff and became responsible for the five Squadrons at Workington, Whitehaven, Millom, Ulverston and Barrow. I didn't command them but their Squadron Leaders reported to me. That was my patch from 1984 until 1991.

Prior to joining the ATC, I'd been a special constable so the only time I came into contact with youngsters was on a Friday or Saturday night when they were fighting outside dance-halls or in pubs. That was the negative aspect but with the ATC you saw the positive side of boys. Here we had youngsters who had been in classroom all day and were still willing to come to the ATC for two hours on a night. My attitude was, 'If they're willing to give their time to come and do that, then I've got to give them something special.' And I really enjoyed doing that and had a very good relationship with the cadets.

For two years I worked for the special constables and the cadets but I resigned from the specials as I couldn't do both jobs. With the cadets I was working a minimum of two nights and one day at a weekend but usually it was about four nights a week and three weekends out of four. By that time I was fully committed to the cadets and apart from being responsible to the squadrons I was the Wing Gliding Liaison Officer and Wing Physical Education Officer, organising all the sports within the wing and the inter-squadron sports.

All that took over my life and then in 1991 I was promoted to Squadron Leader and eighteen months later I became a Wing Commander. That meant I was responsible for twenty-eight squadrons which covered from the Scottish border down to Hesketh Bank on the outskirts of Southport, across to Chorley. Really, I covered everything west of the M6 motorway, except for Chorley and Appleby which were to the East of the M6. In my last year with the cadets, I travelled twenty-two thousand miles soley on ATC duties visiting squadrons. Besides visiting squadrons I've been on about every RAF station in the UK and Germany as Camp Commandant and used to go to camp for two weeks and be in charge of the cadets.

When I look back I wonder how the hell I managed but you become geared up to it and it becomes a way of life. I'd go to work in a morning and have my uniform shirt on plus black tie and trousers. When I finished work at five o'clock, off would come my civvie pullover and on would go the RAF one. Then I'd be driving down to Preston, Blackpool or Hesketh Bank and visiting the squadrons there until half-past-ten at night. I'd get home at about one in the morning and be out for work the same morning. That life style went on and on and I wouldn't have changed it or missed it for anything.

Of course we used to parade on Cenotaph Sundays. There was one we had at Carlisle and I think there'd be about three hundred cadets on parade and going to the service at the Cathedral. I was already sitting there when all these cadets were coming in, that was when everything really hit me. I was so proud and humble as they filled the Cathedral. I'd just wanted to help those youngsters and my efforts had been rewarded.

For youngsters there's the sea cadets, air cadets and the army cadets. They'll all give youngsters something if they're willing to put something in themselves. Girls have now taken over squadrons. Loads of cadets have gone into the forces and made names for themselves. Keeping in touch with these youngsters really is great. But it's been a great life. I thoroughly enjoyed my RAF service and my ATC service. I would recommend them to anybody, I really would.

'Tony and his wife, Nancy, attending his farewell dinner after 19 years with the Air Cadets.

Index